Global Theatre Anthologies: Classical and Modern Plays from India

Global Theatre Anthologies: Classical and Modern Plays from India

The Shattered Thigh
Shakuntala
Chitra
Behind the Veil
The Blind Age (*Andha Yug*)
One Day in the Season of Rain
Whirlpool
The Lone Tusker
Seven Steps Around the Fire

Edited by
NANDI BHATIA *and* R. N. SANDBERG

methuen | drama
LONDON • NEW YORK • OXFORD • NEW DELHI • SYDNEY

METHUEN DRAMA
Bloomsbury Publishing Plc, 50 Bedford Square, London, WC1B 3DP, UK
Bloomsbury Publishing Inc, 1385 Broadway, New York, NY 10018, USA
Bloomsbury Publishing Ireland, 29 Earlsfort Terrace, Dublin 2, D02 AY28, Ireland

BLOOMSBURY, METHUEN DRAMA and the Methuen Drama logo are trademarks of
Bloomsbury Publishing Plc

First published in Great Britain 2025

Copyright © Nandi Bhatia and R. N. Sandberg, 2025
The Shattered Thigh © A. N. D. Haksar, 1993
Shakuntala © Arthur W. Ryder 1912
Chitra © Tagore, 1914
Behind the Veil © Rashid Jahan, 1932
The Blind Age (Andha Yug) © Dharamvir Bharati; translated by Tripurari Sharma, 1953, 1963
One Day in the Season of Rain © Mohan Rakesh; translated Aparna Dharwadker and Vinay Dharwadker, 1958
Whirlpool © Datta Bhagat; translation by George Nagies, Vimal Thorat and Eleanor Zelliot, 1978
The Lone Tusker © K. N. Panikkar; translated by K. S. Narayana Pillai, 1991
Seven Steps Around the Fire © Mahesh Dattani, 1999

The authors have asserted their right under the Copyright, Designs and Patents Act, 1988, to be identified as authors of this work.

For legal purposes the Acknowledgements on p. vi constitute an extension of this copyright page.

Series design by Rebecca Heselton
Map © steve estvanik / Shutterstock

All rights reserved. No part of this publication may be: i) reproduced or transmitted in any form, electronic or mechanical, including photocopying, recording or by means of any information storage or retrieval system without prior permission in writing from the publishers; or ii) used or reproduced in any way for the training, development or operation of artificial intelligence (AI) technologies, including generative AI technologies. The rights holders expressly reserve this publication from the text and data mining exception as per Article 4(3) of the Digital Single Market Directive (EU) 2019/790.

Bloomsbury Publishing Plc does not have any control over, or responsibility for, any third-party websites referred to or in this book. All internet addresses given in this book were correct at the time of going to press. The author and publisher regret any inconvenience caused if addresses have changed or sites have ceased to exist, but can accept no responsibility for any such changes.

No rights in incidental music or songs contained in the work are hereby granted and performance rights for any performance/presentation whatsoever must be obtained from the respective copyright owners.

All rights whatsoever in this play are strictly reserved and application for performance etc. should be made before rehearsals to Permissions Department, Bloomsbury Publishing Plc, 50 Bedford Square, London, WC1B 3DP, UK. No performance may be given unless a licence has been obtained.

A catalogue record for this book is available from the British Library.

A catalog record for this book is available from the Library of Congress.

ISBN: HB: 978-1-3504-0844-9
PB: 978-1-3504-0843-2
ePDF: 978-1-3504-0846-3
eBook: 978-1-3504-0845-6

Series: Global Theatre Anthologies
Series Editor: R. N. Sandberg

Typeset by RefineCatch Limited, Bungay, Suffolk
Printed and bound in Great Britain

For product safety related questions contact productsafety@bloomsbury.com.

To find out more about our authors and books visit and sign up for our newsletters.

Contents

Acknowledgements vi

Introduction 1

The Shattered Thigh by Bhasa 7
Shakuntala by Kalidasa 21
Chitra by Rabindranath Tagore 101
Behind the Veil by Rashid Jahan 117
The Blind Age (Andha Yug) by Dharamvir Bharati 127
One Day in the Season of Rain by Mohan Rakesh 211
Whirlpool by Datta Bhagat 273
The Lone Tusker by K. N. Panikkar 301
Seven Steps Around the Fire by Mahesh Dattani 311

Further Reading 345

Bibliography 347

Acknowledgements

We would like to thank:

Datta Bhagat and Mahesh Dattani for generously granting the rights to include their plays in the collection

Erin Mee for connecting us with Girish Karnad's family

Dr. Saraswathy Ganapathy, Karnad's widow, and Raghu Karnad, his son, for the effort to help us obtain the rights to Karnad's plays. Despite not being successful, the excitement they showed about this project and desire to have his work included reflected the spirit and humanity that comes through the plays.

Kimberly Rampersad for her production of *Chitra* at the Shaw Festival and conversation about the production

Sam Nicholls and Dom O'Hanlon at Bloomsbury for their guidance and efforts throughout the longer than expected process of bringing this volume to publication

Introduction

The Global Theatre Anthology series is designed to introduce readers to plays from around the world. The main goals are to make a range of rich dramatic literature available to English language readers, to show the many ways theatre is conceived and operates, to reveal how techniques and themes play out through particular theatrical cultures, and to stimulate readers' critical thinking and untapped imagination. Beyond these, one hopes readers will gain an appreciation for other cultures, a new perspective on their own, and a great deal of pleasure.

Each volume is a collection of ancient, indigenous, and modern plays from a specific area. By exploring these diverse pieces together, one may begin to see common theatrical elements and themes. The plays have been chosen to reflect these commonalities. Yet, we believe they do give us insight into what may be seen as significant aspects of the region being examined. That is not to say that every play operates in the same way or explores the same issues. There are numerous distinct cultures and societies within a given area. The plays not only grow out of their specific worlds but have been created by the unique voices of their authors. The specificity, the uniqueness, are what make them important, powerful works. Nevertheless, reading these pieces together can stimulate thinking about how theatre can be made in different environments and how the making and concerns can be seen to continue and develop over time.

This second volume in the series collects plays from India, not only the most populous country in the world but one with a multiplicity of theatrical cultures, some of which stretch back millennia. It includes two classical Sanskrit dramas, along with seven twentieth-century plays from these various cultures. These cultures are reflected in the fact that the seven modern pieces were written in six different languages: Hindi, Bengali, Marathi, Malayalam, Urdu, and even English, one of India's official languages. The works range from folk tales to history plays with authors who include a female gynaecologist and India's first literature Nobel Laureate. Taken together, how can these nine pieces help us think about what might be fundamental to Indian drama?

The Sanskrit plays serve as a kind of template for the modern pieces. The *Natyashastra*, the oldest work of Indian dramatic criticism, presents the aims, elements, and stage craft of Sanskrit drama. It provides an understanding of this drama but also amplifies the template for Indian drama as a whole. The *Natyashastra* was compiled sometime between 200 BCE and 200 CE and is generally attributed to the sage Bharata. Indian theatre was a highly developed artform even before this time, with professional writers, actors, and playhouses. Based on the practice of the period, the *Natyashastra* describes everything from the playhouses themselves to acting techniques to costumes and makeup to types of plays and how they work. Plays should begin with an offering to the gods and a benediction, indicating the spiritual nature of the performance. A metatheatrical prologue follows in which the director and actors interact with each other, acknowledging the performance itself. The body of the works can be one to ten acts in length. A benediction closes the performance. The foundational principle of the drama is that of *rasas* – sentiments, flavours, essences, or modes that both drive and are the aims of work. Characters experience these *rasas*, allowing the audience to appreciate them. There were initially eight *rasas*: Erotic, Comic, Pathetic, Furious, Heroic, Terrible, Odious and Marvelous. These each grow out of corresponding emotions or psychological states: love, mirth, sorrow, anger, energy, terror, disgust, and astonishment. Later authors added a ninth *rasa* based on peace and tranquility.

The Shattered Thigh seems to have a single dominant emotion – sorrow or grief, which would lead to the *rasa* of Pathos or compassion. However, there are moments of anger, terror, and disgust too; so even in this short work, several *rasas* are touched upon. The play is driven by these feelings; there is little action. In the Prologue, the Director speaks to the audience trying to make it seem as if the soldiers are returning from a battle that has just happened when in fact the story is from the *Mahabharata*, one of the foundational Hindu epics. So, the audience is acknowledged as present and meant to share in the feelings the play generates. The issues the play grapples with – the destruction of war, loss, grieving, death – are direct and raw. The final moments of the play present three possibilities of how to deal with these challenges: transcendent acceptance, leaving the feelings behind for a better community, or violent revenge.

The Prologue of *Shakuntala* is different from *Shattered Thigh*. The interaction with the audience is direct about presenting a play to them rather than some actual event, and the director and actress use verse at times, he speaking, she singing. Both plays are filled with heightened, poetic language. In *Shakuntala* we can see clearly how the linguistic conventions operate throughout the play. The King frequently speaks in verse. Those considered of lower stations, like the Clown, and women speak primarily in prose – in the original this prose would be Prakrit, the vernacular, rather than Sanskrit, the literary language of the higher status characters. Another convention, prescribed in the *Natyashastra* like the registers of language, is that movement can work non-naturalistically. As the King and Charioteer chase the deer through the woods, there is no chariot; music and dance create the hunt. And a step or two can take a character to a different location, for instance, when the King goes from the woods to the hermitage.

Shakuntala, like *Shattered Thigh*, is based on a story from the *Mahabharata*. Though there is more dramatic action in *Shakuntala*, the principle of *rasas* still drives the play. Here, it is the Erotic and Heroic *rasas* that predominate: the Erotic – love, desire, affection, longing – in the first acts and the Heroic – bravery, charity, forgiveness – in its latter parts. Note how the feelings of the King and the sensuality of Shakuntala and the natural setting, rather than a series of actions, form the basis of the opening acts. The transformation of the King and his reconciliation with Shakuntala in the final act are accomplished by what they feel rather than what they do. How will this focus on *rasas*/feelings as the primary mode creating the drama – along with a metatheatrical frame, heightened language, non-naturalistic staging, historical sources – be seen in the modern works?

And what themes in the Sanskrit plays might be concerns for the modern dramas? The challenge of coping with grief and violence as a solution from *Shattered Thigh*? The expression and legitimacy of romantic love and the nature of caste or social status in *Shakuntala*? The misuses of authority and the problematic impact of gender expectations in both plays?

Tagore's *Chitra*, like the Sanskrit plays, is based on a story from the *Mahabharata*, is written in poetic, heightened language, and begins with a scene that reflects and honours the power of the gods – though there is no direct acknowledgement of the audience. At the centre of the play as in *Shakuntala* is the issue of romantic love, the result of which will be a son, an important heir. In a way, Chitra, like King Dushyanta with Shakuntala, hides her identity from Arjuna to win him over: she has the gods make her beautiful. Is this deception a misuse of power? Dushyanta has withheld his status to let Shakuntala see him for who he is as a person; his abuse of authority will come later when he refuses to accept her as his wife – though it is a curse that causes the abuse. Chitra, physically transformed by the gods, does not want Arjuna to see who she truly is – an 'unfeminine' warrior. Chitra believes in the societal expectations of what a woman should be, just as Shakuntala and her companions seem to in the early acts of her play. But by the end of each play, the strength of the women will be shown as their true nature and the men will not merely accept this, they will recognize its value. Women don't need to be coy, sensual, or beautiful to be worthy, equal partners.

Though the status of women is only one aspect of *Shakuntala* and *Chitra*, it is the primary subject of *Behind the Veil*. The play begins with its central character Mohammadi Begum wishing for death to overtake her because of the burden of being a woman. Like *The Shattered Thigh*, grief, sorrow. and the Pathetic *rasa* are the basis of the play. There is no dramatic action, just Mohammadi Begum grieving her life which feels unbearable. She is suffering physically, like Duryodhan, but the longing for death may be even more from the psychic pain of her powerlessness. Even though she has brought wealth to her marriage, her husband controls her body with continuous demands for sex. Her yearly pregnancies and births have destroyed her body, forcing her to have uterine surgery so her husband can still take his pleasure. We never see the husband, but the abuse of patriarchal authority is clear.

Chitra and *Behind the Veil* are both from the early twentieth century. The real development of modern Indian theatre begins after Independence and the Partition of India and Pakistan. Two plays, both written in Hindi in the 1950s, return to India's historical and cultural roots for their subjects. *The Blind Age (Andha Yug)* uses the larger *Mahabharata* story around *The Shattered Thigh*, the war between the Kauravas and Pandavas, to grapple with the Partition of India and Pakistan. In classic Sanskrit play form with an Invocation and a metatheatrical opening and closing, it depicts the last day of the war as a collapse into an age of darkness. There is no space for love, mirth, or astonishment. The Heroic Duryodhan is never seen. Ashwattama becomes the raging soul of much of the play. The Pathetic, Furious, Terrible, and Odious *rasas* fill the stage. Written in searing, beautiful verse, it's a devastating condemnation of violence, revenge, and division as solutions or ways forward. The authority figures of the play know only abandonment and destruction. *The Blind Age (Andha Yug)* seems to say that battles, particularly the ones within a family, lead only to worse states. The promise of triumph or independence can easily be lost.

Comparatively, *One Day in the Season of Rain* is light and balmy, which is of course a mischaracterization of a play filled with storm and downward spirals. The play is set in the Hindu world of caste status and gender expectations. The historical tale is a refraction of *Shakuntala* with author Kalidasa an actual character, but Mallika the Shakuntala stand-in at the centre. The main events take place offstage and the trajectory of the piece tracks Mallika's feelings and hopes for Kalidas and their relationship. Love and the Erotic *rasa* dominate early. Though Mallika tries to hold on to them, they fade just as the decorations of the house do as the play proceeds. Sorrow and the Pathetic *rasa* undergird much of the play with loss seeming continuous for Mallika, her mother, and ultimately perhaps Kalidas himself. The misuse of authority isn't so much abuse as it is insensitivity and neglect. The self-sacrificing Mallika seems to embrace this as being for the greater good, the creation of Kalidas' art. This may be another kind of gendered expectation, different from the married life that her mother (and Shakuntala and Chitra) want but potentially still resulting in the loss of self. Mallika may love the baby she clutches at the end, but it doesn't stop her tears. It isn't Kalidas' offspring. It won't grow to found a nation. Is it ironic that the play itself has been birthed by the real Kalidasa's creations?

The title *Whirlpool* seems to suggest an eddy's downward spiral and a tone similar to *One Day in the Season of Rain*. But right from the beginning we see that this play is driven by the Comic *rasa*. The Stage Manager and Jester, comic figures who frame the play with their patter, not only comment on the story as it goes along but even become part of the tale in a satiric way. The Jester becomes the judge in the proceedings which will decide characters' fates, the Stage Manager his assistant. Roles are reversed just as the play argues for upending the existing system of authority. In the metatheatrical opening, the Stage Manager and Jester state directly that this is a piece of Dalit literature, which means it's going to show the inhumanity of the caste system. Dalit is a Marathi word derived from Sanskrit which people of the marginalized castes chose to call themselves. The Sanskrit epic that's referenced in the play is the *Ramayana* not the *Mahabharata*, and the influence of Sanskrit drama is evident. There is a convention like walking around the stage to take one to a new location and a mode that emphasizes responses to what has happened and what might happen rather than events happening in the moment. But the piece may be more indebted to another indigenous form, the Maharashtra folk play Tamasa, filled with songs, dances, and comic bits. Yet not all is mirth. Violence has been done and is threatened, not as revenge for loss, but as a means of enforcing the oppressive caste system. At moments, the Furious *rasa* is seen; and, in the end, the two comic players, caught in what may be an unchanging societal caste whirlpool, seem filled with sorrow.

The Lone Tusker uses the traditional art forms of Kerala, *Koothu* and *Koodiyattam*, which combine Sanskrit elements with music, dance, and acting. The central character of the *Chakyar* is a member of a community of traditional Malayalam actors who performed at Hindu temples and were thus part of the priest caste. He narrates and enacts a tale in which he is mistaken for an elephant by two woodsmen who attempt to abuse him. The metatheatrical nature of the piece along with the duping of the woodsmen certainly lean into the Comedic *rasa* but with the *Chakyar* becoming an elephant and the woodsmen joining with him, one wonders if the *rasa* is the Marvelous in its astonishment at the power of theatre and performance. Underneath this seem to be commentary on death, grief, and the possibility of violence being overcome through cooperation. The piece ends with *Bharatavakya*, a kind of benediction honoring Bharata, harking back to the *Natyashastra*.

On one level *Seven Steps Around the Fire*, the final play in the volume, seems as far away as possible from the *Natyashastra* and Sanskrit drama. It's a contemporary murder mystery radio drama, written in English, commissioned by and first broadcast on the BBC (before being successfully produced on multiple stages in India). That commission, however, was to mark the fiftieth anniversary of Indian independence and the historic resonance goes back far further. The opening stage direction is 'Sanskrit mantras fade in, the ones chanted during a Hindu wedding.' In this unseen wedding as in *Shakuntala*, the bride is a 'woman' whose husband will not publicly acknowledge her as his wife before declaring the truth in a most dramatic way. That the 'woman' is an *hijra*, transgender, non-binary, extends and deepens the themes that have been seen in other plays – the legitimacy of romantic love, societal expectations around gender and caste, and the abuse and violence that the powerful inflict on those who they feel threatened by. *Hijra* has its origins in the *Ramayana*, the central character tells us, and the *hijra* sisterhood have traditionally performed at weddings for thousands of years. Like most mysteries, *Seven Steps* focuses on unearthing what has happened and the feelings that come with it. There is terror and disgust, the Terrible and Odious *rasas*; but perhaps, as in *Shakuntala*, the Heroic *rasa* comes to the fore through the central character, a female graduate student doggedly trying to uncover the truth and right the wrongs that have been done to the marginalized community.

Seven Steps is set in Karnataka, the state that was home to Girish Karnad, one of the most important figures in modern Indian theatre. His plays, written in the Kannada language and translated into English by himself, draw on the *Mahabharata*, folk tales, and Indian history, using many of the elements (metatheatrical frame, heightened language, physical movement) and themes (the abuse of authority, expectations around gender and romantic love, violence against the marginalized) that we've traced through the plays in this volume. A play like *Nagamandala* in which a newly married woman is rejected than accepted by her husband through the most magical of inventions would be a powerful companion to *Shakuntala* and *Seven Steps*. Unfortunately, we've been unable to include it, other pieces by Karnad and so many other superb Indian plays. We hope readers will use the Further Reading list at the end of the volume as a guide to exploring those works of Karnad and others.

As you read through the plays in this volume – and others from the list – we hope you'll see the theatrical elements and themes that we've examined. But we must emphasize that each of the plays has its own way of working and can be read for ideas other than the ones this introduction has chosen to highlight. Think of possible alternative interpretations for each of the plays, other themes one might foreground. The idea of community, for instance, is central not just to *Seven Steps* but also to *Behind the Veil* and even *The Shattered Thigh* in a different kind of way. We have chosen the plays in the volume because of their theatrical and thematic commonalities in the hope that readers will think about how these plays are Indian and what that means for theatre in India and beyond. But we also want readers to explore the complexity and richness of these unique plays as individual works. If you responded to them, know they are only an introduction to the wealth of Indian theatrical creations.

References

Bharata-Muni. *The Nāṭyaśāstra*. Translated and with introduction and notes by Manomohan Ghosh. Calcutta: Manisha, 1995.

Bharata-Muni. *The Nāṭyaśāstra*. English Translation with Critical Notes by Adya Rangacharya. New Delhi: Munshiram Manoharlal Publishers, 2010.

The Shattered Thigh (*Urubhangam*)

Bhasa

Translated by A. N. D. Haksar

Bhasa (first to third century CE) is the earliest known Sanskrit playwright. In 1909, a collection of Sanskrit texts were found. Though there is some scholarly disagreement, it is generally believed that thirteen of these are plays by Bhasa. The majority are based on stories from the *Mahabharata* and the *Ramayana*, the two great Indian epics. *The Vision of Vasavadatta* (*Swapnavasavadattam*) is considered Bhasa's finest work, but the one-act *The Shattered Thigh* is unique among Sanskrit plays.

The *Mahabharata* is the story of the Bharata clan. It culminates with the war between the clan's two families, the Kauravas and the Pandavas, as they attempt to avenge wrongs and gain control of the throne. In this battle, the one hundred Kaurava sons are killed and the Pandavas triumph. Bhasa dramatizes the fate of Duryodhan, the eldest and last of the Kaurava sons.

During the period in which Bhasa lived, Bharata authored the *Natyashastra*, which delineated the specifics of Sanskrit plays. They should begin with a benediction, followed by a prologue, one to ten acts, and a closing benediction. Though the emotion of sorrow or grief and the corresponding *rasa* of compassion are among those that can form the drama, death and a tragic ending are not to be shown.

In *The Shattered Thigh*, as in others of his plays, Bhasa references but does not include an opening benediction. Since Sanskrit dramatic conventions preclude violence being shown on stage, the Prologue and exchanges among the soldiers that follow only describe the destruction of the war and the battle between Duryodhan and Bheem (sometimes translated as Bhima). Duryodhan, we're told, fights fairly, not taking advantage when Bheem is on the ground; but Bheem, instructed by the god Krishna, violates the principles of combat, thrusting his mace into Duryodhan's thigh. Bhasa, bringing on Duryodhan's parents, wives, and son, powerfully builds the drama on grief and the *rasa* of compassion; but then, defying convention, he has Duryodhan die on stage. Why might Bhasa have made this choice? Is it a tragic ending? Or might there be other ways to read it? And what to make of the closing benediction by the god Balaram, Krishna's brother? Gods are not to appear on stage and yet here one is - and he is the one who taught both Duryodhan and Bheem to use their weapons and calls for the destruction of enemies. Is this benediction meant to upend the dignity and peace that Duryodhan seems to have achieved?

Reference

A. N. D. Haksar. 'Introduction', *The Shattered Thigh and Other Plays*. Translated by A. N. D. Haksar. India: Penguin, 1993.

Cast in order of appearance

The Producer	*in the Prologue*
His Assistant	*- do -*
Three Soldiers	*of the Kaurava army*
Balaram	*elder brother of Krishna*
Duryodhan	*chief of the Kauravas, eldest son of Dhritarashtra*
Dhritarashtra	*the blind old king*
Gandhari	*wife of Dhritarashtra*
Malavi	*wife of Duryodhan*
Pauravi	*wife of Duryodhan*
Durjaya	*young son of Duryodhan*
Ashwatthama	*son of the Kurus' preceptor*

Other characters mentioned in the play

Vyas	*a famous sage*
Vidur	*a half-brother of Dhritarashtra*

Prologue

After the benediction, enter the **Producer**.

Producer   May Krishna help you surmount your enemies. The same, who took Arjun across the flooded river of his foes. A river whose source was Shakuni, and the torrent Duryodhan. A river full of swords and arrows, with Jayadrath as the water and Karna as the waves, with Bheeshma and Drona as its two banks, and with Ashwatthama and Krip as lurking crocodiles.

And now, distinguished spectators, I have to announce that – but what is that? There seems to be a sound just as I was about to start. Well, let me look.

Voices *off stage*

Voices   We are here! Sir, we are here!

Producer   Ah, I see.

Enter an **Assistant**

Assistant   Sir, from where have these people come? Their limbs are wounded with thrusts of spears and arrows and elephant tusks. They challenge each other as they rush about. It seems they want to die fighting for the sake of glory.

Producer   Don't you understand, sir? Kurukshetra is littered with the corpses of kings. Only Duryodhan remains on the side of blind Dhritarashtra who has already lost a hundred sons. And on the side of Yudhishthir, only Krishna and the Pandava brothers remain. The battlefield is like one of those pictures, full of minute details. Dead elephants and horses, dead kings and soldiers, all killed in combat. And the combat of Bheem and Duryodhan is about to begin. Their warriors are already dead.

Exit.

End of Prologue.

Act I

Enter **Three Soldiers**.

All   We are here! Sir, we are here!

First   This is war. The cauldron of hate and brute force, of pride and glory. Where the nymphs of heaven select their bridegrooms. Where lives are sacrificed, and princes find heroic deathbeds and stairways to paradise.

Second   That's right. The ground is dotted with dead elephants. There are nesting vultures and empty chariots on all sides. The princes are no more. Yet, they still live, such were their deeds in battle.

Third   Quite so. War is a sacred sacrifice. Enmity fans its flames. Elephant trunks are the ritual posts, and arrows the ceremonial grass. Men perish there as sacrificial beasts. Their cries are the sacred chants.

First   Look this side, gentlemen. These nobles lie dead here, struck by each others' shafts. And those birds with bloodstained beaks are trying to loosen the ornaments from their bodies.

Second   And that war-elephant fallen under a hail of darts, its armour pierced. It looks like an arsenal with all the bows and arrows around it.

Third   And there's another sight. Those jackals are eagerly pulling out a dead warrior from his chariot, with all his jewelled quiver and garlands. From the same chariot, would his sisters-in-law have helped him down when he was a bridegroom.

All   Kurukshetra is a terrifying sight today. The ground is a slush with the blood of elephants, horses and men. Broken armour and all kinds of weapons are scattered everywhere.

First   Dead elephants lie like bridges in pools of blood. Others wander crazed, without their drivers. Horses pull empty chariots. Headless trunks writhe and twitch.

Second   Look at those vultures with wings outstretched, like palm leaf fans in the sky. They have pale eyes, and beaks like elephant goads, with bits of flesh on them like coral.

Third   All these dead horses and elephants, soldiers and chieftains are so sharply etched by the harsh glare of sunlight. And so are the scattered spears and arrows, swords and daggers. Like stars fallen on the earth.

First   But even in this condition, the warriors look splendid. Their fearless faces are still like lotuses, lying on land.

Second   Even such warriors cannot resist death, what to say of lesser people.

Third   Death is the soldier's fate.

First   Without doubt.

Second That's not so. It was Arjun who forced death on these proud chiefs, with his sharp arrows and terrible bow.

All Listen, there's a sound. The rumble of a thundercloud? A thunderbolt on a mountain peak? A tremor in the earth below? The crash of waves in a stormy sea? Let's see.

All *move around.*

First Look! The combat between Bheem and Duryodhan has begun. The middle Pandava is incensed, remembering the humiliation of Draupadi. The king is enraged at the killing of his hundred brothers. They are duelling with maces before Vyas and Vidur, Krishna and Balaram, and the other Kuru and Yadava leaders.

Second Bheem's broad chest is like a golden rock. Duryodhan's shoulders are hard as an elephant's trunk. They strike at each other with weapons poised. That sound is the clash of their maces.

Third Look at the king! His face is flushed with anger. His helmet plume quivers as he advances crouching, his arm extended. The blood-spattered mace in his right hand gleams like lightning on Mount Kailash.

First Look at Bheem. His body is covered with blood. It flows from his gashed brow and shoulders. His chest is wet with gouts of blood. Wounded and bleeding from mace blows, he looks like a mountain covered with streams of red mud.

Second Duryodhan swings a fearful mace. He roars as he springs. He is quick to draw his arm and ward the other's blow. He advances striking relentlessly. The king has more skill. But Bheem is stronger.

Third Bheem is like a mountain. He has no match in a fight. But he is wet with blood from that big wound on his head. And look! He has fallen down! Like a mountain peak struck by lightning.

First Bheem Sen has fallen! His legs buckled under that heavy blow. Vyas seems astonished, his face upturned resting on a single finger under the chin.

Second Yudhishthir looks distressed. Vidur is in tears.

Third Arjun plucks at his bow, Gandiv. Krishna stares at the sky.

All Balaram is waving his plough with excitement. He loves his pupil.

First The king is brave. His helmet gleams with gems. He is radiant with daring, with dignity and arrogance. He says mockingly: 'Don't be afraid, Bheem. The brave do not strike someone who is down during battle!'

Second Seeing Bheem Sen thus ridiculed, Krishna now gives him a sign, striking his own thighs.

Third That sign seems to have assured Bheem. Seeing his son's distress, the wind-god has also given him strength. He knits his brow, wipes off the sweat, and grasps his mace 'Chitrangada' with both hands. Then, roaring like a lion at a bull, he stands up again.

First Oh! The combat has started again. The son of Pandu rubs his hands on the ground, bites his lip and roars with rage. But that's a foul! He follows Krishna's sign, but ignores the rules. With a swift and deep two-handed swing he has hurled the mace on the thighs of Gandhari's son!

All Alas! The king has fallen.

Third Seeing the king fallen, his body pale with loss of blood, the blessed Vyas has risen into the sky. Balaram covers his eyes. He is angry for Duryodhan. Meanwhile, on Vyas's advice, Krishna and the Pandavas lead Bheem away.

First Bheem Sen's departure has been noticed by Balaram, even though his eyes were closed. Balaram's headdress quivers. His eyes are bloodshot with anger. As he pulls up his garland and draws his dark garment around his body, he looks like the moon descended on earth.

Second Come, let us also go and attend on the king.

The Others Very good.

Exit all.

Act II

Enter **Balaram**.

Balaram That was not fair, O you kings. He cheated in the contest. He was too proud to care about me or my death-dealing plough. In open battle he brought the mace down on Duryodhan's thighs, and also dragged down the reputation of his own family. Live on, Duryodhan! Till I plunge this plough into Bheem's breast today, and make it full of furrows wet with sweat and blood.

Voice *off stage.*

Voice Please! Please, lord Balaram!

Balram O poor Duryodhan! Even in this plight he follows me. Like a child he drags himself on the ground. His arms are pale with dust. His body is smeared and wet with the bloody cosmetic of war. But he is splendid, like the serpent dragging its tired body through the water, after having been used to churn the ocean.

Enter **Duryodhan**, *with both his thighs broken.*

Duryodhan Here I am. Bheem broke the rules of war. His mace blow shattered my thighs. I drag my half-dead body along the earth with my arms. But please, lord Balaram, please calm your anger. Today, for the first time, this head is on the ground, at your feet. We are finished. And so is the war and the enmity. Now just let the funeral of the Kuru clan proceed.

Balaram O Duryodhan, live on, at least for a little while.

Duryodhan What are you going to do?

Balaram Listen. I will make an offering for your fallen comrades. I will give them the sons of Pandu, their bodies pierced with my plough and smashed with my club.

Duryodhan No, no, sir. Bheem fulfilled his vow. My brothers have gone to heaven. I am in this condition. What will be achieved by fighting?

Balaram Sir, you were cheated before my eyes. That has made me very angry.

Duryodhan You think I was cheated?

Balaram Is there any doubt about it?

Duryodhan O I had put my life on stake. Bheem had the wit to escape from that dreadful fire in the house of lac. He survived the avalanche of rocks in the battle with Kuber. He killed the demon Hidimb. If you think, Balaram, that he beat me today by deceit, that is just not so.

Balaram Should Bheem Sen live, having cheated you in battle?

Duryodhan Was I cheated by Bheem Sen?

Balaram Then by whom have you been brought to this pass?

Duryodhan   Listen. Who defied Indra and took away the wishing tree from paradise? Who sleeps for sport on the ocean for a thousand celestial years? Who is the world's beloved? It was he who suddenly entered Bheem's sharp mace and delivered me to death.

Voices *off stage*

Voices   Move aside, gentlemen, move aside!

Balaram (*looking*)   Oh! That is His Majesty Dhritarashtra with Gandhari, led by Durjaya. The ladies of the inner palace are also with him. His step falters. His heart is full of grief. But it is also full of courage. The gods were fearful at his birth, and blinded him. He distributed his sight among a hundred sons. He still stands proud and upright. His long arms are like columns of gold.

Enter **Dhritarashtra**, **Gandhari**, *two* **Queens** *and* **Durjaya**.

Dhirtarashtra   My son, where are you?

Gandhari   Where are you, my child?

Queens   Great king, where are you?

Dhritarashtra   Alas! My sightless eyes have been blinded even more by tears since I heard today that my son had been struck down by trickery. Gandhari, are you there?

Gandhari   Alas! I am still alive.

Queens   Great king! O Great king!

Duryodhan   Alas! My wives are also weeping. I had hardly noticed the mace's blow before. It is only now that I feel its full force, when my women come into the battlefield with their heads uncovered.

Dhritarashtra   Gandhari, can you see Duryodhan, the pride of our family?

Gandhari   I cannot see him, Your Majesty.

Dhritarashtra   What do you mean? Alas, today I am truly blind, when I cannot even see my son at this time of need. I was the proud father of a hundred splendid sons. Do I not deserve that even one should remain to make my funeral offering?

Gandhari   Suyodhan, my boy, answer me. Say something to console your grief-stricken father.

Balaram   That is queen Gandhari. She always yearned to see her children and grand-children, but kept her eyes bandaged out of devotion to her husband. Now even her fortitude is overcome by grief. That bandage of devotion is wet with tears.

Dhritarashtra   Duryodhan! My son! King of eighteen armies! Where are you?

Duryodhan   A king indeed today!

Dhritarashtra   My firstborn son! Come! Answer me!

Duryodhan   Answer you indeed! I am ashamed at what has happened.

Dhritarashtra Come, my son, greet me.

Duryodhan I am coming. (*Tries to get up, but falls again.*) Alas! This is the second blow. Bheem Sen's mace has today deprived me, both of using my thighs and of saluting my father.

Gandhari Here, my daughters.

Queens We are here, madam.

Gandhari Go to your husband.

Queens We go, ill-fated as we are.

Dhritarashtra Who is this guiding me? Tugging at the hem of my garment?

Durjaya It's me, grandfather. Durjaya.

Dhritarashtra Durjaya! Go, grandson, look to your father.

Durjaya But I am tired, grandfather.

Dhritarashtra Go, rest in your father's lap.

Durjaya I am going. (*Approaching.*) Father, where are you?

Duryodhan Oh, he has come too. Love for a son is always in one's heart. In all conditions. But now it burns me. Durjaya has never known sorrow. He has only known the comfort of his father's lap. What will he say when he sees me defeated?

Durjaya Here's the great king. He's sitting on the ground.

Duryodhan My son! Why have you come?

Durjaya You were away for so long.

Duryodhan Ah! Even in this condition, love for my son burns my heart.

Durjaya I want to sit in your lap. (*Tries to climb on to* **Duryodhan**'*s thighs.*)

Duryodhan (*preventing him*) Durjaya! Durjaya! The pain! Alas! This light of my eyes, delight of my heart, this moon, is now a burning fire.

Durjaya Why don't you let me sit in your lap?

Duryodhan Let it be, my son. Sit anywhere else. From today your old familiar sitting place is not there any more.

Durjaya Why, where is the great king going?

Duryodhan I am going to my brothers.

Durjaya Take me there also.

Duryodhan Tell that to Bheem, my son.

Durjaya Come, great king, you are being called.

Duryodhan By whom, son?

Durjaya   By Her Majesty and His Majesty and all the palace ladies.

Duryodhan   You go, my son. I cannot come.

Durjaya   I'll take you.

Duryodhan   You are still too small, my son.

Durjaya (*walking around*)   Ladies, the great king is here.

Queens   The great king! Alas! Alas!

Dhritarashtra   Where is the great king?

Gandhari   Where is my child?

Durjaya   Here he is, sitting on the ground.

Dhritarashtra   Alas! Is this the great king? He was like a pillar of gold, the king of all kings. And now my poor boy lies on the floor, like a broken doorpost.

Gandhari   Suyodhan, my child. You must be tired.

Duryodhan   My lady, I am your son.

Dhritarashtra   Who is that?

Gandhari   It is I, great king, who gave birth to fearless sons.

Duryodhan   I now feel reborn today. Come father, why this distress now?

Dhritarashtra   Why would I be distressed, son? Your hundred brave brothers were consecrated for battle. They have all perished. With you, I also am dead. (*Falls.*)

Duryodhan   Alas! His Majesty has fallen. Father, you must console the queen.

Dhritarashtra   What consolation can I give her?

Duryodhan   Say I died in battle facing the foe. O father, control your grief for my sake. I have bowed my head only at your feet. I have no care for this fire raging within me. I will go to heaven just as proudly as I was born.

Dhritarashtra   I am old and blind from birth. I have no wish to live. And now this bitter grief for my children has come upon me.

Balaram   Alas! His eyes are closed for ever. He has lost all hope for his son. I can hardly announce myself to him just now.

Duryodhan   My lady, I would like to say something to you.

Gandhari   Speak, my child.

Duryodhan   With folded hands I say to you, if I have done any good at all in this life, be my mother in my future lives also.

Gandhari   You speak indeed my own wish.

Duryodhan   Malavi, you also listen. Blows of the mace have bloodied my brow. The blood on my breast leaves no place for garlands. Look at my arms, with wounds as fine as golden bracelets. But your husband fell in battle without turning his back. You are a warrior's wife. Why should you weep?

Malavi   I am just a girl, your wedded wife. So I weep.

Duryodhan   And you, Pauravi. We performed the various sacrifices enjoined by the scriptures. We looked after the family. Our dependents had no complaints. Our dear brothers, subjugated the enemies. The kings of the eighteen armies were given a hard battle. You are a proud woman. Think of my pride. Wives of such men do not weep.

Pauravi   I have already decided to go with you. So I do not weep.

Duryodhan   Durjaya, you listen also.

Dhritarashtra   Gandhari, what does he say?

Gandhari   My own thoughts.

Duryodhan   You must listen to the Pandavas just as you do to me. Obey the orders of the lady, mother Kunti. Honour Draupadi and the mother of Abhimanyu like your own mother. Look, my son! Duryodhan was your father. He was splendid and glorious. His heart was fired with pride. He fell in battle facing an equal adversary. Just remember this and give up grief. Then, touching the silk on Yudhishthir's strong right arm, you must join the sons of Pandu in offering the funeral water in my name.

Balaram   Ah! Enmity gives way to remorse. Well, the drums and trumpets are silent. Arrows and armour, fans and umbrellas, all lie scattered. The soldiers and charioteers all lie dead. But there is a noise. Frightened crows are wheeling in the sky. From whose bow is that sound?

Ashwatthama's *voice off stage.*

Ashwatthama   I came to this battle with Duryodhan when he raised the bow. I was as eager as a priest coming to the great horse sacrifice. Now I have come again.

Balaram   Oh, that is the preceptor's son coming here. Ashwatthama. Large, clear eyes. Long golden arms. Angrily drawing that terrible blow. He shines like Mount Meru with a rainbow on its peak.

Enter **Ashwatthama**.

Ashwatthama   Listen to me, you warrior kings. Your armies came together in battle like two oceans. Like sharks were the upraised weapons. Few survive, and their life ebbs with each breath. But it was the Kuru King, not I, whose thighs were shattered by deceit. It was the charioteer's son, not I, whose weapons failed. Today, I, the son of Drona, stand alone on this field of victory, my weapons drawn. But, for me also, what is the point of glory in war without the accolade of victory. (*Walking around.*) But, no. The king of the Kurus was cheated when I was busy with my father's funeral. Who will believe it? The lords of eleven armies waited with folded hands upon his words. Bheeshma and my father fought for him in the battle. It is clear that Duryodhan was defeated only by bad luck. Now where is he? (*Walking around and looking.*) Ah! Here is the Kuru King. He has crossed the ocean of war, and now lies in the midst of fallen elephants and horses, chariots and soldiers. His hair is dishevelled. His limbs are wet with blood from mace blows. He lies on this final stony seat, like the sun at sunset, sinking into twilight. (*Approaching him.*) O Kuru King, what is this?

Duryodhan   The fruit of craving, O son of my teacher.

Ashwatthama   Your Majesty, I am going to put aside the proprieties.

Duryodhan   What are you going to do?

Ashwatthama   Krishna wants to fight. I am going to wipe out the sons of Pandu, together with him and his eagle and discus. Like bad lines from a drawing.

Duryodhan   No. No, sir, not that. All those crowned kings are no more. Karna has gone to heaven. Bheeshma has fallen. All my hundred brothers have perished in battle. And we are in this condition. Lay down your bow, sir.

Ashwatthama   Your Majesty, it seems that in the contest when Bheem struck you with the mace and seized you by the hair, he crushed your pride and spirit also, alongwith your thighs.

Duryodhan   No, no. What are kings but pride. It was for the sake of pride that I chose this war. Look, teacher's son, how Draupadi was dragged by the hair at the gambling match, how Abhimanyu was killed in battle while still a boy, how the Pandavas were beaten by a trick of the dice and sent to live in the forest with wild animals. Just think, there is not much they have done to break my spirit and pride.

Ashwatthama   I swear by everything, by you, by the paradise of warriors, by my own soul, I will attack tonight and destroy the Pandavas in battle.

Balaram   This will certainly happen. The preceptor's son has said it.

Ashwatthama   Lord Balaram.

Dhritarashtra   Alas, this conspiracy has a witness.

Ashwatthama   Come here, Durjaya. By this priest's oath, may you be the uncrowned king of all the realm won by your father's strength and valour.

Duryodhan   Bless you! What my heart wanted is done. Now my life is going. Shantanu and all my royal ancestors are here. Here are my brothers with Karna at their head. Here too is Abhimanyu, with his boyish tresses, sitting on Indra's elephant, berating me angrily. Urvashi and the celestial nymphs have come to receive me. Here are the oceans, and the Ganga and other rivers. Death has sent a warrior's car drawn by a thousand swans to fetch me. I come. (*Dies.*)

He is covered with a cloth.

Dhritarashtra   Curse this kingdom, useless with the death of my sons. I go to the forest hermitage where decent people live.

Ashwatthama   And I go, weapon in hand, ready to kill those who sleep tonight.

Benediction.

Balaram   *May the lord of men destroy the enemies and protect us all.*

Exit all.

Shakuntala (*Abhijñānaśākuntala*)
A PLAY IN SEVEN ACTS

Kalidasa

Translated by Arthur W. Ryder

Kalidasa (second to fifth century CE) is considered the foremost Sanskrit poet and playwright. His dates are uncertain, with the fourth to fifth centuries most likely. *Shakuntala* is considered his greatest work and arguably the finest Indian play of any era.

Shakuntala is a court drama with finely honed language, written for an educated, sophisticated audience. The story is from the *Mahabharata*, one of the foundational epics of India and Hinduism. It depicts the origin and wars of the Bharata clan.

The first part of the Shakuntala story in the *Mahabharata* is like the play, though the King is more aggressive in his hunting, almost conducting a war against nature, and the encounter with Shakuntala is more explicitly sexual. Kalidasa makes several changes to the rest of the narrative. Among the most significant are that King Dushyanta's rejection of Shakuntala is the result of a curse rather than a choice on his part, and that the reunion of the couple occurs after an extended period and takes place in the realm of the gods. What do Kalidasa's revisions indicate about the goals of the play? The first change seems to shift the blame from the king – he recognized her but had to hide it for political or societal reasons – to Shakuntala – she brought about the curse because she did not properly welcome the sage Durvasas, perhaps due to being overwhelmed by her feelings for the king. And yet, the play also makes us ask, why has the king left Shakuntala in the forest? Why has he not asked her to come to the court? Beyond this, the period after the rejection primarily focuses on the king's path to reconciliation. So, does he bear the primary responsibility? And what do we make of the fact that he's given Shakuntala a royal ring to guarantee she will be recognized at court? Does he suspect that he won't acknowledge her? And what of the loss of the ring itself? Is it another case of Shakuntala's carelessness due to love sickness? But it happens as she's giving obeisance to the god Indra; so, does that absolve her?

Nobel Laureate Rabindranath Tagore, among many, was influenced by the play, writing a 1920 essay about it in which he said its subject was 'to elevate love from the sphere of physical beauty to the eternal heaven of moral beauty.' The drama does begin on earth and end in the heavens. But the places on earth are not all the same. The first four of the seven acts are set in the forest, the realm of nature and the hermitage, home of the revered ascetic sage Kanva, Shakuntala's adoptive father. The fifth and six acts, in which the disruptive problems occur, take place in the capital, the world of the court in which human rules, rather than those of nature and the gods, seem to determine what happens. And the final act in the heavens, in many ways, seems to be a return to the original setting, a place of nature and simplicity. So, is the ending about elevating from or returning to what is valued? And is moral beauty or morality the central issue? Is the tale one of a fall and the need for penance? If so, whose? Shakuntala's because she allowed herself to be seduced? But wasn't this more Dushyanta's doing? Or perhaps because she married in secret without her father's blessing? But don't we see Kanva giving his daughter only love? Or perhaps it's Dushyanta's fall? Certainly, he falls hard for Shakuntala. But is the play condemning this? The king's first significant actions are to give up hunting and to honor the holy hermitage. As this holy place is of sensuous nature, do his actions seem some kind of violation?

There are many questions arising from the play open to interpretation. There is one, however, that has a simple answer. Why is this story, which might seem merely a charming romance, so important? The couple's child, who is the focus in the final movement of the play, will become the conqueror of all India, known by a new name Bharata – the official name of the Republic of India. This is the origin myth of India itself.

References

P. Lal. *Great Sanskrit Plays*. New York: New Directions, 1964
Kalidasa. *Shakuntala*, in Arthur W. Ryder, ed., *Translations of Shakuntala and Other Works*. London: J. M. Dent & Sons, Ltd, 1912.
Romila Thapar, ed. *Śakuntalā: Text, Readings, Histories*. New Delhi: Kali for Women, 1999.

Dramatis Personæ

King Dushyanta
Bharata *nicknamed 'All-tamer', his son*
Madhavya *a clown, his companion*
His Charioteer
Raivataka *a door-keeper*
Bhadrasena *a general*
Karabhaka *a servant*
Parvatayana *a chamberlain*
Somarata *a chaplain*
Kanva *hermit-father*

Sharngarava } *his pupils*
Sharadvata
Harita

Durvasas *an irascible sage*
The Chief of Police

Suchaka } *policemen*
Januka

A Fisherman

Shakuntala *foster-child of Kanva*

Anusuya } *her friends*
Priyamvada

Gautami *hermit-mother*
Kashyapa *father of the gods*
Aditi *mother of the gods*
Matali *charioteer of heaven's king*
Galava *a pupil in heaven*
Mishrakeshi *a heavenly nymph*

Stage-director and actress (in the prologue), hermits and hermit-women, two court poets, palace attendants, invisible fairies.

The first four acts pass in Kanva's forest hermitage; acts five and six in the king's palace; act seven on a heavenly mountain. The time is perhaps seven years.

Prologue

Benediction Upon Audience

> Eight forms has Shiva, lord of all and king:
> And these are water, first created thing;
> And fire, which speeds the sacrifice begun;
> The priest; and time's dividers, moon and sun;
> The all-embracing ether, path of sound;
> The earth, wherein all seeds of life are found;
> And air, the breath of life: may he draw near,
> Revealed in these, and bless those gathered here.

The Stage-Director Enough of this! (*Turning toward the dressing-room.*) Madam, if you are ready, pray come here. (*Enter an* **Actress**.)

Actress Here I am, sir. What am I to do?

Director Our audience is very discriminating, and we are to offer them a new play, called *Shakuntala and the ring of recognition*, written by the famous Kalidasa. Every member of the cast must be on his mettle.

Actress Your arrangements are perfect. Nothing will go wrong.

Director (*smiling*) To tell the truth, madam,
> Until the wise are satisfied,
> I cannot feel that skill is shown;
> The best-trained mind requires support,
> And does not trust itself alone.

Actress True. What shall we do first?

Director First, you must sing something to please the ears of the audience.

Actress What season of the year shall I sing about?

Director Why, sing about the pleasant summer which has just begun. For at this time of year
> A mid-day plunge will temper heat;
> The breeze is rich with forest flowers;
> To slumber in the shade is sweet;
> And charming are the twilight hours.

Actress (*sings*)
> The siris-blossoms fair,
> With pollen laden,
> Are plucked to deck her hair
> By many a maiden,
> But gently; flowers like these
> Are kissed by eager bees.

Director Well done! The whole theatre is captivated by your song, and sits as if painted. What play shall we give them to keep their good-will?

Actress Why, you just told me we were to give a new play called *Shakuntala and the ring*.

Director Thank you for reminding me. For the moment I had quite forgotten.
Your charming song had carried me away
As the deer enticed the hero of our play.

Exeunt ambo.

Act I The Hunt

Enter, in a chariot, pursuing a deer, **King Dushyanta**, *bow and arrow in hand; and a* **Charioteer**.

Charioteer (*looking at the* **King** *and the deer*)   Your Majesty,
  I see you hunt the spotted deer
  With shafts to end his race,
  As though God Shiva should appear
  In his immortal chase.

King   Charioteer, the deer has led us a long chase. And even now
  His neck in beauty bends
  As backward looks he sends
  At my pursuing car
  That threatens death from far.
  Fear shrinks to half the body small;
  See how he fears the arrow's fall!

  The path he takes is strewed
  With blades of grass half-chewed
  From jaws wide with the stress
  Of fevered weariness.
  He leaps so often and so high,
  He does not seem to run, but fly.
(*In surprise.*) Pursue as I may, I can hardly keep him in sight.

Charioteer   Your Majesty, I have been holding the horses back because the ground was rough. This checked us and gave the deer a lead. Now we are on level ground, and you will easily overtake him.

King   Then let the reins hang loose.

Charioteer   Yes, your Majesty. (*He counterfeits rapid motion.*) Look, your Majesty!
  The lines hang loose; the steeds unreined
  Dart forward with a will.
  Their ears are pricked; their necks are strained;
  Their plumes lie straight and still.
  They leave the rising dust behind;
  They seem to float upon the wind.

King (*joyfully*)   See! The horses are gaining on the deer.
  As onward and onward the chariot flies,
  The small flashes large to my dizzy eyes.
  What is cleft in twain, seems to blur and mate;
  What is crooked in nature, seems to be straight.
  Things at my side in an instant appear
  Distant, and things in the distance, near.

A Voice Behind the Scenes   O King, this deer belongs to the hermitage, and must not be killed.

Charioteer (*listening and looking*)   Your Majesty, here are two hermits, come to save the deer at the moment when your arrow was about to fall.

King (*hastily*)   Stop the chariot.

Charioteer   Yes, your Majesty. (*He does so. Enter a* **Hermit** *with his* **Pupil**.)

Hermit (*lifting his hand*)   O King, this deer belongs to the hermitage.
Why should his tender form expire,
As blossoms perish in the fire?
How could that gentle life endure
The deadly arrow, sharp and sure?

Restore your arrow to the quiver;
To you were weapons lent
The broken-hearted to deliver,
Not strike the innocent.

King (*bowing low*)   It is done. (*He does so.*)

Hermit (*joyfully*)   A deed worthy of you, scion of Puru's race, and shining example of kings. May you beget a son to rule earth and heaven.

King (*bowing low*)   I am thankful for a Brahman's blessing.

The Two Hermits   O King, we are on our way to gather firewood. Here, along the bank of the Malini, you may see the hermitage of Father Kanva, over which Shakuntala presides, so to speak, as guardian deity. Unless other deities prevent, pray enter here and receive a welcome. Besides,
Beholding pious hermit-rites
Preserved from fearful harm,
Perceive the profit of the scars
On your protecting arm.

King   Is the hermit father there?

The Two Hermits   No, he has left his daughter to welcome guests, and has just gone to Somatirtha, to avert an evil fate that threatens her.

King   Well, I will see her. She shall feel my devotion, and report it to the sage.

The Two Hermits   Then we will go on our way. (*Exit* **Hermit** *with* **Pupil**.)

King   Charioteer, drive on. A sight of the pious hermitage will purify us.

Charioteer   Yes, your Majesty. (*He counterfeits motion again.*)

King (*looking about*)   One would know, without being told, that this is the precinct of a pious grove.

Charioteer   How so?

King Do you not see? Why, here
  Are rice-grains, dropped from bills of parrot chicks
  Beneath the trees; and pounding-stones where sticks
  A little almond-oil; and trustful deer
  That do not run away as we draw near;
   And river-paths that are besprinkled yet
  From trickling hermit-garments, clean and wet.
Besides,
  The roots of trees are washed by many a stream
  That breezes ruffle; and the flowers' red gleam
  Is dimmed by pious smoke; and fearless fawns
  Move softly on the close-cropped forest lawns.

Charioteer It is all true.

King (*after a little*) We must not disturb the hermitage. Stop here while I dismount.

Charioteer I am holding the reins. Dismount, your Majesty.

King (*dismounts and looks at himself*) One should wear modest garments on entering a hermitage. Take these jewels and the bow. (*He gives them to the* **Charioteer**.) Before I return from my visit to the hermits, have the horses' backs wet down.

Charioteer Yes, your Majesty. (*Exit.*)

King (*walking and looking about*) The hermitage! Well, I will enter. (*As he does so, he feels a throbbing in his arm.*)
  A tranquil spot! Why should I thrill?
  Love cannot enter there –
  Yet to inevitable things
  Doors open everywhere.

A Voice Behind the Scenes This way, girls!

King (*listening*) I think I hear some one to the right of the grove. I must find out. (*He walks and looks about.*) Ah, here are hermit-girls, with watering-pots just big enough for them to handle. They are coming in this direction to water the young trees. They are charming!
  The city maids, for all their pains,
  Seem not so sweet and good;
  Our garden blossoms yield to these
  Flower-children of the wood.
I will draw back into the shade and wait for them. (*He stands, gazing toward them. Enter* **Shakuntala**, *as described, and her* **Two Friends**.)

First Friend It seems to me, dear, that Father Kanva cares more for the hermitage trees than he does for you. You are delicate as a jasmine blossom, yet he tells you to fill the trenches about the trees.

Shakuntala Oh, it isn't Father's bidding so much. I feel like a real sister to them. (*She waters the trees.*)

Priyamvada Shakuntala, we have watered the trees that blossom in the summertime. Now let's sprinkle those whose flowering-time is past. That will be a better deed, because we shall not be working for a reward.

Shakuntala What a pretty idea! (*She does so.*)

King (*to himself*) And this is Kanva's daughter, Shakuntala. (*In surprise.*) The good Father does wrong to make her wear the hermit's dress of bark.

>The sage who yokes her artless charm
>With pious pain and grief,
>Would try to cut the toughest vine
>With a soft, blue lotus-leaf.

Well, I will step behind a tree and see how she acts with her friends. (*He conceals himself.*)

Shakuntala Oh, Anusuya! Priyamvada has fastened this bark dress so tight that it hurts. Please loosen it. (**Anusuya** *does so.*)

Priyamvada (*laughing*) You had better blame your own budding charms for that.

King She is quite right.
>Beneath the barken dress
>Upon the shoulder tied,
>In maiden loveliness
>Her young breast seems to hide,
>
>As when a flower amid
>The leaves by autumn tossed –
>Pale, withered leaves – lies hid,
>And half its grace is lost.

Yet in truth the bark dress is not an enemy to her beauty. It serves as an added ornament. For
>The meanest vesture glows
>On beauty that enchants:
>The lotus lovelier shows
>Amid dull water-plants;
>
>The moon in added splendour
>Shines for its spot of dark;
>Yet more the maiden slender
>Charms in her dress of bark.

Shakuntala (*looking ahead*) Oh, girls, that mango-tree is trying to tell me something with his branches that move in the wind like fingers. I must go and see him. (*She does so.*)

Priyamvada There, Shakuntala, stand right where you are a minute.

Shakuntala Why?

Priyamvada When I see you there, it looks as if a vine were clinging to the mango-tree.

Shakuntala I see why they call you the flatterer.

King But the flattery is true.
   Her arms are tender shoots; her lips
   Are blossoms red and warm;
   Bewitching youth begins to flower
   In beauty on her form.

Anusuya Oh, Shakuntala! Here is the jasmine-vine that you named Light of the Grove. She has chosen the mango-tree as her husband.

Shakuntala (*approaches and looks at it, joyfully*) What a pretty pair they make. The jasmine shows her youth in her fresh flowers, and the mango-tree shows his strength in his ripening fruit. (*She stands gazing at them.*)

Priyamvada (*smiling*) Anusuya, do you know why Shakuntala looks so hard at the Light of the Grove?

Anusuya No. Why?

Priyamvada She is thinking how the Light of the Grove has found a good tree, and hoping that she will meet a fine lover.

Shakuntala That's what you want for yourself. (*She tips her watering-pot.*)

Anusuya Look, Shakuntala! Here is the spring-creeper that Father Kanva tended with his own hands – just as he did you. You are forgetting her.

Shakuntala I'd forget myself sooner. (*She goes to the creeper and looks at it, joyfully.*) Wonderful! Wonderful! Priyamvada, I have something pleasant to tell you.

Priyamvada What is it, dear?

Shakuntala It is out of season, but the spring-creeper is covered with buds down to the very root.

The Two Friends (*running up*) Really?

Shakuntala Of course. Can't you see?

Priyamvada (*looking at it joyfully*) And I have something pleasant to tell *you*. You are to be married soon.

Shakuntala (*snappishly*) You know that's just what you want for yourself.

Priyamvada I'm not teasing. I really heard Father Kanva say that this flowering vine was to be a symbol of your coming happiness.

Anusuya Priyamvada, that is why Shakuntala waters the spring-creeper so lovingly.

Shakuntala She is my sister. Why shouldn't I give her water? (*She tips her watering-pot.*)

King May I hope that she is the hermit's daughter by a mother of a different caste? But it *must* be so.

   Surely, she may become a warrior's bride;
   Else, why these longings in an honest mind?
   The motions of a blameless heart decide
    Of right and wrong, when reason leaves us blind.

Yet I will learn the whole truth.

Shakuntala (*excitedly*) Oh, oh! A bee has left the jasmine-vine and is flying into my face. (*She shows herself annoyed by the bee.*)

King (*ardently*)
   As the bee about her flies,
   Swiftly her bewitching eyes
   Turn to watch his flight.
   She is practising to-day
   Coquetry and glances' play
   Not from love, but fright.

(*Jealously.*)
   Eager bee, you lightly skim
   O'er the eyelid's trembling rim
   Toward the cheek aquiver.
   Gently buzzing round her cheek,
   Whispering in her ear, you seek
   Secrets to deliver.

   While her hands that way and this
   Strike at you, you steal a kiss,
   Love's all, honeymaker.
   I know nothing but her name,
   Not her caste, nor whence she came –
   You, my rival, take her.

Shakuntala Oh, girls! Save me from this dreadful bee!

The Two Friends (*smiling*) Who are we, that we should save you? Call upon Dushyanta. For pious groves are in the protection of the king.

King A good opportunity to present myself. Have no – (*He checks himself. Aside.*) No, they would see that I am the king. I prefer to appear as a guest.

Shakuntala He doesn't leave me alone! I am going to run away. (*She takes a step and looks about.*) Oh, dear! Oh, dear! He is following me. Please save me.

King (*hastening forward*) Ah!
   A king of Puru's mighty line
   Chastises shameless churls;
   What insolent is he who baits
   These artless hermit-girls?

The girls are a little flurried on seeing the **King**.

Anusuya   It is nothing very dreadful, sir. But our friend (*indicating* **Shakuntala**) was teased and frightened by a bee.

King (*to* **Shakuntala**)   I hope these pious days are happy ones. (**Shakuntala**'s *eyes drop in embarrassment.*)

Anusuya   Yes, now that we receive such a distinguished guest.

Priyamvada   Welcome, sir. Go to the cottage, Shakuntala, and bring fruit. This water will do to wash the feet.

King   Your courteous words are enough to make me feel at home.

Anusuya   Then, sir, pray sit down and rest on this shady bench.

King   You, too, are surely wearied by your pious task. Pray be seated a moment.

Priyamvada (*aside to* **Shakuntala**)   My dear, we must be polite to our guest. Shall we sit down? (*The three girls sit.*)

Shakuntala (*to herself*)   Oh, why do I have such feelings when I see this man? They seem wrong in a hermitage.

King (*looking at the girls*)   It is delightful to see your friendship. For you are all young and beautiful.

Priyamvada (*aside to* **Anusuya**)   Who is he, dear? With his mystery, and his dignity, and his courtesy? He acts like a king and a gentleman.

Anusuya   I am curious too. I am going to ask him. (*Aloud.*) Sir, you are so very courteous that I make bold to ask you something. What royal family do you adorn, sir? What country is grieving at your absence? Why does a gentleman so delicately bred submit to the weary journey into our pious grove?

Shakuntala (*aside*)   Be brave, my heart. Anusuya speaks your very thoughts.

King (*aside*)   Shall I tell at once who I am, or conceal it? (*He reflects.*) This will do. (*Aloud.*) I am a student of Scripture. It is my duty to see justice done in the cities of the king. And I have come to this hermitage on a tour of inspection.

Anusuya   Then we of the hermitage have some one to take care of us. (**Shakuntala** *shows embarrassment.*)

The Two Friends (*observing the demeanour of the pair. Aside to* **Shakuntala**) Oh, Shakuntala! If only Father were here to-day.

Shakuntala   What would he do?

The Two Friends   He would make our distinguished guest happy, if it took his most precious treasure.

Shakuntala (*feigning anger*)   Go away! You mean something. I'll not listen to you.

King   I too would like to ask a question about your friend.

The Two Friends   Sir, your request is a favour to us.

King Father Kanva lives a lifelong hermit. Yet you say that your friend is his daughter. How can that be?

Anusuya Listen, sir. There is a majestic royal sage named Kaushika –

King Ah, yes. The famous Kaushika.

Anusuya Know, then, that he is the source of our friend's being. But Father Kanva is her real father, because he took care of her when she was abandoned.

King You waken my curiosity with the word 'abandoned'. May I hear the whole story?

Anusuya Listen, sir. Many years ago, that royal sage was leading a life of stern austerities, and the gods, becoming strangely jealous, sent the nymph Menaka to disturb his devotions.

King Yes, the gods feel this jealousy toward the austerities of others. And then –

Anusuya Then in the lovely spring-time he saw her intoxicating beauty – (*She stops in embarrassment.*)

King The rest is plain. Surely, she is the daughter of the nymph.

Anusuya Yes.

King It is as it should be.
 To beauty such as this
 No woman could give birth;
 The quivering lightning flash
 Is not a child of earth.

Shakuntala *hangs her head in confusion.*

King (*to himself*) Ah, my wishes become hopes.

Priyamvada (*looking with a smile at* **Shakuntala**) Sir, it seems as if you had more to say. (**Shakuntala** *threatens her friend with her finger.*)

King You are right. Your pious life interests me, and I have another question.

Priyamvada Do not hesitate. We hermit people stand ready to answer all demands.

King My question is this:
 Does she, till marriage only, keep her vow
 As hermit-maid, that shames the ways of love?
 Or must her soft eyes ever see, as now,
 Soft eyes of friendly deer in peaceful grove?

Priyamvada Sir, we are under bonds to lead a life of virtue. But it is her father's wish to give her to a suitable lover.

King (*joyfully to himself*)
 O heart, your wish is won!
 All doubt at last is done;
 The thing you feared as fire,
 Is the jewel of your desire.

Shakuntala (*pettishly*)   Anusuya, I'm going.

Anusuya   What for?

Shakuntala   I am going to tell Mother Gautami that Priyamvada is talking nonsense. (*She rises.*)

Anusuya   My dear, we hermit people cannot neglect to entertain a distinguished guest, and go wandering about.

Shakuntala *starts to walk away without answering.*

King (*aside*)   She is going! (*He starts up as if to detain her, then checks his desires.*) A thought is as vivid as an act, to a lover.
   Though nurture, conquering nature, holds
   Me back, it seems
   As had I started and returned
   In waking dreams.

Priyamvada (*approaching* **Shakuntala**)   You dear, peevish girl! You mustn't go.

Shakuntala (*turns with a frown*)   Why not?

Priyamvada   You owe me the watering of two trees. You can go when you have paid your debt. (*She forces her to come back.*)

King   It is plain that she is already wearied by watering the trees. See!
   Her shoulders droop; her palms are reddened yet;
   Quick breaths are struggling in her bosom fair;
   The blossom o'er her ear hangs limply wet;
   One hand restrains the loose, dishevelled hair.
I therefore remit her debt. (*He gives the* **Two Friends** *a ring. They take it, read the name engraved on it, and look at each other.*)

King   Make no mistake. This is a present – from the king.

Priyamvada   Then, sir, you ought not to part with it. Your word is enough to remit the debt.

Anusuya   Well, Shakuntala, you are set free by this kind gentleman – or rather, by the king himself. Where are you going now?

Shakuntala (*to herself*)   I would never leave him if I could help myself.

Priyamvada   Why don't you go now?

Shakuntala   I am not *your* servant any longer. I will go when I like.

King (*looking at* **Shakuntala**. *To himself*)   Does she feel toward me as I do toward her? At least, there is ground for hope.
   Although she does not speak to me,
   She listens while I speak;
   Her eyes turn not to see my face,
   But nothing else they seek.

A Voice Behind the Scenes   Hermits! Hermits! Prepare to defend the creatures in our pious grove. King Dushyanta is hunting in the neighbourhood.
   The dust his horses' hoofs have raised,
   Red as the evening sky,
   Falls like a locust-swarm on boughs
   Where hanging garments dry.

King (*aside*)   Alas! My soldiers are disturbing the pious grove in their search for me.

A Voice Behind the Scenes   Hermits! Hermits! Here is an elephant who is terrifying old men, women, and children.
   One tusk is splintered by a cruel blow
   Against a blocking tree; his gait is slow,
   For countless fettering vines impede and cling;
   He puts the deer to flight; some evil thing
   He seems, that comes our peaceful life to mar,
   Fleeing in terror from the royal car.

The girls listen and rise anxiously.

King   I have offended sadly against the hermits. I must go back.

The Two Friends   Your Honour, we are frightened by this alarm of the elephant. Permit us to return to the cottage.

Anusuya (*to* **Shakuntala**)   Shakuntala dear, Mother Gautami will be anxious. We must hurry and find her.

Shakuntala (*feigning lameness*)   Oh, oh! I can hardly walk.

King   You must go very slowly. And I will take pains that the hermitage is not disturbed.

The Two Friends   Your honour, we feel as if we knew you very well. Pray pardon our shortcomings as hostesses. May we ask you to seek better entertainment from us another time?

King   You are too modest. I feel honoured by the mere sight of you.

Shakuntala   Anusuya, my foot is cut on a sharp blade of grass, and my dress is caught on an amaranth twig. Wait for me while I loosen it. (*She casts a lingering glance at the* **King**, *and goes out with her* **Two Friends**.)

King (*sighing*)   They are gone. And I must go. The sight of Shakuntala has made me dread the return to the city. I will make my men camp at a distance from the pious grove. But I cannot turn my own thoughts from Shakuntala.
   It is my body leaves my love, not I;
   My body moves away, but not my mind;
   For back to her my struggling fancies fly
   Like silken banners borne against the wind.

Exit.

Act II The Secret

Enter the **Clown**.

Clown (*sighing*) Damn! Damn! Damn! I'm tired of being friends with this sporting king. 'There's a deer!' he shouts, 'There's a boar!' And off he chases on a summer noon through woods where shade is few and far between. We drink hot, stinking water from the mountain streams, flavoured with leaves – nasty! At odd times we get a little tepid meat to eat. And the horses and the elephants make such a noise that I can't even be comfortable at night. Then the hunters and the bird-chasers – damn 'em – wake me up bright and early. They do make an ear-splitting rumpus when they start for the woods. But even that isn't the whole misery. There's a new pimple growing on the old boil. He left us behind and went hunting a deer. And there in a hermitage they say he found – oh, dear! oh, dear! he found a hermit-girl named Shakuntala. Since then he hasn't a thought of going back to town. I lay awake all night, thinking about it. What can I do? Well, I'll see my friend when he is dressed and beautified. (*He walks and looks about.*) Hello! Here he comes, with his bow in his hand, and his girl in his heart. He is wearing a wreath of wild flowers! I'll pretend to be all knocked up. Perhaps I can get a rest that way. (*He stands, leaning on his staff. Enter the* **King**, *as described.*)

King (*to himself*)
  Although my darling is not lightly won,
  She seemed to love me, and my hopes are bright;
  Though love be balked ere joy be well begun,
  A common longing is itself delight.
(*Smiling.*) Thus does a lover deceive himself. He judges his love's feelings by his own desires.
  Her glance was loving – but 'twas not for me;
  Her step was slow – 'twas grace, not coquetry;
  Her speech was short – to her detaining friend.
  In things like these love reads a selfish end!

Clown (*standing as before*) Well, king, I can't move my hand. I can only greet you with my voice.

King (*looking and smiling*) What makes you lame?

Clown Good! You hit a man in the eye, and then ask him why the tears come.

King I do not understand you. Speak plainly.

Clown When a reed bends over like a hunchback, do you blame the reed or the river-current?

King The river-current, of course.

Clown And you are to blame for my troubles.

King How so?

Clown It's a fine thing for you to neglect your royal duties and such a sure job – to live in the woods! What's the good of talking? Here I am, a Brahman, and my joints are all shaken up by this eternal running after wild animals, so that I can't move. Please be good to me. Let us have a rest for just one day.

King (*to himself*) He says this. And I too, when I remember Kanva's daughter, have little desire for the chase. For
  The bow is strung, its arrow near;
  And yet I cannot bend
  That bow against the fawns who share
  Soft glances with their friend.

Clown (*observing the* **King**) He means more than he says. I might as well weep in the woods.

King (*smiling*) What more could I mean? I have been thinking that I ought to take my friend's advice.

Clown (*cheerfully*) Long life to you, then. (*He unstiffens.*)

King Wait. Hear me out.

Clown Well, sir?

King When you are rested, you must be my companion in another task – an easy one.

Clown Crushing a few sweetmeats?

King I will tell you presently.

Clown Pray command my leisure.

King Who stands without? (*Enter the* **Door-Keeper**.)

Door-Keeper I await your Majesty's commands.

King Raivataka, summon the general.

Door-Keeper Yes, your Majesty. (*He goes out, then returns with the* **General**.) Follow me, sir. There is his Majesty, listening to our conversation. Draw near, sir.

General (*observing the* **King**, *to himself*) Hunting is declared to be a sin, yet it brings nothing but good to the king. See!
  He does not heed the cruel sting
  Of his recoiling, twanging string;
  The mid-day sun, the dripping sweat
  Affect him not, nor make him fret;
  His form, though sinewy and spare,
  Is most symmetrically fair;
  No mountain-elephant could be
  More filled with vital strength than he.
(*He approaches.*) Victory to your Majesty! The forest is full of deer-tracks, and beasts of prey cannot be far off. What better occupation could we have?

King Bhadrasena, my enthusiasm is broken. Madhavya has been preaching against hunting.

General (*aside to the* **Clown**) Stick to it, friend Madhavya. I will humour the king a moment. (*Aloud.*) Your Majesty, he is a chattering idiot. Your Majesty may judge by his own case whether hunting is an evil. Consider:

> The hunter's form grows sinewy, strong, and light;
> He learns, from beasts of prey, how wrath and fright
> Affect the mind; his skill he loves to measure
> With moving targets. 'Tis life's chiefest pleasure.

Clown (*angrily*) Get out! Get out with your strenuous life! The king has come to his senses. But you, you son of a slave-wench, can go chasing from forest to forest, till you fall into the jaws of some old bear that is looking for a deer or a jackal.

King Bhadrasena, I cannot take your advice, because I am in the vicinity of a hermitage. So for to-day

> The hornèd buffalo may shake
> The turbid water of the lake;
> Shade-seeking deer may chew the cud,
> Boars trample swamp-grass in the mud;
> The bow I bend in hunting, may
> Enjoy a listless holiday.

General Yes, your Majesty.

King Send back the archers who have gone ahead. And forbid the soldiers to vex the hermitage, or even to approach it. Remember:

> There lurks a hidden fire in each
> Religious hermit-bower;
> Cool sun-stones kindle if assailed
> By any foreign power.

General Yes, your Majesty.

Clown Now will you get out with your strenuous life? (*Exit* **General**.)

King (*to his attendants*) Lay aside your hunting dress. And you, Raivataka, return to your post of duty.

Raivataka Yes, your Majesty. (*Exit.*)

Clown You have got rid of the vermin. Now be seated on this flat stone, over which the trees spread their canopy of shade. I can't sit down till you do.

King Lead the way.

Clown Follow me. (*They walk about and sit down.*)

King Friend Madhavya, you do not know what vision is. You have not seen the fairest of all objects.

Clown I see you, right in front of me.

King Yes, every one thinks himself beautiful. But I was speaking of Shakuntala, the ornament of the hermitage.

Clown (*to himself*) I mustn't add fuel to the flame. (*Aloud.*) But you can't have her because she is a hermit-girl. What is the use of seeing her?

King Fool!
    And is it selfish longing then,
    That draws our souls on high
    Through eyes that have forgot to wink,
    As the new moon climbs the sky?
Besides, Dushyanta's thoughts dwell on no forbidden object.

Clown Well, tell me about her.

King Sprung from a nymph of heaven
    Wanton and gay,
    Who spurned the blessing given,
    Going her way;
    By the stern hermit taken
    In her most need:
    So fell the blossom shaken,
    Flower on a weed.

Clown (*laughing*) You are like a man who gets tired of good dates and longs for sour tamarind. All the pearls of the palace are yours, and you want this girl!

King My friend, you have not seen her, or you could not talk so.

Clown She must be charming if she surprises *you*.

King Oh, my friend, she needs not many words.
    She is God's vision, of pure thought
    Composed in His creative mind;
    His reveries of beauty wrought
    The peerless pearl of womankind.
    So plays my fancy when I see
    How great is God, how lovely she.

Clown How the women must hate her!

King This too is in my thought.
    She seems a flower whose fragrance none has tasted,
    A gem uncut by workman's tool,
    A branch no desecrating hands have wasted,
    Fresh honey, beautifully cool.

    No man on earth deserves to taste her beauty,
    Her blameless loveliness and worth,
    Unless he has fulfilled man's perfect duty –
    And is there such a one on earth?

Clown Marry her quick, then, before the poor girl falls into the hands of some oily-headed hermit.

King She is dependent on her father, and he is not here.

Clown But how does she feel toward you?

King My friend, hermit-girls are by their very nature timid. And yet
When I was near, she could not look at me;
She smiled – but not to me – and half denied it;
She would not show her love for modesty,
Yet did not try so very hard to hide it.

Clown Did you want her to climb into your lap the first time she saw you?

King But when she went away with her friends, she almost showed that she loved me.
When she had hardly left my side,
'I cannot walk', the maiden cried,
And turned her face, and feigned to free
The dress not caught upon the tree.

Clown She has given you some memories to chew on. I suppose that is why you are so in love with the pious grove.

King My friend, think of some pretext under which we may return to the hermitage.

Clown What pretext do you need? Aren't you the king?

King What of that?

Clown Collect the taxes on the hermits' rice.

King Fool! It is a very different tax which these hermits pay – one that outweighs heaps of gems.
The wealth we take from common men,
Wastes while we cherish;
These share with us such holiness
As ne'er can perish.

Voices Behind the Scenes Ah, we have found him.

King (*listening*) The voices are grave and tranquil. These must be hermits. (*Enter the* **Door-Keeper**.)

Door-Keeper Victory, O King. There are two hermit-youths at the gate.

King Bid them enter at once.

Door-Keeper Yes, your Majesty. (*He goes out, then returns with the* **Youths**.) Follow me.

First Youth (*looking at the* **King**) A majestic presence, yet it inspires confidence. Nor is this wonderful in a king who is half a saint. For to him
The splendid palace serves as hermitage;
His royal government, courageous, sage,
Adds daily to his merit; it is given

> To him to win applause from choirs of heaven
> Whose anthems to his glory rise and swell,
> Proclaiming him a king, and saint as well.

Second Youth My friend, is this Dushyanta, friend of Indra?

First Youth It is.

Second Youth
> Nor is it wonderful that one whose arm
> Might bolt a city gate, should keep from harm
> The whole broad earth dark-belted by the sea;
> For when the gods in heaven with demons fight,
> Dushyanta's bow and Indra's weapon bright
> Are their reliance for the victory.

The Two Youths (*approaching*) Victory, O King!

King (*rising*) I salute you.

The Two Youths All hail! (*They offer fruit.*)

King (*receiving it and bowing low*) May I know the reason of your coming?

The Two Youths The hermits have learned that you are here, and they request –

King They command rather.

The Two Youths The powers of evil disturb our pious life in the absence of the hermit-father. We therefore ask that you will remain a few nights with your charioteer to protect the hermitage.

King I shall be most happy to do so.

Clown (*to the* **King**) You rather seem to like being collared this way.

King Raivataka, tell my charioteer to drive up, and to bring the bow and arrows.

Raivataka Yes, your Majesty. (*Exit*)

The Two Youths
> Thou art a worthy scion of
> The kings who ruled our nation
> And found, defending those in need,
> Their truest consecration.

King Pray go before. And I will follow straightway.

The Two Youths Victory, O King! (*Exeunt.*)

King Madhavya, have you no curiosity to see Shakuntala?

Clown I *did* have an unending curiosity, but this talk about the powers of evil has put an end to it.

King Do not fear. You will be with me.

Clown I'll stick close to your chariot-wheel. (*Enter the* **Door-Keeper**.)

Door-Keeper Your Majesty, the chariot is ready, and awaits your departure to victory. But one Karabhaka has come from the city, a messenger from the queen-mother.

King (*respectfully*) Sent by my mother?

Door-Keeper Yes.

King Let him enter.

Door-Keeper (*goes out and returns with* **Karabhaka**) Karabhaka, here is his Majesty. You may draw near.

Karabhaka (*approaching and bowing low*) Victory to your Majesty. The queen-mother sends her commands –

King What are her commands?

Karabhaka She plans to end a fasting ceremony on the fourth day from to-day. And on that occasion her dear son must not fail to wait upon her.

King On the one side is my duty to the hermits, on the other my mother's command. Neither may be disregarded. What is to be done?

Clown (*laughing*) Stay half-way between, like Trishanku.

King In truth, I am perplexed.
    Two inconsistent duties sever
    My mind with cruel shock,
    As when the current of a river
    Is split upon a rock.
(*He reflects.*) My friend, the queen-mother has always felt toward you as toward a son. Do you return, tell her what duty keeps me here, and yourself perform the offices of a son.

Clown You don't think I am afraid of the devils?

King (*smiling*) O mighty Brahman, who could suspect it?

Clown But I want to travel like a prince.

King I will send all the soldiers with you, for the pious grove must not be disturbed.

Clown (*strutting*) Aha! Look at the heir-apparent!

King (*to himself*) The fellow is a chatterbox. He might betray my longing to the ladies of the palace. Good, then! (*He takes the* **Clown** *by the hand. Aloud.*) Friend Madhavya, my reverence for the hermits draws me to the hermitage. Do not think that I am really in love with the hermit-girl. Just think:
    A king, and a girl of the calm hermit-grove,
    Bred with the fawns, and a stranger to love!
    Then do not imagine a serious quest;
    The light words I uttered were spoken in jest.

Clown Oh, I understand that well enough.

Exeunt ambo.

Act III The Love-Making

Enter a **Pupil**, *with sacred grass for the sacrifice.*

Pupil (*with meditative astonishment*)   How great is the power of King Dushyanta! Since his arrival our rites have been undisturbed.

> He does not need to bend the bow;
> For every evil thing,
> Awaiting not the arrow, flees
> From the twanging of the string.

Well, I will take this sacred grass to the priests, to strew the altar. (*He walks and looks about, then speaks to some one not visible.*) Priyamvada, for whom are you carrying this cuscus-salve and the fibrous lotus-leaves? (*He listens.*) What do you say? That Shakuntala has become seriously ill from the heat, and that these things are to relieve her suffering? Give her the best of care, Priyamvada. She is the very life of the hermit-father. And I will give Gautami the holy water for her. (*Exit. Enter the lovelorn* **King**.)

King (*with a meditative sigh*).

> I know that stern religion's power
> Keeps guardian watch my maiden o'er;
> Yet all my heart flows straight to her
> Like water to the valley-floor.

Oh, mighty Love, thine arrows are made of flowers. How can they be so sharp? (*He recalls something.*) Ah, I understand.

> Shiva's devouring wrath still burns in thee,
> As burns the eternal fire beneath the sea;
> Else how couldst thou, thyself long since consumed,
> Kindle the fire that flames so ruthlessly?

Indeed, the moon and thou inspire confidence, only to deceive the host of lovers.

> Thy shafts are blossoms; coolness streams
> From moon-rays: thus the poets sing;
> But to the lovelorn, falsehood seems
> To lurk in such imagining;
> The moon darts fire from frosty beams;
> Thy flowery arrows cut and sting.

And yet

> If Love will trouble her
> Whose great eyes madden me,
> I greet him unafraid,
> Though wounded ceaselessly.

O mighty god, wilt thou not show me mercy after such reproaches?

> With tenderness unending
> I cherished thee when small,
> In vain – thy bow is bending;

On me thine arrows fall.
My care for thee to such a plight
Has brought me; and it serves me right.

I have driven off the powers of evil, and the hermits have dismissed me. Where shall I go now to rest from my weariness? (*He sighs.*) There is no rest for me except in seeing her whom I love. (*He looks up.*) She usually spends these hours of midday heat with her friends on the vine-wreathed banks of the Malini. I will go there. (*He walks and looks about.*) I believe the slender maiden has just passed through this corridor of young trees. For

The stems from which she gathered flowers
Are still unhealed;
The sap where twigs were broken off
Is uncongealed.

(*He feels a breeze stirring.*) This is a pleasant spot, with the wind among the trees.

Limbs that love's fever seizes,
Their fervent welcome pay
To lotus-fragrant breezes
That bear the river-spray.

(*He studies the ground.*) Ah, Shakuntala must be in this reedy bower. For

In white sand at the door
Fresh footprints appear,
The toe lightly outlined,
The heel deep and clear.

I will hide among the branches, and see what happens. (*He does so. Joyfully.*) Ah, my eyes have found their heaven. Here is the darling of my thoughts, lying upon a flower-strewn bench of stone, and attended by her two friends. I will hear what they say to each other. (*He stands gazing. Enter* **Shakuntala** *with her* **Two Friends**.)

The Two Friends (*fanning her*)   Do you feel better, dear, when we fan you with these lotus-leaves?

Shakuntala (*wearily*)   Oh, are you fanning me, my dear girls? (*The* **Two Friends** *look sorrowfully at each other.*)

King   She is seriously ill. (*Doubtfully.*) Is it the heat, or is it as I hope? (*Decidedly.*) It *must* be so.

With salve upon her breast,
With loosened lotus-chain,
My darling, sore oppressed,
Is lovely in her pain.

Though love and summer heat
May work an equal woe,
No maiden seems so sweet
When summer lays her low.

Priyamvada (*aside to* **Anusuya**)   Anusuya, since she first saw the good king, she has been greatly troubled. I do not believe her fever has any other cause.

Anusuya I suspect you are right. I am going to ask her. My dear, I must ask you something. You are in a high fever.

King It is too true.
    Her lotus-chains that were as white
    As moonbeams shining in the night,
    Betray the fever's awful pain,
    And fading, show a darker stain.

Shakuntala (*half rising*) Well, say whatever you like.

Anusuya Shakuntala dear, you have not told us what is going on in your mind. But I have heard old, romantic stories, and I can't help thinking that you are in a state like that of a lady in love. Please tell us what hurts you. We have to understand the disease before we can even try to cure it.

King Anusuya expresses my own thoughts.

Shakuntala It hurts me terribly. I can't tell you all at once.

Priyamvada Anusuya is right, dear. Why do you hide your trouble? You are wasting away every day. You are nothing but a beautiful shadow.

King Priyamvada is right. See!
    Her cheeks grow thin; her breast and shoulders fail;
    Her waist is weary and her face is pale:
    She fades for love; oh, pitifully sweet!
    As vine-leaves wither in the scorching heat.

Shakuntala (*sighing*) I could not tell any one else. But I shall be a burden to you.

The Two Friends That is why we insist on knowing, dear. Grief must be shared to be endured.

King
    To friends who share her joy and grief
    She tells what sorrow laid her here;
    She turned to look her love again
    When first I saw her – yet I fear!

Shakuntala Ever since I saw the good king who protects the pious grove – (*She stops and fidgets.*)

The Two Friends Go on, dear.

Shakuntala I love him, and it makes me feel like this.

The Two Friends Good, good! You have found a lover worthy of your devotion. But of course, a great river always runs into the sea.

King (*joyfully*) I have heard what I longed to hear.
    'Twas love that caused the burning pain;
    'Tis love that eases it again;
    As when, upon a sultry day,
    Rain breaks, and washes grief away.

Shakuntala Then, if you think best, make the good king take pity upon me. If not, remember that I was.

King Her words end all doubt.

Priyamvada (*aside to* **Anusuya**) Anusuya, she is far gone in love and cannot endure any delay.

Anusuya Priyamvada, can you think of any scheme by which we could carry out her wishes quickly and secretly?

Priyamvada We must plan about the 'secretly'. The 'quickly' is not hard.

Anusuya How so?

Priyamvada Why, the good king shows his love for her in his tender glances, and he has been wasting away, as if he were losing sleep.

King It is quite true.
   The hot tears, flowing down my cheek
   All night on my supporting arm
   And on its golden bracelet, seek
   To stain the gems and do them harm.

   The bracelet slipping o'er the scars
   Upon the wasted arm, that show
   My deeds in hunting and in wars,
   All night is moving to and fro.

Priyamvada (*reflecting*) Well, she must write him a love-letter. And I will hide it in a bunch of flowers and see that it gets into the king's hand as if it were a relic of the sacrifice.

Anusuya It is a pretty plan, dear, and it pleases me. What does Shakuntala say?

Shakuntala I suppose I must obey orders.

Priyamvada Then compose a pretty little love-song, with a hint of yourself in it.

Shakuntala I'll try. But my heart trembles, for fear he will despise me.

King
   Here stands the eager lover, and you pale
   For fear lest he disdain a love so kind:
   The seeker may find fortune, or may fail;
   But how could fortune, seeking, fail to find?
And again:
   The ardent lover comes, and yet you fear
   Lest he disdain love's tribute, were it brought,
   The hope of which has led his footsteps here –
   Pearls need not seek, for they themselves are sought.

The Two Friends You are too modest about your own charms. Would anybody put up a parasol to keep off the soothing autumn moonlight?

Shakuntala (*smiling*)   I suppose I shall have to obey orders. (*She meditates.*)

King   It is only natural that I should forget to wink when I see my darling. For
One clinging eyebrow lifted,
As fitting words she seeks,
Her face reveals her passion
For me in glowing cheeks.

Shakuntala   Well, I have thought out a little song. But I haven't anything to write with.

Priyamvada   Here is a lotus-leaf, glossy as a parrot's breast. You can cut the letters in it with your nails.

Shakuntala   Now listen, and tell me whether it makes sense.

The Two Friends   Please.

Shakuntala (*reads*)
I know not if I read your heart aright;
Why, pitiless, do you distress me so?
I only know that longing day and night
Tosses my restless body to and fro,
That yearns for you, the source of all its woe.

King (*advancing*)
Though Love torments you, slender maid,
Yet he consumes me quite,
As daylight shuts night-blooming flowers
And slays the moon outright.

The Two Friends (*perceive the* **King** *and rise joyfully*)   Welcome to the wish that is fulfilled without delay. (**Shakuntala** *tries to rise.*)

King
Do not try to rise, beautiful Shakuntala.
Your limbs from which the strength is fled,
That crush the blossoms of your bed
And bruise the lotus-leaves, may be
Pardoned a breach of courtesy.

Shakuntala (*sadly to herself*)   Oh, my heart, you were so impatient, and now you find no answer to make.

Anusuya   Your Majesty, pray do this stone bench the honour of sitting upon it. (**Shakuntala** *edges away.*)

King (*seating himself*)   Priyamvada, I trust your friend's illness is not dangerous.

Priyamvada (*smiling*)   A remedy is being applied and it will soon be better. It is plain, sir, that you and she love each other. But I love her too, and I must say something over again.

King   Pray do not hesitate. It always causes pain in the end, to leave unsaid what one longs to say.

Priyamvada   Then listen, sir.

King   I am all attention.

Priyamvada   It is the king's duty to save hermit-folk from all suffering. Is not that good Scripture?

King   There is no text more urgent.

Priyamvada   Well, our friend has been brought to this sad state by her love for you. Will you not take pity on her and save her life?

King   We cherish the same desire. I feel it a great honour.

Shakuntala (*with a jealous smile*)   Oh, don't detain the good king. He is separated from the court ladies, and he is anxious to go back to them.

King
Bewitching eyes that found my heart,
You surely see
It could no longer live apart,
Nor faithless be.
I bear Love's arrows as I can;
Wound not with doubt a wounded man.

Anusuya   But, your Majesty, we hear that kings have many favourites. You must act in such a way that our friend may not become a cause of grief to her family.

King   What more can I say?
Though many queens divide my court,
But two support the throne;
Your friend will find a rival in
The sea-girt earth alone.

The Two Friends   We are content. (**Shakuntala** *betrays her joy.*)

Priyamvada (*aside to* **Anusuya**)   Look, Anusuya! See how the dear girl's life is coming back moment by moment – just like a peahen in summer when the first rainy breezes come.

Shakuntala   You must please ask the king's pardon for the rude things we said when we were talking together.

The Two Friends (*smiling*)   Anybody who says it was rude, may ask his pardon. Nobody else feels guilty.

Shakuntala   Your Majesty, pray forgive what we said when we did not know that you were present. I am afraid that we say a great many things behind a person's back.

King (*smiling*)
Your fault is pardoned if I may
Relieve my weariness

By sitting on the flower-strewn couch
Your fevered members press.

Priyamvada   But that will not be enough to satisfy him.

Shakuntala (*feigning anger*)   Stop! You are a rude girl. You make fun of me when I am in this condition.

Anusuya (*looking out of the arbour*)   Priyamvada, there is a little fawn, looking all about him. He has probably lost his mother and is trying to find her. I am going to help him.

Priyamvada   He is a frisky little fellow. You can't catch him alone. I'll go with you. (*They start to go.*)

Shakuntala   I will not let you go and leave me alone.

The Two Friends (*smiling*)   You alone, when the king of the world is with you! (*Exeunt.*)

Shakuntala   Are my friends gone?

King (*looking about*)   Do not be anxious, beautiful Shakuntala. Have you not a humble servant here, to take the place of your friends? Then tell me:
Shall I employ the moistened lotus-leaf
To fan away your weariness and grief?
Or take your lily feet upon my knee
And rub them till you rest more easily?

Shakuntala   I will not offend against those to whom I owe honour. (*She rises weakly and starts to walk away.*)

King (*detaining her*)   The day is still hot, beautiful Shakuntala, and you are feverish.
Leave not the blossom-dotted couch
To wander in the midday heat,
With lotus-petals on your breast,
With fevered limbs and stumbling feet.

He lays his hand upon her.

Shakuntala   Oh, don't! Don't! For I am not mistress of myself. Yet what can I do now? I had no one to help me but my friends.

King   I am rebuked.

Shakuntala   I was not thinking of your Majesty. I was accusing fate.

King   Why accuse a fate that brings what you desire?

Shakuntala   Why not accuse a fate that robs me of self-control and tempts me with the virtues of another?

King (*to himself*)
Though deeply longing, maids are coy
And bid their wooers wait;

Though eager for united joy
In love, they hesitate.

Love cannot torture them, nor move
Their hearts to sudden mating;
Perhaps they even torture love
By their procrastinating.

Shakuntala *moves away.*

King   Why should I not have my way? (*He approaches and seizes her dress.*)

Shakuntala   Oh, sir! Be a gentleman. There are hermits wandering about.

King   Do not fear your family, beautiful Shakuntala. Father Kanva knows the holy law. He will not regret it.
   For many a hermit maiden who
   By simple, voluntary rite
   Dispensed with priest and witness, yet
   Found favour in her father's sight.
(*He looks about.*) Ah, I have come into the open air. (*He leaves* **Shakuntala** *and retraces his steps.*)

Shakuntala (*takes a step, then turns with an eager gesture*)   O King, I cannot do as you would have me. You hardly know me after this short talk. But oh, do not forget me.

King
   When evening comes, the shadow of the tree
   Is cast far forward, yet does not depart;
   Even so, belovèd, wheresoe'er you be,
   The thought of you can never leave my heart.

Shakuntala (*takes a few steps. To herself*)   Oh, oh! When I hear him speak so, my feet will not move away. I will hide in this amaranth hedge and see how long his love lasts. (*She hides and waits.*)

King   Oh, my belovèd, my love for you is my whole life, yet you leave me and go away without a thought.
   Your body, soft as siris-flowers,
   Engages passion's utmost powers;
   How comes it that your heart is hard
   As stalks that siris-blossoms guard?

Shakuntala   When I hear this, I have no power to go.

King   What have I to do here, where she is not? (*He gazes on the ground.*) Ah, I cannot go.
   The perfumed lotus-chain
   That once was worn by her
   Fetters and keeps my heart
   A hopeless prisoner. (*He lifts it reverently.*)

Shakuntala (*looking at her arm*)   Why, I was so weak and ill that when the lotus-bracelet fell off, I did not even notice it.

King (*laying the lotus-bracelet on his heart*)   Ah!
   Once, dear, on your sweet arm it lay,
   And on my heart shall ever stay;
   Though you disdain to give me joy,
   I find it in a lifeless toy.

Shakuntala   I cannot hold back after that. I will use the bracelet as an excuse for my coming. (*She approaches.*)

King (*seeing her. Joyfully*)   The queen of my life! As soon as I complained, fate proved kind to me.
   No sooner did the thirsty bird
   With parching throat complain,
   Than forming clouds in heaven stirred
   And sent the streaming rain.

Shakuntala (*standing before the* **King**)   When I was going away, sir, I remembered that this lotus-bracelet had fallen from my arm, and I have come back for it. My heart seemed to tell me that you had taken it. Please give it back, or you will betray me, and yourself too, to the hermits.

King   I will restore it on one condition.

Shakuntala   What condition?

King   That I may myself place it where it belongs.

Shakuntala (*to herself*)   What can I do? (*She approaches.*)

King   Let us sit on this stone bench. (*They walk to the bench and sit down.*)

King (*taking* **Shakuntala**'s *hand*)   Ah!
   When Shiva's anger burned the tree
   Of love in quenchless fire,
   Did heavenly fate preserve a shoot
   To deck my heart's desire?

Shakuntala (*feeling his touch*)   Hasten, my dear, hasten.

King (*joyfully to himself*)   Now I am content. She speaks as a wife to her husband. (*Aloud.*) Beautiful Shakuntala, the clasp of the bracelet is not very firm. May I fasten it in another way?

Shakuntala (*smiling*)   If you like.

King (*artfully delaying before he fastens it*)   See, my beautiful girl!
   The lotus-chain is dazzling white
   As is the slender moon at night.
   Perhaps it was the moon on high
   That joined her horns and left the sky,

Believing that your lovely arm
Would, more than heaven, enhance her charm.

Shakuntala   I cannot see it. The pollen from the lotus over my ear has blown into my eye.

King (*smiling*)   Will you permit me to blow it away?

Shakuntala   I should not like to be an object of pity. But why should I not trust you?

King   Do not have such thoughts. A new servant does not transgress orders.

Shakuntala   It is this exaggerated courtesy that frightens me.

King (*to himself*)   I shall not break the bonds of this sweet servitude. (*He starts to raise her face to his.* **Shakuntala** *resists a little, then is passive.*)

King   Oh, my bewitching girl, have no fear of me.

Shakuntala *darts a glance at him, then looks down. The* **King** *raises her face. Aside.*

King   Her sweetly trembling lip
With virgin invitation
Provokes my soul to sip
Delighted fascination.

Shakuntala   You seem slow, dear, in fulfilling your promise.

King   The lotus over your ear is so near your eye, and so like it, that I was confused. (*He gently blows her eye.*)

Shakuntala   Thank you. I can see quite well now. But I am ashamed not to make any return for your kindness.

King   What more could I ask?
It ought to be enough for me
To hover round your fragrant face;
Is not the lotus-haunting bee
Content with perfume and with grace?

Shakuntala   But what does he do if he is not content?

King   This! This! (*He draws her face to his.*)

A Voice Behind the Scenes   O sheldrake bride, bid your mate farewell. The night is come.

Shakuntala (*listening excitedly*)   Oh, my dear, this is Mother Gautami, come to inquire about me. Please hide among the branches.

The **King** *conceals himself. Enter* **Gautami**, *with a bowl in her hand.*

Gautami   Here is the holy water, my child. (*She sees* **Shakuntala** *and helps her to rise.*) So ill, and all alone here with the gods?

Shakuntala   It was just a moment ago that Priyamvada and Anusuya went down to the river.

Gautami (*sprinkling* **Shakuntala** *with the holy water*) May you live long and happy, my child. Has the fever gone down? (*She touches her.*)

Shakuntala There is a difference, mother.

Gautami The sun is setting. Come, let us go to the cottage.

Shakuntala (*weakly rising. To herself*) Oh, my heart, you delayed when your desire came of itself. Now see what you have done. (*She takes a step, then turns around. Aloud.*) O bower that took away my pain, I bid you farewell until another blissful hour. (*Exeunt* **Shakuntala** *and* **Gautami**.)

King (*advancing with a sigh.*) The path to happiness is strewn with obstacles.
   Her face, adorned with soft eye-lashes,
   Adorable with trembling flashes
   Of half-denial, in memory lingers;
   The sweet lips guarded by her fingers,
   The head that drooped upon her shoulder –
   Why was I not a little bolder?
Where shall I go now? Let me stay a moment in this bower where my belovèd lay. (*He looks about.*)
   The flower-strewn bed whereon her body tossed;
   The bracelet, fallen from her arm and lost;
   The dear love-missive, in the lotus-leaf
   Cut by her nails: assuage my absent grief
   And occupy my eyes – I have no power,
   Though she is gone, to leave the reedy bower.
(*He reflects.*) Alas! I did wrong to delay when I had found my love. So now
   If she will grant me but one other meeting,
   I'll not delay; for happiness is fleeting;
   So plans my foolish, self-defeated heart;
   But when she comes, I play the coward's part.

A Voice Behind the Scenes O King!
   The flames rise heavenward from the evening altar;
   And round the sacrifices, blazing high,
   Flesh-eating demons stalk, like red cloud-masses,
   And cast colossal shadows on the sky.

King (*listens. Resolutely*) Have no fear, hermits. I am here.

Exit.

Act IV Shakuntala's Departure

Scene I

Enter the **Two Friends**, *gathering flowers.*

Anusuya Priyamvada, dear Shakuntala has been properly married by the voluntary ceremony and she has a husband worthy of her. And yet I am not quite satisfied.

Priyamvada Why not?

Anusuya The sacrifice is over and the good king was dismissed to-day by the hermits. He has gone back to the city and there he is surrounded by hundreds of court ladies. I wonder whether he will remember poor Shakuntala or not.

Priyamvada You need not be anxious about that. Such handsome men are sure to be good. But there is something else to think about. I don't know what Father will have to say when he comes back from his pilgrimage and hears about it.

Anusuya I believe that he will be pleased.

Priyamvada Why?

Anusuya Why not? You know he wanted to give his daughter to a lover worthy of her. If fate brings this about of itself, why shouldn't Father be happy?

Priyamvada I suppose you are right. (*She looks at her flower-basket.*) My dear, we have gathered flowers enough for the sacrifice.

Anusuya But we must make an offering to the gods that watch over Shakuntala's marriage. We had better gather more.

Priyamvada Very well. (*They do so.*)

A Voice Behind the Scenes Who will bid me welcome?

Anusuya (*listening*) My dear, it sounds like a guest announcing himself.

Priyamvada Well, Shakuntala is near the cottage. (*Reflecting.*) Ah, but to-day her heart is far away. Come, we must do with the flowers we have. (*They start to walk away.*)

The Voice
   Do you dare despise a guest like me?
   Because your heart, by loving fancies blinded,
   Has scorned a guest in pious life grown old,
   Your lover shall forget you though reminded,
   Or think of you as of a story told.

The two girls listen and show dejection.

Priyamvada   Oh, dear! The very thing has happened. The dear, absent-minded girl has offended some worthy man.

Anusuya (*looking ahead*)   My dear, this is no ordinary somebody. It is the great sage Durvasas, the irascible. See how he strides away!

Priyamvada   Nothing burns like fire. Run, fall at his feet, bring him back, while I am getting water to wash his feet.

Anusuya   I will. (*Exit.*)

Priyamvada (*stumbling*)   There! I stumbled in my excitement, and the flower-basket fell out of my hand. (*She collects the scattered flowers.* **Anusuya** *returns.*)

Anusuya   My dear, he is anger incarnate. Who could appease him? But I softened him a little.

Priyamvada   Even that is a good deal for him. Tell me about it.

Anusuya   When he would not turn back, I fell at his feet and prayed to him. 'Holy sir', I said, 'remember her former devotion and pardon this offence. Your daughter did not recognise your great and holy power to-day.'

Priyamvada   And then –

Anusuya   Then he said: 'My words must be fulfilled. But the curse shall be lifted when her lover sees a gem which he has given her for a token.' And so he vanished.

Priyamvada   We can breathe again. When the good king went away, he put a ring, engraved with his own name, on Shakuntala's finger to remember him by. That will save her.

Anusuya   Come, we must finish the sacrifice for her. (*They walk about.*)

Priyamvada (*gazing*)   Just look, Anusuya! There is the dear girl, with her cheek resting on her left hand. She looks like a painted picture. She is thinking about him. How could she notice a guest when she has forgotten herself?

Anusuya   Priyamvada, we two must keep this thing to ourselves. We must be careful of the dear girl. You know how delicate she is.

Priyamvada   Would any one sprinkle a jasmine-vine with scalding water? (*Exeunt ambo.*)

Scene II.—*Early Morning*

Enter a **Pupil** *of Kanva, just risen from sleep.*

Pupil   Father Kanva has returned from his pilgrimage, and has bidden me find out what time it is. I will go into the open air and see how much of the night remains. (*He walks and looks about.*) See! The dawn is breaking. For already

   The moon behind the western mount is sinking;

The eastern sun is heralded by dawn;
From heaven's twin lights, their fall and glory linking,
Brave lessons of submission may be drawn.

And again:

Night-blooming lilies, when the moon is hidden,
Have naught but memories of beauty left.
Hard, hard to bear! Her lot whom heaven has bidden
To live alone, of love and lover reft.

And again:

On jujube-trees the blushing dewdrops falter;
The peacock wakes and leaves the cottage thatch;
A deer is rising near the hoof-marked altar,
And stretching, stands, the day's new life to catch.

And yet again:

The moon that topped the loftiest mountain ranges,
That slew the darkness in the midmost sky,
Is fallen from heaven, and all her glory changes:
So high to rise, so low at last to lie!

Anusuya (*entering hurriedly. To herself*)   That is just what happens to the innocent. Shakuntala has been treated shamefully by the king.

Pupil   I will tell Father Kanva that the hour of morning sacrifice is come. (*Exit.*)

Anusuya   The dawn is breaking. I am awake bright and early. But what shall I do now that I am awake? My hands refuse to attend to the ordinary morning tasks. Well, let love take its course. For the dear, pure-minded girl trusted him – the traitor! Perhaps it is not the good king's fault. It must be the curse of Durvasas. Otherwise, how could the good king say such beautiful things, and then let all this time pass without even sending a message? (*She reflects.*) Yes, we must send him the ring he left as a token. But whom shall we ask to take it? The hermits are unsympathetic because they have never suffered. It seemed as if her friends were to blame and so, try as we might, we could not tell Father Kanva that Shakuntala was married to Dushyanta and was expecting a baby. Oh, what shall we do? (*Enter* **Priyamvada**.)

Priyamvada   Hurry, Anusuya, hurry! We are getting Shakuntala ready for her journey.

Anusuya (*astonished*)   What do you mean, my dear?

Priyamuada   Listen. I just went to Shakuntala, to ask if she had slept well.

Anusuya   And then –

Priyamvada   I found her hiding her face for shame, and Father Kanva was embracing her and encouraging her. 'My child', he said, 'I bring you joy. The offering fell straight in the sacred fire, and auspicious smoke rose toward the sacrificer. My pains for you have proved like instruction given to a good student; they have brought me no regret. This very day I shall give you an escort of hermits and send you to your husband.'

Anusuya But, my dear, who told Father Kanva about it?

Priyamvada A voice from heaven that recited a verse when he had entered the fire-sanctuary.

Anusuya (*astonished*) What did it say?

Priyamvada Listen. (*Speaking in good Sanskrit.*)
  Know, Brahman, that your child,
  Like the fire-pregnant tree,
  Bears kingly seed that shall be born
  For earth's prosperity.

Anusuya (*hugging* **Priyamvada**) I am so glad, dear. But my joy is half sorrow when I think that Shakuntala is going to be taken away this very day.

Priyamvada We must hide our sorrow as best we can. The poor girl must be made happy to-day.

Anusuya Well, here is a cocoa-nut casket, hanging on a branch of the mango-tree. I put flower-pollen in it for this very purpose. It keeps fresh, you know. Now you wrap it in a lotus-leaf, and I will get yellow pigment and earth from a sacred spot and blades of panic grass for the happy ceremony. (**Priyamvada** *does so. Exit* **Anusuya**.)

A Voice Behind the Scenes Gautami, bid the worthy Sharngarava and Sharadvata make ready to escort my daughter Shakuntala.

Priyamvada (*listening*) Hurry, Anusuya, hurry! They are calling the hermits who are going to Hastinapura. (*Enter* **Anusuya**, *with materials for the ceremony.*)

Anusuya Come, dear, let us go. (*They walk about.*)

Priyamvada (*looking ahead*) There is Shakuntala. She took the ceremonial bath at sunrise, and now the hermit-women are giving her rice-cakes and wishing her happiness. Let's go to her. (*They do so. Enter* **Shakuntala** *with attendants as described, and* **Gautami**.)

Shakuntala Holy women, I salute you.

Gautami My child, may you receive the happy title 'queen', showing that your husband honours you.

Hermit-Women My dear, may you become the mother of a hero. (*Exeunt all but* **Gautami**.)

The Two Friends (*approaching*) Did you have a good bath, dear?

Shakuntala Good morning, girls. Sit here.

The Two Friends (*seating themselves*) Now stand straight, while we go through the happy ceremony.

Shakuntala It has happened often enough, but I ought to be very grateful to-day. Shall I ever be adorned by my friends again? (*She weeps.*)

The Two Friends You ought not to weep, dear, at this happy time. (*They wipe the tears away and adorn her.*)

Priyamvada You are so beautiful, you ought to have the finest gems. It seems like an insult to give you these hermitage things. (*Enter* **Harita**, *a hermit-youth with ornaments.*)

Harita Here are ornaments for our lady. (*The women look at them in astonishment.*)

Gautami Harita, my son, whence come these things?

Harita From the holy power of Father Kanva.

Gautami A creation of his mind?

Harita Not quite. Listen. Father Kanva sent us to gather blossoms from the trees for Shakuntala, and then
>One tree bore fruit, a silken marriage dress
>That shamed the moon in its white loveliness;
>Another gave us lac-dye for the feet;
>From others, fairy hands extended, sweet
>Like flowering twigs, as far as to the wrist,
>And gave us gems, to adorn her as we list.

Priyamvada (*looking at* **Shakuntala**) A bee may be born in a hole in a tree, but she likes the honey of the lotus.

Gautami This gracious favour is a token of the queenly happiness which you are to enjoy in your husband's palace. (**Shakuntala** *shows embarrassment.*)

Harita Father Kanva has gone to the bank of the Malini, to perform his ablutions. I will tell him of the favour shown us by the trees. (*Exit.*)

Anusuya My dear, we poor girls never saw such ornaments. How shall we adorn you? (*She stops to think, and to look at the ornaments.*) But we have seen pictures. Perhaps we can arrange them right.

Shakuntala I know how clever you are. (*The* **Two Friends** *adorn her. Enter* **Kanva**, *returning after his ablutions.*)

Kanva
>Shakuntala must go to-day;
>I miss her now at heart;
>I dare not speak a loving word
>Or choking tears will start.
>
>My eyes are dim with anxious thought;
>Love strikes me to the life:
>And yet I strove for pious peace –
>I have no child, no wife.
>
>What must a father feel, when come
>The pangs of parting from his child at home? (*He walks about.*)

The Two Friends   There, Shakuntala, we have arranged your ornaments. Now put on this beautiful silk dress. (**Shakuntala** *rises and does so.*)

Gautami   My child, here is your father. The eyes with which he seems to embrace you are overflowing with tears of joy. You must greet him properly. (**Shakuntala** *makes a shamefaced reverence.*)

Kanva   My child,
> Like Sharmishtha, Yayati's wife,
> Win favour measured by your worth;
> And may you bear a kingly son
> Like Puru, who shall rule the earth.

Gautami   My child, this is not a prayer, but a benediction.

Kanva   My daughter, walk from left to right about the fires in which the offering has just been thrown. (*All walk about.*)
> The holy fires around the altar kindle,
> And at their margins sacred grass is piled;
> Beneath their sacrificial odours dwindle
> Misfortunes. May the fires protect you, child!

Shakuntala *walks about them from left to right.*

Kanva   Now you may start, my daughter. (*He glances about.*) Where are Sharngarava and Sharadvata? (*Enter the* **Two Pupils**.)

The Two Pupils   We are here, Father.

Kanva   Sharngarava, my son, lead the way for your sister.

Sharngarava   Follow me. (*They all walk about.*)

Kanva   O trees of the pious grove, in which the fairies dwell,
> She would not drink till she had wet
> Your roots, a sister's duty,
> Nor pluck your flowers; she loves you yet
> Far more than selfish beauty.
>
> 'Twas festival in her pure life
> When budding blossoms showed;
> And now she leaves you as a wife –
> Oh, speed her on her road!

Sharngarava (*listening to the song of koïl-birds*)   Father,
> The trees are answering your prayer
> In cooing cuckoo-song,
> Bidding Shakuntala farewell,
> Their sister for so long.

Invisible beings,
> May lily-dotted lakes delight your eye;
> May shade-trees bid the heat of noonday cease;

May soft winds blow the lotus-pollen nigh;
May all your path be pleasantness and peace.

All listen in astonishment.

Gautami My child, the fairies of the pious grove bid you farewell. For they love the household. Pay reverence to the holy ones.

Shakuntala (*does so. Aside to* **Priyamvada**) Priyamvada, I long to see my husband, and yet my feet will hardly move. It is hard, hard to leave the hermitage.

Priyamvada You are not the only one to feel sad at this farewell. See how the whole grove feels at parting from you.
   The grass drops from the feeding doe;
   The peahen stops her dance;
   Pale, trembling leaves are falling slow,
   The tears of clinging plants.

Shakuntala (*recalling something*) Father, I must say good-bye to the spring-creeper, my sister among the vines.

Kanva I know your love for her. See! Here she is at your right hand.

Shakuntala (*approaches the vine and embraces it*) Vine sister, embrace me too with your arms, these branches. I shall be far away from you after to-day. Father, you must care for her as you did for me.

Kanva
   My child, you found the lover who
   Had long been sought by me;
   No longer need I watch for you;
   I'll give the vine a lover true,
   This handsome mango-tree.
And now start on your journey.

Shakuntala (*going to the* **Two Friends**) Dear girls, I leave her in your care too.

The Two Friends But who will care for poor us? (*They shed tears.*)

Kanva Anusuya! Priyamvada! Do not weep. It is you who should cheer Shakuntala. (*All walk about.*)

Shakuntala Father, there is the pregnant doe, wandering about near the cottage. When she becomes a happy mother, you must send some one to bring me the good news. Do not forget.

Kanva I shall not forget, my child.

Shakuntala (*stumbling*) Oh, oh! Who is it that keeps pulling at my dress, as if to hinder me? (*She turns round to see.*)

Kanva
   It is the fawn whose lip, when torn
   By kusha-grass, you soothed with oil;

The fawn who gladly nibbled corn
Held in your hand; with loving toil
You have adopted him, and he
Would never leave you willingly.

Shakuntala My dear, why should you follow me when I am going away from home? Your mother died when you were born and I brought you up. Now I am leaving you, and Father Kanva will take care of you. Go back, dear! Go back! (*She walks away, weeping.*)

Kanva Do not weep, my child. Be brave. Look at the path before you.
Be brave, and check the rising tears
That dim your lovely eyes;
Your feet are stumbling on the path
That so uneven lies.

Sharngarava Holy Father, the Scripture declares that one should accompany a departing loved one only to the first water. Pray give us your commands on the bank of this pond, and then return.

Kanva Then let us rest in the shade of this fig-tree. (*All do so.*) What commands would it be fitting for me to lay on King Dushyanta? (*He reflects.*)

Anusuya My dear, there is not a living thing in the whole hermitage that is not grieving to-day at saying good-bye to you. Look!
The sheldrake does not heed his mate
Who calls behind the lotus-leaf;
He drops the lily from his bill
And turns on you a glance of grief.

Kanva Son Sharngarava, when you present Shakuntala to the king, give him this message from me.
Remembering my religious worth,
Your own high race, the love poured forth
By her, forgetful of her friends,
Pay her what honour custom lends
To all your wives. And what fate gives
Beyond, will please her relatives.

Sharngarava I will not forget your message, Father.

Kanva (*turning to* **Shakuntala**) My child, I must now give you my counsel. Though I live in the forest, I have some knowledge of the world.

Sharngarava True wisdom, Father, gives insight into everything.

Kanva My child, when you have entered your husband's home,
Obey your elders; and be very kind
To rivals; never be perversely blind
And angry with your husband, even though he
Should prove less faithful than a man might be;

Be as courteous to servants as you may,
Not puffed with pride in this your happy day:
Thus does a maiden grow into a wife;
But self-willed women are the curse of life.
But what does Gautami say?

Gautami This is advice sufficient for a bride. (*To* **Shakuntala**.) You will not forget, my child.

Kanva Come, my daughter, embrace me and your friends.

Shakuntala Oh, Father! Must my friends turn back too?

Kanva My daughter, they too must some day be given in marriage. Therefore they may not go to court. Gautami will go with you.

Shakuntala (*throwing her arms about her father*) I am torn from my father's breast like a vine stripped from a sandal-tree on the Malabar hills. How can I live in another soil? (*She weeps.*)

Kanva My daughter, why distress yourself so?
A noble husband's honourable wife,
You are to spend a busy, useful life
In the world's eye; and soon, as eastern skies
Bring forth the sun, from you there shall arise
A child, a blessing and a comfort strong –
You will not miss me, dearest daughter, long.

Shakuntala (*falling at his feet*) Farewell, Father.

Kanva My daughter, may all that come to you which I desire for you.

Shakuntala (*going to her* **Two Friends**) Come, girls! Embrace me, both of you together.

The Two Friends (*do so*) Dear, if the good king should perhaps be slow to recognise you, show him the ring with his own name engraved on it.

Shakuntala Your doubts make my heart beat faster.

The Two Friends Do not be afraid, dear. Love is timid.

Sharngarava (*looking about*) Father, the sun is in mid-heaven. She must hasten.

Shakuntala (*embracing* **Kanva** *once more*) Father, when shall I see the pious grove again?

Kanva My daughter,
When you have shared for many years
The king's thoughts with the earth,
When to a son who knows no fears
You shall have given birth,
When, trusted to the son you love,
Your royal labours cease,

Come with your husband to the grove
And end your days in peace.

Gautami My child, the hour of your departure is slipping by. Bid your father turn back. No, she would never do that. Pray turn back, sir.

Kanva Child, you interrupt my duties in the pious grove.

Shakuntala Yes, Father. You will be busy in the grove. You will not miss me. But oh! I miss you.

Kanva How can you think me so indifferent? (*He sighs.*)
My lonely sorrow will not go,
For seeds you scattered here
Before the cottage door, will grow;
And I shall see them, dear.
Go. And peace go with you. (*Exit* **Shakuntala***, with* **Gautami***,* **Sharngarava***, and* **Sharadvata***.*)

The Two Friends (*gazing long after her. Mournfully*) Oh, oh! Shakuntala is lost among the trees.

Kanva Anusuya! Priyamvada! Your companion is gone. Choke down your grief and follow me. (*They start to go back.*)

The Two Friends Father, the grove seems empty without Shakuntala.

Kanva So love interprets. (*He walks about, sunk in thought.*) Ah! I have sent Shakuntala away, and now I am myself again. For
A girl is held in trust, another's treasure;
To arms of love my child to-day is given;
And now I feel a calm and sacred pleasure;
I have restored the pledge that came from heaven.

Exeunt omnes.

Act V Shakuntala's Rejection

Enter a **Chamberlain**.

Chamberlain (*sighing*)   Alas! To what a state am I reduced!
 I once assumed the staff of reed
 For custom's sake alone,
 As officer to guard at need
 The ladies round the throne.
 But years have passed away and made
 It serve, my tottering steps to aid.

The king is within. I will tell him of the urgent business which demands his attention. (*He takes a few steps.*) But what is the business? (*He recalls it.*) Yes, I remember. Certain hermits, pupils of Kanva, desire to see his Majesty. Strange, strange!
 The mind of age is like a lamp
 Whose oil is running thin;
 One moment it is shining bright,
 Then darkness closes in.
(*He walks and looks about.*) Here is his Majesty.
 He does not seek – until a father's care
 Is shown his subjects – rest in solitude;
 As a great elephant recks not of the sun
 Until his herd is sheltered in the wood.
In truth, I hesitate to announce the coming of Kanva's pupils to the king. For he has this moment risen from the throne of justice. But kings are never weary. For
 The sun unyokes his horses never;
 Blows night and day the breeze;
 Shesha upholds the world forever:
 And kings are like to these.

He walks about. Enter the **King**, *the* **Clown**, *and retinue according to rank.*

King (*betraying the cares of office*)   Every one is happy on attaining his desire – except a king. His difficulties increase with his power. Thus:
 Security slays nothing but ambition;
 With great possessions, troubles gather thick;
 Pain grows, not lessens, with a king's position,
 As when one's hand must hold the sunshade's stick.

Two court **Poets** *behind the scenes:* Victory to your Majesty.

First Poet
 The world you daily guard and bless,
 Not heeding pain or weariness;
 Thus is your nature made.
 A tree will brave the noonday, when

    The sun is fierce, that weary men
    May rest beneath its shade.

Second Poet
    Vice bows before the royal rod;
    Strife ceases at your kingly nod;
    You are our strong defender.
    Friends come to all whose wealth is sure,
    But you, alike to rich and poor,
    Are friend both strong and tender.

King (*listening*)   Strange! I was wearied by the demands of my office, but this renews my spirit.

Clown   Does a bull forget that he is tired when you call him the leader of the herd?

King (*smiling*)   Well, let us sit down. (*They seat themselves, and the retinue arranges itself. A lute is heard behind the scenes.*)

Clown (*listening*)   My friend, listen to what is going on in the music-room. Some one is playing a lute, and keeping good time. I suppose Lady Hansavati is practising.

King   Be quiet. I wish to listen.

Chamberlain (*looks at the* **King**)   Ah, the king is occupied. I must await his leisure. (*He stands aside.*)

A song behind the scenes
    You who kissed the mango-flower,
    Honey-loving bee,
    Gave her all your passion's power,
    Ah, so tenderly!

    How can you be tempted so
    By the lily, pet?
    Fresher honey's sweet, I know;
    But can you forget?

King   What an entrancing song!

Clown   But, man, don't you understand what the words mean?

King (*smiling*)   I was once devoted to Queen Hansavati. And the rebuke comes from her. Friend Madhavya, tell Queen Hansavati in my name that the rebuke is a very pretty one.

Clown   Yes, sir. (*He rises.*) But, man, you are using another fellow's fingers to grab a bear's tail-feathers with. I have about as much chance of salvation as a monk who hasn't forgotten his passions.

King   Go. Soothe her like a gentleman.

Clown   I suppose I must. (*Exit.*)

King (*to himself*) Why am I filled with wistfulness on hearing such a song? I am not separated from one I love. And yet

> In face of sweet presentment
> Or harmonies of sound,
> Man e'er forgets contentment,
> By wistful longings bound.
>
> There must be recollections
> Of things not seen on earth,
> Deep nature's predilections,
> Loves earlier than birth.

He shows the wistfulness that comes from unremembered things.

Chamberlain (*approaching*) Victory to your Majesty. Here are hermits who dwell in the forest at the foot of the Himalayas. They bring women with them, and they carry a message from Kanva. What is your pleasure with regard to them?

King (*astonished*) Hermits? Accompanied by women? From Kanva?

Chamberlain Yes.

King Request my chaplain Somarata in my name to receive these hermits in the manner prescribed by Scripture, and to conduct them himself before me. I will await them in a place fit for their reception.

Chamberlain Yes, your Majesty. (*Exit.*)

King (*rising*) Vetravati, conduct me to the fire-sanctuary.

Portress Follow me, your Majesty. (*She walks about.*) Your Majesty, here is the terrace of the fire-sanctuary. It is beautiful, for it has just been swept, and near at hand is the cow that yields the milk of sacrifice. Pray ascend it.

King (*ascends and stands leaning on the shoulder of an attendant*) Vetravati, with what purpose does Father Kanva send these hermits to me?

> Do leaguèd powers of sin conspire
> To balk religion's pure desire?
> Has wrong been done to beasts that roam
> Contented round the hermits' home?
> Do plants no longer bud and flower,
> To warn me of abuse of power?
> These doubts and more assail my mind,
> But leave me puzzled, lost, and blind.

Portress How could these things be in a hermitage that rests in the fame of the king's arm? No, I imagine they have come to pay homage to their king, and to congratulate him on his pious rule.

Enter the **Chaplain** *and the* **Chamberlain**, *conducting the two pupils of* **Kanva**, *with* **Gautami** *and* **Shakuntala**.

Chamberlain Follow me, if you please.

Sharngarava Friend Sharadvata,
  The king is noble and to virtue true;
  None dwelling here commit the deed of shame;
  Yet we ascetics view the worldly crew
  As in a house all lapped about with flame.

Sharadvata Sharngarava, your emotion on entering the city is quite just. As for me,
  Free from the world and all its ways,
  I see them spending worldly days
  As clean men view men smeared with oil,
  As pure men, those whom passions soil,
  As waking men view men asleep,
  As free men, those in bondage deep.

Chaplain That is why men like you are great.

Shakuntala (*observing an evil omen*) Oh, why does my right eye throb?

Gautami Heaven avert the omen, my child. May happiness wait upon you. (*They walk about.*)

Chaplain (*indicating the* **King**) O hermits, here is he who protects those of every station and of every age. He has already risen, and awaits you. Behold him.

Sharngarava Yes, it is admirable, but not surprising. For
  Fruit-laden trees bend down to earth;
  The water-pregnant clouds hang low;
  Good men are not puffed up by power –
  The unselfish are by nature so.

Portress Your Majesty, the hermits seem to be happy. They give you gracious looks.

King (*observing* **Shakuntala**) Ah!
  Who is she, shrouded in the veil
  That dims her beauty's lustre,
  Among the hermits like a flower
  Round which the dead leaves cluster?

Portress Your Majesty, she is well worth looking at.

King Enough! I must not gaze upon another's wife.

Shakuntala (*laying her hand on her breast. Aside*) Oh, my heart, why tremble so? Remember his constant love and be brave.

Chaplain (*advancing*) Hail, your Majesty. The hermits have been received as Scripture enjoins. They have a message from their teacher. May you be pleased to hear it.

King (*respectfully*) I am all attention.

The two pupils (*raising their right hands*)   Victory, O King.

King (*bowing low*)   I salute you all.

The two pupils   All hail.

King   Does your pious life proceed without disturbance?

The two pupils
    How could the pious duties fail
    While you defend the right?
    Or how could darkness' power prevail
    O'er sunbeams shining bright?

King (*to himself*)   Indeed, my royal title is no empty one. (*Aloud.*) Is holy Kanva in health?

Sharngarava   O King, those who have religious power can command health. He asks after your welfare and sends this message.

King   What are his commands?

Sharngarava   He says: 'Since you have met this my daughter and have married her, I give you my glad consent. For
    You are the best of worthy men, they say;
    And she, I know, Good Works personified;
    The Creator wrought for ever and a day,
    In wedding such a virtuous groom and bride.
She is with child. Take her and live with her in virtue.'

Gautami   Bless you, sir. I should like to say that no one invites me to speak.

King   Speak, mother.

Gautami
    Did she with father speak or mother?
    Did you engage her friends in speech?
    Your faith was plighted each to other;
    Let each be faithful now to each.

Shakuntala   What will my husband say?

King (*listening with anxious suspicion*)   What is this insinuation?

Shakuntala (*to herself*)   Oh, oh! So haughty and so slanderous!

Sharngarava   'What is this insinuation?' What is your question? Surely you know the world's ways well enough.
    Because the world suspects a wife
    Who does not share her husband's lot,
    Her kinsmen wish her to abide
    With him, although he love her not.

King   You cannot mean that this young woman is my wife.

Shakuntala (*sadly to herself*)   Oh, my heart, you feared it, and now it has come.

Sharngarava   O King,
A king, and shrink when love is done,
Turn coward's back on truth, and flee!

King   What means this dreadful accusation?

Sharngarava (*furiously*)
O drunk with power! We might have known
That you were steeped in treachery.

King   A stinging rebuke!

Gautami (*to* **Shakuntala**)   Forget your shame, my child. I will remove your veil. Then your husband will recognise you. (*She does so.*)

King (*observing* **Shakuntala**. *To himself*)
As my heart ponders whether I could ever
Have wed this woman that has come to me
In tortured loveliness, as I endeavour
To bring it back to mind, then like a bee

That hovers round a jasmine flower at dawn,
While frosty dews of morning still o'erweave it,
And hesitates to sip ere they be gone,
I cannot taste the sweet, and cannot leave it.

Portress (*to herself*)   What a virtuous king he is! Would any other man hesitate when he saw such a pearl of a woman coming of her own accord?

Sharngarava   Have you nothing to say, O King?

King   Hermit, I have taken thought. I cannot believe that this woman is my wife. She is plainly with child. How can I take her, confessing myself an adulterer?

Shakuntala (*to herself*)   Oh, oh, oh! He even casts doubt on our marriage. The vine of my hope climbed high, but it is broken now.

Sharngarava   Not so.
You scorn the sage who rendered whole
His child befouled, and choked his grief,
Who freely gave you what you stole
And added honour to a thief!

Sharadvata   Enough, Sharngarava. Shakuntala, we have said what we were sent to say. You hear his words. Answer him.

Shakuntala (*to herself*)   He loved me so. He is so changed. Why remind him? Ah, but I must clear my own character. Well, I will try. (*Aloud.*) My dear husband – (*She stops.*) No, he doubts my right to call him that. Your Majesty, it was pure love that opened my poor heart to you in the hermitage. Then you were kind to me and gave me your promise. Is it right for you to speak so now, and to reject me?

King (*stopping his ears*)   Peace, peace!
   A stream that eats away the bank,
   Grows foul, and undermines the tree.
   So you would stain your honour, while
   You plunge me into misery.

Shakuntala   Very well. If you have acted so because you really fear to touch another man's wife, I will remove your doubts with a token you gave me.

King   An excellent idea!

Shakuntala (*touching her finger*)   Oh, oh! The ring is lost. (*She looks sadly at* **Gautami**.)

Gautami   My child, you worshipped the holy Ganges at the spot where Indra descended. The ring must have fallen there.

King   Ready wit, ready wit!

Shakuntala   Fate is too strong for me there. I will tell you something else.

King   Let me hear what you have to say.

Shakuntala   One day, in the bower of reeds, you were holding a lotus-leaf cup full of water.

King   I hear you.

Shakuntala   At that moment the fawn came up, my adopted son. Then you took pity on him and coaxed him. 'Let him drink first', you said. But he did not know you, and he would not come to drink water from your hand. But he liked it afterwards, when I held the very same water. Then you smiled and said: 'It is true. Every one trusts his own sort. You both belong to the forest.'

King   It is just such women, selfish, sweet, false, that entice fools.

Gautami   You have no right to say that. She grew up in the pious grove. She does not know how to deceive.

King   Old hermit woman,
   The female's untaught cunning may be seen
   In beasts, far more in women selfish-wise;
   The cuckoo's eggs are left to hatch and rear
   By foster-parents, and away she flies.

Shakuntala (*angrily*)   Wretch! You judge all this by your own false heart. Would any other man do what you have done? To hide behind virtue, like a yawning well covered over with grass!

King (*to himself*)   But her anger is free from coquetry, because she has lived in the forest. See!
   Her glance is straight; her eyes are flashing red;
   Her speech is harsh, not drawlingly well-bred;
   Her whole lip quivers, seems to shake with cold;

Her frown has straightened eyebrows arching bold.
No, she saw that I was doubtful, and her anger was feigned. Thus
> When I refused but now
> Hard-heartedly, to know
> Of love or secret vow,
> Her eyes grew red; and so,
> Bending her arching brow,
> She fiercely snapped Love's bow.

(*Aloud.*) My good girl, Dushyanta's conduct is known to the whole kingdom, but not this action.

Shakuntala   Well, well. I had my way. I trusted a king, and put myself in his hands. He had a honey face and a heart of stone. (*She covers her face with her dress and weeps.*)

Sharngarava   Thus does unbridled levity burn.
> Be slow to love, but yet more slow
> With secret mate;
> With those whose hearts we do not know,
> Love turns to hate.

King   Why do you trust this girl, and accuse me of an imaginary crime?

Sharngarava (*disdainfully*)   You have learned your wisdom upside down.
> It would be monstrous to believe
> A girl who never lies;
> Trust those who study to deceive
> And think it very wise.

King   Aha, my candid friend! Suppose I were to admit that I am such a man. What would happen if I deceived the girl?

Sharngarava   Ruin.

King   It is unthinkable that ruin should fall on Puru's line.

Sharngarava   Why bandy words? We have fulfilled our Father's bidding. We are ready to return.
> Leave her or take her, as you will;
> She is your wife;
> Husbands have power for good or ill
> O'er woman's life.

Gautami, lead the way. (*They start to go.*)

Shakuntala   He has deceived me shamelessly. And will you leave me too? (*She starts to follow.*)

Gautami (*turns around and sees her*)   Sharngarava, my son, Shakuntala is following us, lamenting piteously. What can the poor child do with a husband base enough to reject her?

Sharngarava (*turns angrily*)   You self-willed girl! Do you dare show independence? (**Shakuntala** *shrinks in fear.*) Listen.
> If you deserve such scorn and blame,
> What will your father with your shame?
> But if you know your vows are pure,
> Obey your husband and endure.

Remain. We must go.

King   Hermit, why deceive this woman? Remember:
> Night-blossoms open to the moon,
> Day-blossoms to the sun;
> A man of honour ever strives
> Another's wife to shun.

Sharngarava   O King, suppose you had forgotten your former actions in the midst of distractions. Should you now desert your wife – you who fear to fail in virtue?

King   I ask *you* which is the heavier sin:
> Not knowing whether I be mad
> Or falsehood be in her,
> Shall I desert a faithful wife
> Or turn adulterer?

Chaplain (*considering*)   Now if this were done –

King   Instruct me, my teacher.

Chaplain   Let the woman remain in my house until her child is born.

King   Why this?

Chaplain   The chief astrologers have told you that your first child was destined to be an emperor. If the son of the hermit's daughter is born with the imperial birthmarks, then welcome her and introduce her into the palace. Otherwise, she must return to her father.

King   It is good advice, my teacher.

Chaplain (*rising*)   Follow me, my daughter.

Shakuntala   O mother earth, give me a grave! (*Exit weeping, with the* **Chaplain***, the hermits, and* **Gautami***. The* **King***, his memory clouded by the curse, ponders on* **Shakuntala***.*)

Voices Behind the Scenes   A miracle! A miracle!

King (*listening*)   What does this mean? (*Enter the* **Chaplain***.*)

Chaplain (*in amazement*)   Your Majesty, a wonderful thing has happened.

King   What?

Chaplain   When Kanva's pupils had departed,
> She tossed her arms, bemoaned her plight,

Accused her crushing fate –

King What then?

Chaplain
Before our eyes a heavenly light
In woman's form, but shining bright,
Seized her and vanished straight.

All betray astonishment.

King My teacher, we have already settled the matter. Why speculate in vain? Let us seek repose.

Chaplain Victory to your Majesty. (*Exit.*)

King Vetravati, I am bewildered. Conduct me to my apartment.

Portress Follow me, your Majesty.

King (*walks about. To himself*)
With a hermit-wife I had no part,
All memories evade me;
And yet my sad and stricken heart
Would more than half persuade me.

Exeunt omnes.

Act VI Separation from Shakuntala

Scene I.—*In the street before the Palace*

Enter the **Chief of Police**, **Two Policemen**, *and a* **Fisherman** *with his hands bound behind his back.*

The Two Policemen (*striking the man*) Now, pickpocket, tell us where you found this ring. It is the king's ring, with letters engraved on it, and it has a magnificent great gem.

Fisherman (*showing fright*) Be merciful, kind gentlemen. I am not guilty of such a crime.

First Policeman No, I suppose the king thought you were a pious Brahman, and made you a present of it.

Fisherman Listen, please. I am a fisherman, and I live on the Ganges, at the spot where Indra came down.

Second Policeman You thief, we didn't ask for your address or your social position.

Chief Let him tell a straight story, Suchaka. Don't interrupt.

The Two Policemen Yes, chief. Talk, man, talk.

Fisherman I support my family with things you catch fish with – nets, you know, and hooks, and things.

Chief (*laughing*) You have a sweet trade.

Fisherman Don't say that, master.
  You can't give up a lowdown trade
  That your ancestors began;
  A butcher butchers things, and yet
  He's the tenderest-hearted man.

Chief Go on. Go on.

Fisherman Well, one day I was cutting up a carp. In its maw I see this ring with the magnificent great gem. And then I was just trying to sell it here when you kind gentlemen grabbed me. That is the only way I got it. Now kill me, or find fault with me.

Chief (*smelling the ring*) There is no doubt about it, Januka. It has been in a fish's maw. It has the real perfume of raw meat. Now we have to find out how he got it. We must go to the palace.

The Two Policemen (*to the* **Fisherman**) Move on, you cutpurse, move on. (*They walk about.*)

Chief Suchaka, wait here at the big gate until I come out of the palace. And don't get careless.

The Two Policemen Go in, chief. I hope the king will be nice to you.

Chief Good-bye. (*Exit.*)

Suchaka Januka, the chief is taking his time.

Januka You can't just drop in on a king.

Suchaka Januka, my fingers are itching (*indicating the* **Fisherman**) to kill this cutpurse.

Fisherman Don't kill a man without any reason, master.

Januka (*looking ahead*) There is the chief, with a written order from the king. (*To the* **Fisherman**.) Now you will see your family, or else you will feed the crows and jackals. (*Enter the* **Chief**.)

Chief Quick! Quick! (*He breaks off.*)

Fisherman Oh, oh! I'm a dead man. (*He shows dejection.*)

Chief Release him, you. Release the fishnet fellow. It is all right, his getting the ring. Our king told me so himself.

Suchaka All right, chief. He is a dead man come back to life. (*He releases the* **Fisherman**.)

Fisherman (*bowing low to the* **Chief**) Master, I owe you my life. (*He falls at his feet.*)

Chief Get up, get up! Here is a reward that the king was kind enough to give you. It is worth as much as the ring. Take it. (*He hands the* **Fisherman** *a bracelet.*)

Fisherman (*joyfully taking it*) Much obliged.

Januka He *is* much obliged to the king. Just as if he had been taken from the stake and put on an elephant's back.

Suchaka Chief, the reward shows that the king thought a lot of the ring. The gem must be worth something.

Chief No, it wasn't the fine gem that pleased the king. It was this way.

The Two Policemen Well?

Chief I think, when the king saw it, he remembered somebody he loves. You know how dignified he is usually. But as soon as he saw it, he broke down for a moment.

Suchaka You have done the king a good turn, chief.

Januka All for the sake of this fish-killer, it seems to me. (*He looks enviously at the* **Fisherman**.)

Fisherman Take half of it, masters, to pay for something to drink.

Januka Fisherman, you are the biggest and best friend I've got. The first thing we want, is all the brandy we can hold. Let's go where they keep it. (*Exeunt omnes.*)

Scene II.—*In the Palace Gardens*

Enter **Mishrakeshi**, *flying through the air.*

Mishrakeshi I have taken my turn in waiting upon the nymphs. And now I will see what this good king is doing. Shakuntala is like a second self to me, because she is the daughter of Menaka. And it was she who asked me to do this. (*She looks about.*) It is the day of the spring festival. But I see no preparations for a celebration at court. I might learn the reason by my power of divination. But I must do as my friend asked me. Good! I will make myself invisible and stand near these girls who take care of the garden. I shall find out that way. (*She descends to earth. Enter a* **Maid**, *gazing at a mango branch, and behind her, a second.*)

First Maid
>First mango-twig, so pink, so green,
>First living breath of spring,
>You are sacrificed as soon as seen,
>A festival offering.

Second Maid What are you chirping about to yourself, little cuckoo?

First Maid Why, little bee, you know that the cuckoo goes crazy with delight when she sees the mango-blossom.

Second Maid (*joyfully*) Oh, has the spring really come?

First Maid Yes, little bee. And this is the time when you too buzz about in crazy joy.

Second Maid Hold me, dear, while I stand on tiptoe and offer this blossom to Love, the divine.

First Maid If I do, you must give me half the reward of the offering.

Second Maid That goes without saying, dear. We two are one. (*She leans on her friend and takes the mango-blossom.*) Oh, see! The mango-blossom hasn't opened, but it has broken the sheath, so it is fragrant. (*She brings her hands together.*) I worship mighty Love.
>O mango-twig I give to
>Love As arrow for his bow,
>Most sovereign of his arrows five,
>Strike maiden-targets low.

She throws the twig. Enter the **Chamberlain**.

Chamberlain (*angrily*) Stop, silly girl. The king has strictly forbidden the spring festival. Do you dare pluck the mango-blossoms?

The Two Maids (*frightened*)   Forgive us, sir. We did not know.

Chamberlain   What! You have not heard the king's command, which is obeyed even by the trees of spring and the creatures that dwell in them. See!
  The mango branches are in bloom,
  Yet pollen does not form;
  The cuckoo's song sticks in his throat,
  Although the days are warm;

  The amaranth-bud is formed, and yet
  Its power of growth is gone;
  The love-god timidly puts by
  The arrow he has drawn.

Mishrakeshi   There is no doubt of it. This good king has wonderful power.

First Maid   A few days ago, sir, we were sent to his Majesty by his brother-in-law Mitravasu to decorate the garden. That is why we have heard nothing of this affair.

Chamberlain   You must not do so again.

The Two Maids   But we are curious. If we girls may know about it, pray tell us, sir. Why did his Majesty forbid the spring festival?

Mishrakeshi   Kings are fond of celebrations. There must be some good reason.

Chamberlain (*to himself*)   It is in everybody's mouth. Why should I not tell it? (*Aloud.*) Have you heard the gossip concerning Shakuntala's rejection?

The Two Maids   Yes, sir. The king's brother-in-law told us, up to the point where the ring was recovered.

Chamberlain   There is little more to tell. When his Majesty saw the ring, he remembered that he had indeed contracted a secret marriage with Shakuntala, and had rejected her under a delusion. And then he fell a prey to remorse.
  He hates the things he loved; he intermits
  The daily audience, nor in judgment sits;
  Spends sleepless nights in tossing on his bed;
  At times, when he by courtesy is led
  To address a lady, speaks another name,
  Then stands for minutes, sunk in helpless shame.

Mishrakeshi   I am glad to hear it.

Chamberlain   His Majesty's sorrow has forbidden the festival.

The Two Maids   It is only right.

A Voice Behind the Scenes   Follow me.

Chamberlain (*listening*)   Ah, his Majesty approaches. Go, and attend to your duties. (*Exeunt the* **Two Maids**. *Enter the* **King**, *wearing a dress indicative of remorse; the* **Clown**, *and the* **Portress**.)

Chamberlain (*observing the* **King**) A beautiful figure charms in whatever state. Thus, his Majesty is pleasing even in his sorrow. For
   All ornament is laid aside; he wears
   One golden bracelet on his wasted arm;
   His lip is scorched by sighs; and sleepless cares
   Redden his eyes. Yet all can work no harm
   On that magnificent beauty, wasting, but
   Gaining in brilliance, like a diamond cut.

Mishrakeshi (*observing the* **King**) No wonder Shakuntala pines for him, even though he dishonoured her by his rejection of her.

King (*walks about slowly, sunk in thought*)
   Alas! My smitten heart, that once lay sleeping,
   Heard in its dreams my fawn-eyed love's laments,
   And wakened now, awakens but to weeping,
   To bitter grief, and tears of penitence.

Mishrakeshi That is the poor girl's fate.

Clown (*to himself*) He has got his Shakuntala-sickness again. I wish I knew how to cure him.

Chamberlain (*advancing*) Victory to your Majesty. I have examined the garden. Your Majesty may visit its retreats.

King Vetravati, tell the minister Pishuna in my name that a sleepless night prevents me from mounting the throne of judgment. He is to investigate the citizens' business and send me a memorandum.

Portress Yes, your Majesty. (*Exit.*)

King And you, Parvatayana, return to your post of duty.

Chamberlain Yes, your Majesty. (*Exit.*)

Clown You have got rid of the vermin. Now amuse yourself in this garden. It is delightful with the passing of the cold weather.

King (*sighing*) My friend, the proverb makes no mistake. Misfortune finds the weak spot. See!
   No sooner did the darkness lift
   That clouded memory's power,
   Than the god of love prepared his bow
   And shot the mango-flower.

   No sooner did the ring recall
   My banished maiden dear,
   No sooner do I vainly weep
   For her, than spring is here.

Clown Wait a minute, man. I will destroy Love's arrow with my stick. (*He raises his stick and strikes at the mango branch.*)

King (*smiling*) Enough! I see your pious power. My friend, where shall I sit now to comfort my eyes with the vines? They remind me somehow of her.

Clown Well, you told one of the maids, the clever painter, that you would spend this hour in the bower of spring-creepers. And you asked her to bring you there the picture of the lady Shakuntala which you painted on a tablet.

King It is my only consolation. Lead the way to the bower of spring-creepers.

Clown Follow me. (*They walk about.* **Mishrakeshi** *follows.*) Here is the bower of spring-creepers, with its jewelled benches. Its loneliness seems to bid you a silent welcome. Let us go in and sit down. (*They do so.*)

Mishrakeshi I will hide among the vines and see the dear girl's picture. Then I shall be able to tell her how deep her husband's love is. (*She hides.*)

King (*sighing*) I remember it all now, my friend. I told you how I first met Shakuntala. It is true, you were not with me when I rejected her. But I had told you of her at the first. Had you forgotten, as I did?

Mishrakeshi This shows that a king should not be separated a single moment from some intimate friend.

Clown No, I didn't forget. But when you had told the whole story, you said it was a joke and there was nothing in it. And I was fool enough to believe you. No, this is the work of fate.

Mishrakeshi It must be.

King (*after meditating a moment*) Help me, my friend.

Clown But, man, this isn't right at all. A good man never lets grief get the upper hand. The mountains are calm even in a tempest.

King My friend, I am quite forlorn. I keep thinking of her pitiful state when I rejected her. Thus:
   When I denied her, then she tried
   To join her people. 'Stay', one cried,
   Her father's representative.
   She stopped, she turned, she could but give
   A tear-dimmed glance to heartless me –
   That arrow burns me poisonously.

Mishrakeshi How his fault distresses him!

Clown Well, I don't doubt it was some heavenly being that carried her away.

King Who else would dare to touch a faithful wife? Her friends told me that Menaka was her mother. My heart persuades me that it was she, or companions of hers, who carried Shakuntala away.

Mishrakeshi His madness was wonderful, not his awakening reason.

Clown But in that case, you ought to take heart. You will meet her again.

King How so?

Clown Why, a mother or a father cannot long bear to see a daughter separated from her husband.

King My friend,
   And was it phantom, madness, dream,
   Or fatal retribution stern?
   My hopes fell down a precipice
   And never, never will return.

Clown Don't talk that way. Why, the ring shows that incredible meetings do happen.

King (*looking at the ring*) This ring deserves pity. It has fallen from a heaven hard to earn.
   Your virtue, ring, like mine,
   Is proved to be but small;
   Her pink-nailed finger sweet
   You clasped. How could you fall?

Mishrakeshi If it were worn on any other hand, it would deserve pity. My dear girl, you are far away. I am the only one to hear these delightful words.

Clown Tell me how you put the ring on her finger.

Mishrakeshi He speaks as if prompted by my curiosity.

King Listen, my friend. When I left the pious grove for the city, my darling wept and said: 'But how long will you remember us, dear?'

Clown And then you said –

King Then I put this engraved ring on her finger, and said to her –

Clown Well, what?

King
   Count every day one letter of my name;
   Before you reach the end, dear,
   Will come to lead you to my palace halls
   A guide whom I shall send, dear.
Then, through my madness, it fell out cruelly.

Mishrakeshi It was too charming an agreement to be frustrated by fate.

Clown But how did it get into a carp's mouth, as if it had been a fish-hook?

King While she was worshipping the Ganges at Shachitirtha, it fell.

Clown I see.

Mishrakeshi That is why the virtuous king doubted his marriage with poor Shakuntala. Yet such love does not ask for a token. How could it have been?

King Well, I can only reproach this ring.

Clown (*smiling*) And I will reproach this stick of mine. Why are you crooked when I am straight?

King (*not hearing him*)
>How could you fail to linger
>On her soft, tapering finger,
>And in the water fall?

And yet
>Things lifeless know not beauty;
>But I – I scorned my duty,
>The sweetest task of all.

Mishrakeshi He has given the answer which I had ready.

Clown But that is no reason why I should starve to death.

King (*not heeding*) O my darling, my heart burns with repentance because I abandoned you without reason. Take pity on me. Let me see you again. (*Enter a* **Maid** *with a tablet.*)

Maid Your Majesty, here is the picture of our lady. (*She produces the tablet.*)

King (*gazing at it*) It is a beautiful picture. See!
>A graceful arch of brows above great eyes;
>Lips bathed in darting, smiling light that flies
>Reflected from white teeth; a mouth as red
>As red karkandhu-fruit; love's brightness shed
>O'er all her face in bursts of liquid charm –
>The picture speaks, with living beauty warm.

Clown (*looking at it*) The sketch is full of sweet meaning. My eyes seem to stumble over its uneven surface. What more can I say? I expect to see it come to life, and I feel like speaking to it.

Mishrakeshi The king is a clever painter. I seem to see the dear girl before me.

King My friend,
>What in the picture is not fair,
>Is badly done;
>Yet something of her beauty there,
>I feel, is won.

Mishrakeshi This is natural, when love is increased by remorse.

King (*sighing*)
>I treated her with scorn and loathing ever;
>Now o'er her pictured charms my heart will burst:

> A traveller I, who scorned the mighty river,
> And seeks in the mirage to quench his thirst.

Clown There are three figures in the picture, and they are all beautiful. Which one is the lady Shakuntala?

Mishrakeshi The poor fellow never saw her beauty. His eyes are useless, for she never came before them.

King Which one do you think?

Clown (*observing closely*) I think it is this one, leaning against the creeper which she has just sprinkled. Her face is hot and the flowers are dropping from her hair; for the ribbon is loosened. Her arms droop like weary branches; she has loosened her girdle, and she seems a little fatigued. This, I think, is the lady Shakuntala, the others are her friends.

King You are good at guessing. Besides, here are proofs of my love.
> See where discolorations faint
> Of loving handling tell;
> And here the swelling of the paint
> Shows where my sad tears fell.

Chaturika, I have not finished the background. Go, get the brushes.

Maid Please hold the picture, Madhavya, while I am gone.

King I will hold it. (*He does so. Exit* **Maid**.)

Clown What are you going to add?

Mishrakeshi Surely, every spot that the dear girl loved.

King Listen, my friend.
> The stream of Malini, and on its sands
> The swan-pairs resting; holy foot-hill lands
> Of great Himalaya's sacred ranges, where
> The yaks are seen; and under trees that bear
> Bark hermit-dresses on their branches high,
> A doe that on the buck's horn rubs her eye.

Clown (*aside*) To hear him talk, I should think he was going to fill up the picture with heavy-bearded hermits.

King And another ornament that Shakuntala loved I have forgotten to paint.

Clown What?

Mishrakeshi Something natural for a girl living in the forest.

King
> The siris-blossom, fastened o'er her ear,
> Whose stamens brush her cheek;
> The lotus-chain like autumn moonlight soft
> Upon her bosom meek.

Clown   But why does she cover her face with fingers lovely as the pink water-lily? She seems frightened. (*He looks more closely.*) I see. Here is a bold, bad bee. He steals honey, and so he flies to her lotus-face.

King   Drive him away.

Clown   It is your affair to punish evil-doers.

King   True. O welcome guest of the flowering vine, why do you waste your time in buzzing here?
   Your faithful, loving queen,
   Perched on a flower, athirst,
   Is waiting for you still,
   Nor tastes the honey first.

Mishrakeshi   A gentlemanly way to drive him off!

Clown   This kind are obstinate, even when you warn them.

King (*angrily*)   Will you not obey my command? Then listen:
   'Tis sweet as virgin blossoms on a tree,
   The lip I kissed in love-feasts tenderly;
   Sting that dear lip, O bee, with cruel power,
   And you shall be imprisoned in a flower.

Clown   Well, he doesn't seem afraid of your dreadful punishment. (*Laughing. To himself.*) The man is crazy, and I am just as bad, from associating with him.

King   Will he not go, though I warn him?

Mishrakeshi   Love works a curious change even in a brave man.

Clown (*aloud*)   It is only a picture, man.

King   A picture?

Mishrakeshi   I too understand it now. But to him, thoughts are real experiences.

King   You have done an ill-natured thing.
   When I was happy in the sight,
   And when my heart was warm,
   You brought sad memories back, and made
   My love a painted form.

He sheds a tear.

Mishrakeshi   Fate plays strangely with him.

King   My friend, how can I endure a grief that has no respite?
   I cannot sleep at night
   And meet her dreaming;
   I cannot see the sketch
   While tears are streaming.

Mishrakeshi My friend, you have indeed atoned – and in her friend's presence – for the pain you caused by rejecting dear Shakuntala. (*Enter the maid* **Chaturika**.)

Maid Your Majesty, I was coming back with the box of paint-brushes –

King Well?

Maid I met Queen Vasumati with the maid Pingalika. And the queen snatched the box from me, saying: 'I will take it to the king myself.'

Clown How did you escape?

Maid The queen's dress caught on a vine. And while her maid was setting her free, I excused myself in a hurry.

A Voice Behind the Scenes Follow me, your Majesty.

Clown (*listening*) Man, the she-tiger of the palace is making a spring on her prey. She means to make one mouthful of the maid.

King My friend, the queen has come because she feels touched in her honour. You had better take care of this picture.

Clown 'And yourself', you might add. (*He takes the picture and rises.*) If you get out of the trap alive, call for me at the Cloud Balcony. And I will hide the thing there so that nothing but a pigeon could find it. (*Exit on the run.*)

Mishrakeshi Though his heart is given to another, he is courteous to his early flame. He is a constant friend.

Enter the **Portress** *with a document.*

Portress Victory to your Majesty.

King Vetravati, did you not meet Queen Vasumati?

Portress Yes, your Majesty. But she turned back when she saw that I carried a document.

King The queen knows times and seasons. She will not interrupt business.

Portress Your Majesty, the minister sends word that in the press of various business he has attended to only one citizen's suit. This he has reduced to writing for your Majesty's perusal.

King Give me the document. (*The* **Portress** *does so.*)

King (*reads*) 'Be it known to his Majesty. A seafaring merchant named Dhanavriddhi has been lost in a shipwreck. He is childless, and his property, amounting to several millions, reverts to the crown. Will his Majesty take action?' (*Sadly.*) It is dreadful to be childless. Vetravati, he had great riches. There must be several wives. Let inquiry be made. There may be a wife who is with child.

Portress We have this moment heard that a merchant's daughter of Saketa is his wife. And she is soon to become a mother.

King The child shall receive the inheritance. Go, inform the minister.

Portress Yes, your Majesty. (*She starts to go.*)

King Wait a moment.

Portress (*turning back*) Yes, your Majesty.

King After all, what does it matter whether he have issue or not?
Let King Dushyanta be proclaimed
To every sad soul kin
That mourns a kinsman loved and lost,
Yet did not plunge in sin.

Portress The proclamation shall be made. (*She goes out and soon returns.*) Your Majesty, the royal proclamation was welcomed by the populace as is a timely shower.

King (*sighing deeply*) Thus, when issue fails, wealth passes, on the death of the head of the family, to a stranger. When I die, it will be so with the glory of Puru's line.

Portress Heaven avert the omen!

King Alas! I despised the happiness that offered itself to me.

Mishrakeshi Without doubt, he has dear Shakuntala in mind when he thus reproaches himself.

King
Could I forsake the virtuous wife
Who held my best, my future life
And cherished it for glorious birth,
As does the seed-receiving earth?

Mishrakeshi She will not long be forsaken.

Maid (*to the* **Portress**) Mistress, the minister's report has doubled our lord's remorse. Go to the Cloud Balcony and bring Madhavya to dispel his grief.

Portress A good suggestion. (*Exit.*)

King Alas! The ancestors of Dushyanta are in a doubtful case.
For I am childless, and they do not know,
When I am gone, what child of theirs will bring
The scriptural oblation; and their tears
Already mingle with my offering.

Mishrakeshi He is screened from the light, and is in darkness.

Maid Do not give way to grief, your Majesty. You are in the prime of your years, and the birth of a son to one of your other wives will make you blameless before your ancestors. (*To herself.*) He does not heed me. The proper medicine is needed for any disease.

King (*betraying his sorrow*) Surely,
The royal line that flowed

A river pure and grand,
   Dies in the childless king,
   Like streams in desert sand.

He swoons.

Maid (*in distress*)   Oh, sir, come to yourself.

Mishrakeski   Shall I make him happy now? No, I heard the mother of the gods consoling Shakuntala. She said that the gods, impatient for the sacrifice, would soon cause him to welcome his true wife. I must delay no longer. I will comfort dear Shakuntala with my tidings. (*Exit through the air.*)

A Voice Behind the Scenes   Help, help!

King (*comes to himself and listens*)   It sounds as if Madhavya were in distress.

Maid   Your Majesty, I hope that Pingalika and the other maids did not catch poor Madhavya with the picture in his hands.

King   Go, Chaturika. Reprove the queen in my name for not controlling her servants.

Maid   Yes, your Majesty. (*Exit.*)

The Voice   Help, help!

King   The Brahman's voice seems really changed by fear. Who waits without? (*Enter the* **Chamberlain**.)

Chamberlain   Your Majesty commands?

King   See why poor Madhavya is screaming so.

Chamberlain   I will see. (*He goes out, and returns trembling.*)

King   Parvatayana, I hope it is nothing very dreadful.

Chamberlain   I hope not.

King   Then why do you tremble so? For
   Why should the trembling, born
   Of age, increasing, seize
   Your limbs and bid them shake
   Like fig-leaves in the breeze?

Chamberlain   Save your friend, O King!

King   From what?

Chamberlain   From great danger.

King   Speak plainly, man.

Chamberlain   On the Cloud Balcony, open to the four winds of heaven –

King   What has happened there?

Chamberlain
>While he was resting on its height,
>Which palace peacocks in their flight
>Can hardly reach, he seemed to be
>Snatched up – by what, we could not see.

King (*rising quickly*)   My very palace is invaded by evil creatures. To be a king, is to be a disappointed man.
>The moral stumblings of mine own,
>The daily slips, are scarcely known;
>Who then that rules a kingdom, can
>Guide every deed of every man?

The Voice   Hurry, hurry!

King (*hears the voice and quickens his steps*)   Have no fear, my friend.

The Voice   Have no fear! When something has got me by the back of the neck, and is trying to break my bones like a piece of sugar-cane!

King (*looks about*)   A bow! a bow! (*Enter a* **Greek Woman** *with a bow.*)

Greek Woman   A bow and arrows, your Majesty. And here are the finger-guards. (*The* **King** *takes the bow and arrows.*)

Another Voice Behind the Scenes
>Writhe, while I drink the red blood flowing clear
>And kill you, as a tiger kills a deer;
>Let King Dushyanta grasp his bow; but how
>Can all his kingly valour save you now?

King (*angrily*)   He scorns me, too! In one moment, miserable demon, you shall die. (*Stringing his bow.*) Where is the stairway, Parvatayana?

Chamberlain   Here, your Majesty. (*All make haste.*)

King (*looking about*)   There is no one here.

The Clown's Voice   Save me, save me! I see you, if you can't see me. I am a mouse in the claws of the cat. I am done for.

King   You are proud of your invisibility. But shall not my arrow see you? Stand still. Do not hope to escape by clinging to my friend.
>My arrow, flying when the bow is bent,
>Shall slay the wretch and spare the innocent;
>When milk is mixed with water in a cup,
>Swans leave the water, and the milk drink up.

He takes aim. Enter **Matali** *and the* **Clown**.

Matali   O King, as Indra, king of the gods, commands,
>Seek foes among the evil powers alone;
>For them your bow should bend;

Not cruel shafts, but glances soft and kind
Should fall upon a friend.

King (*hastily withdrawing the arrow*)   It is Matali. Welcome to the charioteer of heaven's king.

Clown   Well! He came within an inch of butchering me. And you welcome him.

Matali (*smiling*)   Hear, O King, for what purpose Indra sends me to you.

King   I am all attention.

Matali   There is a host of demons who call themselves Invincible – the brood of Kalanemi.

King   So Narada has told me.

Matali
Heaven's king is powerless; you shall smite
His foes in battle soon;
Darkness that overcomes the day,
Is scattered by the moon.

Take your bow at once, enter my heavenly chariot, and set forth for victory.

King   I am grateful for the honour which Indra shows me. But why did you act thus toward Madhavya?

Matali   I will tell you. I saw that you were overpowered by some inner sorrow, and acted thus to rouse you. For
The spurnèd snake will swell his hood;
Fire blazes when 'tis stirred;
Brave men are roused to fighting mood
By some insulting word.

King   Friend Madhavya, I must obey the bidding of heaven's king. Go, acquaint the minister Pishuna with the matter, and add these words of mine:
Your wisdom only shall control
The kingdom for a time;
My bow is strung; a distant goal
Calls me, and tasks sublime.

Clown   Very well. (*Exit.*)

Matali   Enter the chariot. (*The* **King** *does so.*)

Exeunt omnes.

Act VII

Enter, in a chariot that flies through the air, the **King** *and* **Matali**.

King Matali, though I have done what Indra commanded, I think myself an unprofitable servant, when I remember his most gracious welcome.

Matali O King, know that each considers himself the other's debtor. For
> You count the service given
> Small by the welcome paid,
> Which to the king of heaven
> Seems mean for such brave aid.

King Ah, no! For the honour given me at parting went far beyond imagination. Before the gods, he seated me beside him on his throne. And then
> He smiled, because his son Jayanta's heart
> Beat quicker, by the self-same wish oppressed,
> And placed about my neck the heavenly wreath
> Still fragrant from the sandal on his breast.

Matali But what do you not deserve from heaven's king? Remember:
> Twice, from peace-loving Indra's sway
> The demon-thorn was plucked away:
> First, by Man-lion's crooked claws;
> Again, by your smooth shafts to-day.

King This merely proves Indra's majesty. Remember:
> All servants owe success in enterprise
> To honour paid before the great deed's done;
> Could dawn defeat the darkness otherwise
> Than resting on the chariot of the sun?

Matali The feeling becomes you. (*After a little.*) See, O King! Your glory has the happiness of being published abroad in heaven.
> With colours used by nymphs of heaven
> To make their beauty shine,
> Gods write upon the surface given
> Of many a magic vine,
> As worth their song, the simple story
> Of those brave deeds that made your glory.

King Matali, when I passed before, I was intent on fighting the demons, and did not observe this region. Tell me. In which path of the winds are we?

Matali
> It is the windpath sanctified
> By holy Vishnu's second stride;
> Which, freed from dust of passion, ever
> Upholds the threefold heavenly river;

And, driving them with reins of light,
Guides the stars in wheeling flight.

King That is why serenity pervades me, body and soul. (*He observes the path taken by the chariot.*) It seems that we have descended into the region of the clouds.

Matali How do you perceive it?

King
Plovers that fly from mountain-caves,
Steeds that quick-flashing lightning laves,
And chariot-wheels that drip with spray –
A path o'er pregnant clouds betray.

Matali You are right. And in a moment you will be in the world over which you bear rule.

King (*looking down*) Matali, our quick descent gives the world of men a mysterious look. For
The plains appear to melt and fall
From mountain peaks that grow more tall;
The trunks of trees no longer hide
Nor in their leafy nests abide;
The river network now is clear,
For smaller streams at last appear:
It seems as if some being threw
The world to me, for clearer view.

Matali You are a good observer, O King. (*He looks down, awe-struck.*) There is a noble loveliness in the earth.

King Matali, what mountain is this, its flanks sinking into the eastern and into the western sea? It drips liquid gold like a cloud at sunset.

Matali O King, this is Gold Peak, the mountain of the fairy centaurs. Here it is that ascetics most fully attain to magic powers. See!
The ancient sage, Marichi's son,
Child of the Uncreated One,
Father of superhuman life,
Dwells here austerely with his wife.

King (*reverently*) I must not neglect the happy chance. I cannot go farther until I have walked humbly about the holy one.

Matali It is a worthy thought, O King. (*The chariot descends.*) We have come down to earth.

King (*astonished*) Matali,
The wheels are mute on whirling rim;
Unstirred, the dust is lying there;
We do not bump the earth, but skim:
Still, still we seem to fly through air.

Matali Such is the glory of the chariot which obeys you and Indra.

King In which direction lies the hermitage of Marichi's son?

Matali (*pointing*) See!
Where stands the hermit, horridly austere,
Whom clinging vines are choking, tough and sore;
Half-buried in an ant-hill that has grown
About him, standing post-like and alone;
Sun-staring with dim eyes that know no rest,
The dead skin of a serpent on his breast:
So long he stood unmoved, insensate there
That birds build nests within his mat of hair.

King (*gazing*) All honour to one who mortifies the flesh so terribly.

Matali (*checking the chariot*) We have entered the hermitage of the ancient sage, whose wife Aditi tends the coral-trees.

King Here is deeper contentment than in heaven. I seem plunged in a pool of nectar.

Matali (*stopping the chariot*) Descend, O King.

King (*descending*) But how will you fare?

Matali The chariot obeys the word of command. I too will descend. (*He does so.*) Before you, O King, are the groves where the holiest hermits lead their self-denying life.

King I look with amazement both at their simplicity and at what they might enjoy.
Their appetites are fed with air
Where grows whatever is most fair;
They bathe religiously in pools
Which golden lily-pollen cools;
They pray within a jewelled home,
Are chaste where nymphs of heaven roam:
They mortify desire and sin
With things that others fast to win.

Matali The desires of the great aspire high. (*He walks about and speaks to some one not visible.*) Ancient Shakalya, how is Marichi's holy son occupied? (*He listens.*) What do you say? That he is explaining to Aditi, in answer to her question, the duties of a faithful wife? My matter must await a fitter time. (*He turns to the* **King**.) Wait here, O King, in the shade of the ashoka tree, till I have announced your coming to the sire of Indra.

King Very well. (*Exit* **Matali***. The* **King***'s arm throbs, a happy omen.*)
I dare not hope for what I pray;
Why thrill – in vain?
For heavenly bliss once thrown away
Turns into pain.

A Voice Behind the Scenes   Don't! You mustn't be so foolhardy. Oh, you are always the same.

King (*listening*)   No naughtiness could feel at home in this spot. Who draws such a rebuke upon himself? (*He looks towards the sound. In surprise.*) It is a child, but no child in strength. And two hermit-women are trying to control him.

>He drags a struggling lion cub,
>The lioness' milk half-sucked, half-missed,
>Towzles his mane, and tries to drub
>Him tame with small, imperious fist.

Enter a small **Boy**, *as described, and two* **Hermit-Women**.

Boy   Open your mouth, cub. I want to count your teeth.

First Woman   Naughty boy, why do you torment our pets? They are like children to us. Your energy seems to take the form of striking something. No wonder the hermits call you All-tamer.

King   Why should my heart go out to this boy as if he were my own son? (*He reflects.*) No doubt my childless state makes me sentimental.

Second Woman   The lioness will spring at you if you don't let her baby go.

Boy (*smiling*)   Oh, I'm dreadfully scared. (*He bites his lip.*)

King (*in surprise*)
>The boy is seed of fire
>Which, when it grows, will burn;
>A tiny spark that soon
>To awful flame may turn.

First Woman   Let the little lion go, dear. I will give you another plaything.

Boy   Where is it? Give it to me. (*He stretches out his hand.*)

King (*looking at the hand*)   He has one of the imperial birthmarks! For
>Between the eager fingers grow
>The close-knit webs together drawn,
>Like some lone lily opening slow
>To meet the kindling blush of dawn.

Second Woman   Suvrata, we can't make him stop by talking. Go. In my cottage you will find a painted clay peacock that belongs to the hermit-boy Mankanaka. Bring him that.

First Woman   I will. (*Exit.*)

Boy   Meanwhile I'll play with this one.

Hermit-Woman (*looks and laughs*)   Let him go.

King   My heart goes out to this willful child. (*Sighing.*)
>They show their little buds of teeth
>In peals of causeless laughter;
>They hide their trustful heads beneath

Your heart. And stumbling after
Come sweet, unmeaning sounds that sing
To you. The father warms
And loves the very dirt they bring
Upon their little forms.

Hermit-Woman (*shaking her finger*)   Won't you mind me? (*She looks about.*) Which one of the hermit-boys is here? (*She sees the* **King**.) Oh, sir, please come here and free this lion cub. The little rascal is tormenting him, and I can't make him let go.

King   Very well. (*He approaches, smiling.*) O little son of a great sage!
Your conduct in this place apart,
Is most unfit;
'Twould grieve your father's pious heart
And trouble it.

To animals he is as good
As good can be;
You spoil it, like a black snake's brood
In sandal tree.

Hermit-Woman   But, sir, he is not the son of a hermit.

King   So it would seem, both from his looks and his actions. But in this spot, I had no suspicion of anything else. (*He loosens the* **Boy**'s *hold on the cub, and touching him, says to himself.*)
It makes me thrill to touch the boy,
The stranger's son, to me unknown;
What measureless content must fill
The man who calls the child his own!

Hermit-Woman (*looking at the two*)   Wonderful! wonderful!

King   Why do you say that, mother?

Hermit-Woman   I am astonished to see how much the boy looks like you, sir. You are not related. Besides, he is a perverse little creature and he does not know you. Yet he takes no dislike to you.

King (*caressing the* **Boy**)   Mother, if he is not the son of a hermit, what is his family?

Hermit-Woman   The family of Puru.

King (*to himself*)   He is of one family with me! Then could my thought be true? (*Aloud.*) But this is the custom of Puru's line:
In glittering palaces they dwell
While men, and rule the country well;
Then make the grove their home in age,
And die in austere hermitage.
But how could human beings, of their own mere motion, attain this spot?

Hermit-Woman   You are quite right, sir. But the boy's mother was related to a nymph, and she bore her son in the pious grove of the father of the gods.

King (*to himself*)   Ah, a second ground for hope. (*Aloud.*) What was the name of the good king whose wife she was?

Hermit-Woman   Who would speak his name? He rejected his true wife.

King (*to himself*)   This story points at me. Suppose I ask the boy for his mother's name. (*He reflects.*) No, it is wrong to concern myself with one who may be another's wife.

Enter the **First Woman**, *with the clay peacock.*

First Woman   Look, All-tamer. Here is the bird, the *shakunta*. Isn't the *shakunta* lovely?

Boy (*looks about*)   Where is my mamma? (*The* **Two Women** *burst out laughing.*)

First Woman   It sounded like her name, and deceived him. He loves his mother.

Second Woman   She said: 'See how pretty the peacock is.' That is all.

King (*to himself*)   His mother's name is Shakuntala! But names are alike. I trust this hope may not prove a disappointment in the end, like a mirage.

Boy   I like this little peacock, sister. Can it fly? (*He seizes the toy.*)

First Woman (*looks at the boy. Anxiously*)   Oh, the amulet is not on his wrist.

King   Do not be anxious, mother. It fell while he was struggling with the lion cub. (*He starts to pick it up.*)

The Two Women   Oh, don't, don't! (*They look at him.*) He has touched it! (*Astonished, they lay their hands on their bosoms, and look at each other.*)

King   Why did you try to prevent me?

First Woman   Listen, your Majesty. This is a divine and most potent charm, called the Invincible. Marichi's holy son gave it to the baby when the birth-ceremony was performed. If it falls on the ground, no one may touch it except the boy's parents or the boy himself.

King   And if another touch it?

First Woman   It becomes a serpent and stings him.

King   Did you ever see this happen to any one else?

Both Women   More than once.

King (*joyfully*)   Then why may I not welcome my hopes fulfilled at last? (*He embraces the* **Boy**.)

Second Woman   Come, Suvrata. Shakuntala is busy with her religious duties. We must go and tell her what has happened. (*Exeunt ambo.*)

Boy Let me go. I want to see my mother.

King My son, you shall go with me to greet your mother.

Boy Dushyanta is my father, not you.

King (*smiling*) You show I am right by contradicting me.

Enter **Shakuntala**, *wearing her hair in a single braid.*

Shakuntala (*doubtfully*) I have heard that All-tamer's amulet did not change when it should have done so. But I do not trust my own happiness. Yet perhaps it is as Mishrakeshi told me. (*She walks about.*)

King (*looking at* **Shakuntala**. *With plaintive joy*) It is she. It is Shakuntala.
   The pale, worn face, the careless dress,
   The single braid,
   Show her still true, me pitiless,
   The long vow paid.

Shakuntala (*seeing the* **King** *pale with remorse. Doubtfully*) It is not my husband. Who is the man that soils my boy with his caresses? The amulet should protect him.

Boy (*running to his mother*) Mother, he is a man that belongs to other people. And he calls me his son.

King My darling, the cruelty I showed you has turned to happiness. Will you not recognise me?

Shakuntala (*to herself*) Oh, my heart, believe it. Fate struck hard, but its envy is gone and pity takes its place. It is my husband.

King
   Black madness flies;
   Comes memory;
   Before my eyes
   My love I see.

   Eclipse flees far;
   Light follows soon;
   The loving star
   Draws to the moon.

Shakuntala Victory, victo – (*Tears choke her utterance.*)

King
   The tears would choke you, sweet, in vain;
   My soul with victory is fed,
   Because I see your face again –
   No jewels, but the lips are red.

Boy Who is he, mother?

Shakuntala Ask fate, my child. (*She weeps.*)

King
    Dear, graceful wife, forget;
    Let the sin vanish;
    Strangely did madness strive
    Reason to banish.

    Thus blindness works in men,
    Love's joy to shake;
    Spurning a garland, lest
    It prove a snake. (*He falls at her feet.*)

Shakuntala   Rise, my dear husband. Surely, it was some old sin of mine that broke my happiness – though it has turned again to happiness. Otherwise, how could you, dear, have acted so? You are so kind. (*The* **King** *rises.*) But what brought back the memory of your suffering wife?

King   I will tell you when I have plucked out the dart of sorrow.
    'Twas madness, sweet, that could let slip
    A tear to burden your dear lip;
    On graceful lashes seen to-day, (*He does so.*)

Shakuntala (*sees more clearly and discovers the ring*)   My husband, it is the ring!

King   Yes. And when a miracle recovered it, my memory returned.

Shakuntala   That was why it was so impossible for me to win your confidence.

King   Then let the vine receive her flower, as earnest of her union with spring.

Shakuntala   I do not trust it. I would rather you wore it.

Enter **Matali**.

Matali   I congratulate you, O King, on reunion with your wife and on seeing the face of your son.

King   My desires bear sweeter fruit because fulfilled through a friend. Matali, was not this matter known to Indra?

Matali (*smiling*)   What is hidden from the gods? Come. Marichi's holy son, Kashyapa, wishes to see you.

King   My dear wife, bring our son. I could not appear without you before the holy one.

Shakuntala   I am ashamed to go before such parents with my husband.

King   It is the custom in times of festival. Come.

They walk about. **Kashyapa** *appears seated, with* **Aditi**.

Kashyapa (*looking at the* **King**)   Aditi,
    'Tis King Dushyanta, he who goes before
    Your son in battle, and who rules the earth,

Whose bow makes Indra's weapon seem no more
Than a fine plaything, lacking sterner worth.

Aditi　His valour might be inferred from his appearance.

Matali　O King, the parents of the gods look upon you with a glance that betrays parental fondness. Approach them.

King　Matali,
　Sprung from the Creator's children, do I see
　Great Kashyapa and Mother Aditi?
　The pair that did produce the sun in heaven,
　To which each year twelve changing forms are given;
　That brought the king of all the gods to birth,
　Who rules in heaven, in hell, and on the earth;
　That Vishnu, than the Uncreated higher,
　Chose as his parents with a fond desire.

Matali　It is indeed they.

King (*falling before them*)　Dushyanta, servant of Indra, does reverence to you both.

Kashyapa　My son, rule the earth long.

Aditi　And be invincible. (**Shakuntala** *and her son fall at their feet.*)

Kashyapa　My daughter,
　Your husband equals Indra, king
　Of gods; your son is like his son;
　No further blessing need I bring:
　Win bliss such as his wife has won.

Aditi　My child, keep the favour of your husband. And may this fine boy be an honour to the families of both parents. Come, let us be seated. (*All seat themselves.*)

Kashyapa (*indicating one after the other*)
　Faithful Shakuntala, the boy,
　And you, O King, I see
　A trinity to bless the world –
　Faith, Treasure, Piety.

King　Holy one, your favour shown to us is without parallel. You granted the fulfilment of our wishes before you called us to your presence. For, holy one,
　The flower comes first, and then the fruit;
　The clouds appear before the rain;
　Effect comes after cause; but you
　First helped, then made your favour plain.

Matali　O King, such is the favour shown by the parents of the world.

King　Holy one, I married this your maid-servant by the voluntary ceremony. When after a time her relatives brought her to me, my memory failed and I rejected her. In so doing, I sinned against Kanva, who is kin to you. But afterwards, when I saw the

ring, I perceived that I had married her. And this seems very wonderful to me.
>   Like one who doubts an elephant,
>   Though seeing him stride by,
>   And yet believes when he has seen
>   The footprints left; so I.

Kashyapa   My son, do not accuse yourself of sin. Your infatuation was inevitable. Listen.

King   I am all attention.

Kashyapa   When the nymph Menaka descended to earth and received Shakuntala, afflicted at her rejection, she came to Aditi. Then I perceived the matter by my divine insight. I saw that the unfortunate girl had been rejected by her rightful husband because of Durvasas' curse. And that the curse would end when the ring came to light.

King (*with a sigh of relief. To himself*)   Then I am free from blame.

Shakuntala (*to herself*)   Thank heaven! My husband did not reject me of his own accord. He really did not remember me. I suppose I did not hear the curse in my absent-minded state, for my friends warned me most earnestly to show my husband the ring.

Kashyapa   My daughter, you know the truth. Do not now give way to anger against your rightful husband. Remember:
>   The curse it was that brought defeat and pain;
>   The darkness flies; you are his queen again.
>   Reflections are not seen in dusty glass,
>   Which, cleaned, will mirror all the things that pass.

King   It is most true, holy one.

Kashyapa   My son, I hope you have greeted as he deserves the son whom Shakuntala has borne you, for whom I myself have performed the birth-rite and the other ceremonies.

King   Holy one, the hope of my race centres in him.

Kashyapa   Know then that his courage will make him emperor.
>   Journeying over every sea,
>   His car will travel easily;
>   The seven islands of the earth
>   Will bow before his matchless worth;
>   Because wild beasts to him were tame,
>   All-tamer was his common name;
>   As Bharata he shall be known,
>   For he will bear the world alone.

King   I anticipate everything from him, since you have performed the rites for him.

Aditi   Kanva also should be informed that his daughter's wishes are fulfilled. But Menaka is waiting upon me here and cannot be spared.

Shakuntala (*to herself*)   The holy one has expressed my own desire.

Kashyapa   Kanva knows the whole matter through his divine insight. (*He reflects.*) Yet he should hear from us the pleasant tidings, how his daughter and her son have been received by her husband. Who waits without? (*Enter a* **Pupil**.)

Pupil   I am here, holy one.

Kashyapa   Galava, fly through the air at once, carrying pleasant tidings from me to holy Kanva. Tell him how Durvasas' curse has come to an end, how Dushyanta recovered his memory, and has taken Shakuntala with her child to himself.

Pupil   Yes, holy one. (*Exit.*)

Kashyapa (*to the* **King**)   My son, enter with child and wife the chariot of your friend Indra, and set out for your capital.

King   Yes, holy one.

Kashyapa   For now
   May Indra send abundant rain,
   Repaid by sacrificial gain;
   With aid long mutually given,
   Rule you on earth, and he in heaven.

King   Holy one, I will do my best.

Kashyapa   What more, my son, shall I do for you?

King   Can there be more than this? Yet may this prayer be fulfilled.
   May kingship benefit the land,
   And wisdom grow in scholars' band;
   May Shiva see my faith on earth
   And make me free of all rebirth.

Exeunt omnes.

Chitra: A Play in One Act (1913)

Rabindranath Tagore

Translated by Tagore

Rabindranath Tagore (1861–1941) was a poet, playwright, philosopher, novelist, musician, artist and short story writer, most famously remembered for *Gitanjali* and his enormous contribution to the Bengal Renaissance. He became the first non-European to win the Nobel Prize in 1913 and continues to be revered for his eloquent language. While critical of British rule, he debunked narrow notions of nationalism, emphasizing the virtues of humanism instead. Deeply committed to education, he left a tremendous legacy through the Viswa Bharati University, which he founded in Shantiniketan, located in West Bengal, India.

Chitra was published in 1913 and was produced by Elliot S. Wheeler and David Widger. In 2022 the play was performed at The Shaw Festival Theatre in Niagara on the Lake in Canada under the direction of Kimberley Rampersad. It draws on the story of the warrior princess Chitrangada from the *Mahabharata* and her love and admiration for the great warrior Arjuna, a *Kshatriya*, aristocratic warrior caste, who must uphold his sense of duty to his people. Thus, it uses mythology to raise broad questions about duty and truth, questions that are addressed through several conflicts between material beauty and inner truth, the duty to oneself and the people, and illusion and reality. Such conflicts are captured through dialogue between gods (Madana – the 'Lord of Love' and Vasanta – 'King of the Seasons'), high caste men and women (Arjuna, a Kuru prince, and a *Kshatriya* warrior, and Chitra, a princess and daughter of the King of Manipur), and villagers. Tagore presents a luscious landscape through lyrical language and vivid imagery of trees, dreams, illusions, crickets, silence, birds and flowers, which, while depicting the contradictions between 'Heaven and earth, time and space, pleasure and pain, death, and life', also suggest Tagore's deep investment in returning to Hindu mythology as an important resource for articulating ideals regarding one's duty to the nation, especially at a time of intensifying anti-colonial nationalism.

Tagore is known for his representation of strong, fierce and independent women. Chitra, who has 'left the seclusion of a woman's chamber' embodies the playwright's feminist vision through her valour and courage, and the art of argumentation through which she exhorts Arjuna to embrace love and beauty in all its imperfection. Tagore's vision aligns with the vision of nationalist and social reformers who, at the time that he was writing, promoted women's education, learning, and intelligence through a revival of mythological stories as examples of India's 'golden age' where women provided guidance and exercised social agency. This is visible in how Arjuna imagines Chitra – as a 'Goddess of Victory', and a 'watchful lioness'. Does the play, however, in highlighting the achievements of Chitra and Arjuna, glorify upper-caste *Kshatriya* men and women as the leaders of the nation? What is the role of the gods and nature in promoting the theme of the play?

Reference

Tagore, Rabindranath. *Chitra*. New York: The Macmillan Company, 1916.

TO

MRS. WILLIAM VAUGHN MOODY

Preface

THIS lyrical drama was written about twenty-five years ago. It is based on the following story from the Mahabharata.

In the course of his wanderings, in fulfilment of a vow of penance, Arjuna came to Manipur. There he saw Chitrangada, the beautiful daughter of Chitravahana, the king of the country. Smitten with her charms, he asked the king for the hand of his daughter in marriage. Chitravahana asked him who he was, and learning that he was Arjuna the Pandara, told him that Prabhanjana, one of his ancestors in the kingly line of Manipur, had long been childless. In order to obtain an heir, he performed severe penances. Pleased with these austerities, the god Shiva gave him this boon, that he and his successors should each have one child. It so happened that the promised child had invariably been a son. He, Chitravahana, was the first to have only a daughter Chitrangada to perpetuate the race. He had, therefore, always treated her as a son and had made her his heir.

Continuing, the king said:

'The one son that will be born to her must be the perpetuator of my race. That son will be the price that I shall demand for this marriage. You can take her, if you like, on this condition.'

Arjuna promised and took Chitrangada to wife, and lived in her father's capital for three years. When a son was born to them, he embraced her with affection, and taking leave of her and her father, set out again on his travels.

The Characters

Gods
  Madana *(Eros)*
  Vasanta *(Lycoris)*

Mortals
  Chitra, *daughter of the King of Manipur*
  Arjuna, *a prince of the house of the Kurus. He is of the Kshatriya or 'warrior caste', and during the action is living as a Hermit retired in the forest*

Villagers from an outlying district of Manipur.

NOTE. – The dramatic poem 'Chitra' has been performed in India without scenery – the actors being surrounded by the audience. Proposals for its production here having been made to him, he went through this translation and provided stage directions, but wished these omitted if it were printed as a book.

Scene I

Chitra   ART thou the god with the five darts, the Lord of Love?

Madana   I am he who was the first born in the heart of the Creator. I bind in bonds of pain and bliss the lives of men and women!

Chitra   I know, I know what that pain is and those bonds. – And who art thou, my lord?

Vasanta   I am his friend – Vasanta – the King of the Seasons. Death and decrepitude would wear the world to the bone but that I follow them and constantly attack them. I am Eternal Youth.

Chitra   I bow to thee, Lord Vasanta.

Madana   But what stern vow is thine, fair stranger? Why dost thou wither thy fresh youth with penance and mortification? Such a sacrifice is not fit for the worship of love. Who art thou and what is thy prayer?

Chitra   I am Chitra, the daughter of the kingly house of Manipur. With godlike grace Lord Shiva promised to my royal grandsire an unbroken line of male descent. Nevertheless, the divine word proved powerless to change the spark of life in my mother's womb – so invincible was my nature, woman though I be.

Madana   I know, that is why thy father brings thee up as his son. He has taught thee the use of the bow and all the duties of a king.

Chitra   Yes, that is why I am dressed in man's attire and have left the seclusion of a woman's chamber. I know no feminine wiles for winning hearts. My hands are strong to bend the bow, but I have never learnt Cupid's archery, the play of eyes.

Madana   That requires no schooling, fair one. The eye does its work untaught, and he knows how well, who is struck in the heart.

Chitra   One day in search of game I roved alone to the forest on the bank of the Purna river. Tying my horse to a tree trunk I entered a dense thicket on the track of a deer. I found a narrow sinuous path meandering through the dusk of the entangled boughs, the foliage vibrated with the chirping of crickets, when of a sudden I came upon a man lying on a bed of dried leaves, across my path. I asked him haughtily to move aside, but he heeded not. Then with the sharp end of my bow I pricked him in contempt. Instantly he leapt up with straight, tall limbs, like a sudden tongue of fire from a heap of ashes. An amused smile flickered round the corners of his mouth, perhaps at the sight of my boyish countenance. Then for the first time in my life I felt myself a woman, and knew that a man was before me.

Madana   At the auspicious hour I teach the man and the woman this supreme lesson to know themselves. What happened after that?

Chitra   With fear and wonder I asked him 'Who are you?' 'I am Arjuna', he said, 'of the great Kuru clan'. I stood petrified like a statue, and forgot to do him obeisance.

Was this indeed Arjuna, the one great idol of my dreams! Yes, I had long ago heard how he had vowed a twelve-years' celibacy. Many a day my young ambition had spurred me on to break my lance with him, to challenge him in disguise to single combat, and prove my skill in arms against him. Ah, foolish heart, whither fled thy presumption? Could I but exchange my youth with all its aspirations for the clod of earth under his feet, I should deem it a most precious grace. I know not in what whirlpool of thought I was lost, when suddenly I saw him vanish through the trees. O foolish woman, neither didst thou greet him, nor speak a word, nor beg forgiveness, but stoodest like a barbarian boor while he contemptuously walked away! . . . Next morning I laid aside my man's clothing. I donned bracelets, anklets, waist-chain, and a gown of purple red silk. The unaccustomed dress clung about my shrinking shame; but I hastened on my quest, and found Arjuna in the forest temple of Shiva.

Madana   Tell me the story to the end. I am the heart-born god, and I understand the mystery of these impulses.

Chitra   Only vaguely can I remember what things I said, and what answer I got. Do not ask me to tell you all. Shame fell on me like a thunderbolt, yet could not break me to pieces, so utterly hard, so like a man am I. His last words as I walked home pricked my ears like red hot needles. 'I have taken the vow of celibacy. I am not fit to be thy husband!' Oh, the vow of a man! Surely thou knowest, thou god of love, that unnumbered saints and sages have surrendered the merits of their life-long penance at the feet of a woman. I broke my bow in two and burnt my arrows in the fire. I hated my strong, lithe arm, scored by drawing the bowstring. O Love, god Love, thou hast laid low in the dust the vain pride of my manlike strength; and all my man's training lies crushed under thy feet. Now teach me thy lessons; give me the power of the weak and the weapon of the unarmed hand.

Madana   I will be thy friend. I will bring the world-conquering Arjuna a captive before thee, to accept his rebellion's sentence at thy hand.

Chitra   Had I but the time needed, I could win his heart by slow degrees, and ask no help of the gods. I would stand by his side as a comrade, drive the fierce horses of his war-chariot, attend him in the pleasures of the chase, keep guard at night at the entrance of his tent, and help him in all the great duties of a Kshatriya, rescuing the weak, and meting out justice where it is due. Surely at last the day would have come for him to look at me and wonder, 'What boy is this? Has one of my slaves in a former life followed me like my good deeds into this?' I am not the woman who nourishes her despair in lonely silence, feeding it with nightly tears and covering it with the daily patient smile, a widow from her birth. The flower of my desire shall never drop into the dust before it has ripened to fruit. But it is the labour of a life time to make one's true self known and honoured. Therefore I have come to thy door, thou world-vanquishing Love, and thou, Vasanta, youthful Lord of the Seasons, take from my young body this primal injustice, an unattractive plainness. For a single day make me superbly beautiful, even as beautiful as was the sudden blooming of love in my heart. Give me but one brief day of perfect beauty, and I will answer for the days that follow.

Madana Lady, I grant thy prayer.

Vasanta Not for the short span of a day, but for one whole year the charm of spring blossoms shall nestle round thy limbs.

Scene II

Arjuna WAS I dreaming or was what I saw by the lake truly there? Sitting on the mossy turf, I mused over bygone years in the sloping shadows of the evening, when slowly there came out from the folding darkness of foliage an apparition of beauty in the perfect form of a woman, and stood on a white slab of stone at the water's brink. It seemed that the heart of the earth must heave in joy under her bare white feet. Methought the vague veilings of her body should melt in ecstasy into air as the golden mist of dawn melts from off the snowy peak of the eastern hill. She bowed herself above the shining mirror of the lake and saw the reflection of her face. She started up in awe and stood still; then smiled, and with a careless sweep of her left arm unloosed her hair and let it trail on the earth at her feet. She bared her bosom and looked at her arms, so flawlessly modelled, and instinct with an exquisite caress. Bending her head she saw the sweet blossoming of her youth and the tender bloom and blush of her skin. She beamed with a glad surprise. So, if the white lotus bud on opening her eyes in the morning were to arch her neck and see her shadow in the water, would she wonder at herself the livelong day. But a moment after the smile passed from her face and a shade of sadness crept into her eyes. She bound up her tresses, drew her veil over her arms, and sighing slowly, walked away like a beauteous evening fading into the night. To me the supreme fulfilment of desire seemed to have been revealed in a flash and then to have vanished. . . . But who is it that pushes the door?

Enter **Chitra**, *dressed as a woman.*

Ah! it is she. Quiet, my heart! . . . Fear me not, lady! I am a Kshatriya.

Chitra Honoured sir, you are my guest. I live in this temple. I know not in what way I can show you hospitality.

Arjuna Fair lady, the very sight of you is indeed the highest hospitality. If you will not take it amiss I would ask you a question.

Chitra You have permission.

Arjuna What stern vow keeps you immured in this solitary temple, depriving all mortals of a vision of so much loveliness?

Chitra I harbour a secret desire in my heart, for the fulfilment of which I offer daily prayers to Lord Shiva.

Arjuna Alas, what can you desire, you who are the desire of the whole world! From the easternmost hill on whose summit the morning sun first prints his fiery foot to the end of the sunset land have I travelled. I have seen whatever is most precious, beautiful and great on the earth. My knowledge shall be yours, only say for what or for whom you seek.

Chitra He whom I seek is known to all.

Arjuna Indeed! Who may this favourite of the gods be, whose fame has captured your heart?

Chitra Sprung from the highest of all royal houses, the greatest of all heroes is he.

Arjuna Lady, offer not such wealth of beauty as is yours on the altar of false reputation. Spurious fame spreads from tongue to tongue like the fog of the early dawn before the sun rises. Tell me who in the highest of kingly lines is the supreme hero?

Chitra Hermit, you are jealous of other men's fame. Do you not know that all over the world the royal house of the Kurus is the most famous?

Arjuna The house of the Kurus!

Chitra And have you never heard of the greatest name of that far-famed house?

Arjuna From your own lips let me hear it.

Chitra Arjuna, the conqueror of the world. I have culled from the mouths of the multitude that imperishable name and hidden it with care in my maiden heart. Hermit, why do you look perturbed? Has that name only a deceitful glitter? Say so, and I will not hesitate to break this casket of my heart and throw the false gem to the dust.

Arjuna Be his name and fame, his bravery and prowess false or true, for mercy's sake do not banish him from your heart – for he kneels at your feet even now.

Chitra You, Arjuna!

Arjuna Yes, I am he, the love-hungered guest at your door.

Chitra Then it is not true that Arjuna has taken a vow of chastity for twelve long years?

Arjuna But you have dissolved my vow even as the moon dissolves the night's vow of obscurity.

Chitra Oh, shame upon you! What have you seen in me that makes you false to yourself? Whom do you seek in these dark eyes, in these milk-white arms, if you are ready to pay for her the price of your probity? Not my true self, I know. Surely this cannot be love, this is not man's highest homage to woman! Alas, that this frail disguise, the body, should make one blind to the light of the deathless spirit! Yes, now indeed, I know, Arjuna, the fame of your heroic manhood is false.

Arjuna Ah, I feel how vain is fame, the pride of prowess! Everything seems to me a dream. You alone are perfect; you are the wealth of the world, the end of all poverty, the goal of all efforts, the one woman! Others there are who can be but slowly known. While to see you for a moment is to see perfect completeness once and for ever.

Chitra Alas, it is not I, not I, Arjuna! It is the deceit of a god. Go, go, my hero, go. Woo not falsehood, offer not your great heart to an illusion. Go.

Scene III

Chitra No, impossible. To face that fervent gaze that almost grasps you like clutching hands of the hungry spirit within; to feel his heart struggling to break its bounds urging its passionate cry through the entire body – and then to send him away like a beggar – no, impossible.

Enter **Madana** *and* **Vasanta**.

Ah, god of love, what fearful flame is this with which thou hast enveloped me! I burn, and I burn whatever I touch.

Madana I desire to know what happened last night.

Chitra At evening I lay down on a grassy bed strewn with the petals of spring flowers, and recollected the wonderful praise of my beauty I had heard from Arjuna; – drinking drop by drop the honey that I had stored during the long day. The history of my past life like that of my former existences was forgotten. I felt like a flower, which has but a few fleeting hours to listen to all the humming flatteries and whispered murmurs of the woodlands and then must lower its eyes from the Sky, bend its head and at a breath give itself up to the dust without a cry, thus ending the short story of a perfect moment that has neither past nor future.

Vasanta A limitless life of glory can bloom and spend itself in a morning.

Madana Like an endless meaning in the narrow span of a song.

Chitra The southern breeze caressed me to sleep. From the flowering Malati bower overhead silent kisses dropped over my body. On my hair, my breast, my feet, each flower chose a bed to die on. I slept. And, suddenly in the depth of my sleep, I felt as if some intense eager look, like tapering fingers of flame, touched my slumbering body. I started up and saw the Hermit standing before me. The moon had moved to the west, peering through the leaves to espy this wonder of divine art wrought in a fragile human frame. The air was heavy with perfume; the silence of the night was vocal with the chirping of crickets; the reflections of the trees hung motionless in the lake; and with his staff in his hand he stood, tall and straight and still, like a forest tree. It seemed to me that I had, on opening my eyes, died to all realities of life and undergone a dream birth into a shadow land. Shame slipped to my feet like loosened clothes. I heard his call – 'Beloved, my most beloved!' And all my forgotten lives united as one and responded to it. I said, 'Take me, take all I am!' And I stretched out my arms to him. The moon set behind the trees. One curtain of darkness covered all. Heaven and earth, time and space, pleasure and pain, death and life merged together in an unbearable ecstasy. . . . With the first gleam of light, the first twitter of birds, I rose up and sat leaning on my left arm. He lay asleep with a vague smile about his lips like the crescent moon in the morning. The rosy red glow of the dawn fell upon his noble forehead. I sighed and stood up. I drew together the leafy lianas to screen the streaming sun from his face. I looked about me and saw the same old earth. I remembered what I used to be, and ran and ran like a deer afraid of her own shadow, through the forest path strewn with shephali flowers. I found a lonely nook, and sitting down covered my face with both hands, and tried to weep and cry. But no tears came to my eyes.

Madana   Alas, thou daughter of mortals! I stole from the divine Storehouse the fragrant wine of heaven, filled with it one earthly night to the brim, and placed it in thy hand to drink – yet still I hear this cry of anguish!

Chitra (*bitterly*)   Who drank it? The rarest completion of life's desire, the first union of love was proffered to me, but was wrested from my grasp? This borrowed beauty, this falsehood that enwraps me, will slip from me taking with it the only monument of that sweet union, as the petals fall from an overblown flower; and the woman ashamed of her naked poverty will sit weeping day and night. Lord Love, this cursed appearance companions me like a demon robbing me of all the prizes of love – all the kisses for which my heart is athirst.

Madana   Alas, how vain thy single night had been! The barque of joy came in sight, but the waves would not let it touch the shore.

Chitra   Heaven came so close to my hand that I forgot for a moment that it had not reached me. But when I woke in the morning from my dream I found that my body had become my own rival. It is my hateful task to deck her every day, to send her to my beloved and see her caressed by him. O god, take back thy boon!

Madana   But if I take it from you how can you stand before your lover? To snatch away the cup from his lips when he has scarcely drained his first draught of pleasure, would not that be cruel? With what resentful anger he must regard thee then?

Chitra   That would be better far than this. I will reveal my true self to him, a nobler thing than this disguise. If he rejects it, if he spurns me and breaks my heart, I will bear even that in silence.

Vasanta   Listen to my advice. When with the advent of autumn the flowering season is over then comes the triumph of fruitage. A time will come of itself when the heat-cloyed bloom of the body will droop and Arjuna will gladly accept the abiding fruitful truth in thee. O child, go back to thy mad festival.

Scene IV

Chitra   WHY do you watch me like that, my warrior?

Arjuna   I watch how you weave that garland. Skill and grace, the twin brother and sister, are dancing playfully on your finger tips. I am watching and thinking.

Chitra   What are you thinking, sir?

Arjuna   I am thinking that you, with this same lightness of touch and sweetness, are weaving my days of exile into an immortal wreath, to crown me when I return home.

Chitra   Home! But this love is not for a home!

Arjuna   Not for a home?

Chitra   No. Never talk of that. Take to your home what is abiding and strong. Leave the little wild flower where it was born; leave it beautifully to die at the day's end among all fading blossoms and decaying leaves. Do not take it to your palace hall to fling it on the stony floor which knows no pity for things that fade and are forgotten.

Arjuna   Is ours that kind of love?

Chitra   Yes, no other! Why regret it? That which was meant for idle days should never outlive them. Joy turns into pain when the door by which it should depart is shut against it. Take it and keep it as long as it lasts. Let not the satiety of your evening claim more than the desire of your morning could earn. . . . The day is done. Put this garland on. I am tired. Take me in your arms, my love. Let all vain bickerings of discontent die away at the sweet meeting of our lips.

Arjuna   Hush! Listen, my beloved, the sound of prayer bells from the distant village temple steals upon the evening air across the silent trees!

Scene V

Vasanta   I CANNOT keep pace with thee, my friend! I am tired. It is a hard task to keep alive the fire thou hast kindled. Sleep overtakes me, the fan drops from my hand, and cold ashes cover the glow of the fire. I start up again from my slumber and with all my might rescue the weary flame. But this can go on no longer.

Madana   I know, thou art as fickle as a child. Ever restless is thy play in heaven and on earth. Things that thou for days buildest up with endless detail thou dost shatter in a moment without regret. But this work of ours is nearly finished. Pleasure-winged days fly fast, and the year, almost at its end, swoons in rapturous bliss.

Scene VI

Arjuna   I WOKE in the morning and found that my dreams had distilled a gem. I have no casket to inclose it, no king's crown whereon to fix it, no chain from which to hang it, and yet have not the heart to throw it away. My Kshatriya's right arm, idly occupied in holding it, forgets its duties.

Enter **Chitra**.

Chitra   Tell me your thoughts, sir!

Arjuna   My mind is busy with thoughts of hunting today. See, how the rain pours in torrents and fiercely beats upon the hillside. The dark shadow of the clouds hangs heavily over the forest, and the swollen stream, like reckless youth, overleaps all barriers with mocking laughter. On such rainy days we five brothers would go to the Chitraka forest to chase wild beasts. Those were glad times. Our hearts danced to the drumbeat of rumbling clouds. The woods resounded with the screams of peacocks. Timid deer could not hear our approaching steps for the patter of rain and the noise of waterfalls; the leopards would leave their tracks on the wet earth, betraying their lairs. Our sport over, we dared each other to swim across turbulent streams on our way back home. The restless spirit is on me. I long to go hunting.

Chitra First run down the quarry you are now following. Are you quite certain that the enchanted deer you pursue must needs be caught? No, not yet. Like a dream the wild creature eludes you when it seems most nearly yours. Look how the wind is chased by the mad rain that discharges a thousand arrows after it. Yet it goes free and unconquered. Our sport is like that, my love! You give chase to the fleet-footed spirit of beauty, aiming at her every dart you have in your hands. Yet this magic deer runs ever free and untouched.

Arjuna My love, have you no home where kind hearts are waiting for your return? A home which you once made sweet with your gentle service and whose light went out when you left it for this wilderness?

Chitra Why these questions? Are the hours of unthinking pleasure over? Do you not know that I am no more than what you see before you? For me there is no vista beyond. The dew that hangs on the tip of a Kinsuka petal has neither name nor destination. It offers no answer to any question. She whom you love is like that perfect bead of dew.

Arjuna Has she no tie with the world? Can she be merely like a fragment of heaven dropped on the earth through the carelessness of a wanton god?

Chitra Yes.

Arjuna Ah, that is why I always seem about to lose you. My heart is unsatisfied, my mind knows no peace. Come closer to me, unattainable one! Surrender yourself to the bonds of name and home and parentage. Let my heart feel you on all sides and live with you in the peaceful security of love.

Chitra Why this vain effort to catch and keep the tints of the clouds, the dance of the waves, the smell of the flowers?

Arjuna Mistress mine, do not hope to pacify love with airy nothings. Give me something to clasp, something that can last longer than pleasure, that can endure even through suffering.

Chitra Hero mine, the year is not yet full, and you are tired already! Now I know that it is Heaven's blessing that has made the flower's term of life short. Could this body of mine have drooped and died with the flowers of last spring it surely would have died with honour. Yet, its days are numbered, my love. Spare it not, press it dry of honey, for fear your beggar's heart come back to it again and again with unsated desire, like a thirsty bee when summer blossoms lie dead in the dust.

Scene VII

Madana TONIGHT is thy last night.

Vasanta The loveliness of your body will return tomorrow to the inexhaustible stores of the spring. The ruddy tint of thy lips freed from the memory of Arjuna's kisses, will bud anew as a pair of fresh asoka leaves, and the soft, white glow of thy skin will be born again in a hundred fragrant jasmine flowers.

Chitra O gods, grant me this my prayer! Tonight, in its last hour let my beauty flash its brightest, like the final flicker of a dying flame.

Madana Thou shalt have thy wish.

Scene VIII

Villagers WHO will protect us now?

Arjuna Why, by what danger are you threatened?

Villagers The robbers are pouring from the northern hills like a mountain flood to devastate our village.

Arjuna Have you in this kingdom no warden?

Villagers Princess Chitra was the terror of all evil doers. While she was in this happy land we feared natural deaths, but had no other fears. Now she has gone on a pilgrimage, and none knows where to find her.

Arjuna Is the warden of this country a woman?

Villagers Yes, she is our father and mother in one.

[Exeunt.]

Enter **Chitra**.

Chitra Why are you sitting all alone?

Arjuna I am trying to imagine what kind of woman Princess Chitra may be. I hear so many stories of her from all sorts of men.

Chitra Ah, but she is not beautiful. She has no such lovely eyes as mine, dark as death. She can pierce any target she will, but not our hero's heart.

Arjuna They say that in valour she is a man, and a woman in tenderness.

Chitra That, indeed, is her greatest misfortune. When a woman is merely a woman; when she winds herself round and round men's hearts with her smiles and sobs and services and caressing endearments; then she is happy. Of what use to her are learning and great achievements? Could you have seen her only yesterday in the court of the Lord Shiva's temple by the forest path, you would have passed by without deigning to look at her. But have you grown so weary of woman's beauty that you seek in her for a man's strength?

With green leaves wet from the spray of the foaming waterfall, I have made our noonday bed in a cavern dark as night. There the cool of the soft green mosses thick on the black and dripping stone, kisses your eyes to sleep. Let me guide you thither.

Arjuna Not today, beloved.

Chitra Why not today?

Arjuna I have heard that a horde of robbers has neared the plains. Needs must I go and prepare my weapons to protect the frightened villagers.

Chitra You need have no fear for them. Before she started on her pilgrimage, Princess Chitra had set strong guards at all the frontier passes.

Arjuna Yet permit me for a short while to set about a Kshatriya's work. With new glory will I ennoble this idle arm, and make of it a pillow more worthy of your head.

Chitra What if I refuse to let you go, if I keep you entwined in my arms? Would you rudely snatch yourself free and leave me? Go then! But you must know that the liana, once broken in two, never joins again. Go, if your thirst is quenched. But, if not, then remember that the goddess of pleasure is fickle, and waits for no man. Sit for a while, my lord! Tell me what uneasy thoughts tease you. Who occupied your mind today? Is it Chitra?

Arjuna Yes, it is Chitra. I wonder in fulfilment of what vow she has gone on her pilgrimage. Of what could she stand in need?

Chitra Her needs? Why, what has she ever had, the unfortunate creature? Her very qualities are as prison walls, shutting her woman's heart in a bare cell. She is obscured, she is unfulfilled. Her womanly love must content itself dressed in rags; beauty is denied her. She is like the spirit of a cheerless morning, sitting upon the stony mountain peak, all her light blotted out by dark clouds. Do not ask me of her life. It will never sound sweet to man's ear.

Arjuna I am eager to learn all about her. I am like a traveller come to a strange city at midnight. Domes and towers and garden-trees look vague and shadowy, and the dull moan of the sea comes fitfully through the silence of sleep. Wistfully he waits for the morning to reveal to him all the strange wonders. Oh, tell me her story.

Chitra What more is there to tell?

Arjuna I seem to see her, in my mind's eye, riding on a white horse, proudly holding the reins in her left hand, and in her right a bow, and like the Goddess of Victory dispensing glad hope all round her. Like a watchful lioness she protects the litter at her dugs with a fierce love. Woman's arms, though adorned with naught but unfettered strength, are beautiful! My heart is restless, fair one, like a serpent reviving from his long winter's sleep. Come, let us both race on swift horses side by side, like twin orbs of light sweeping through space. Out from this slumbrous prison of green gloom, this dank, dense cover of perfumed intoxication, choking breath.

Chitra Arjuna, tell me true, if, now at once, by some magic I could shake myself free from this voluptuous softness, this timid bloom of beauty shrinking from the rude and healthy touch of the world, and fling it from my body like borrowed clothes, would you be able to bear it? If I stand up straight and strong with the strength of a daring heart spurning the wiles and arts of twining weakness, if I hold my head high like a tall young mountain fir, no longer trailing in the dust like a liana, shall I then appeal to man's eye? No, no, you could not endure it. It is better that I should keep spread about me all the dainty playthings of fugitive youth, and wait for you in patience. When it pleases you to return, I will smilingly pour out for you the wine of pleasure in the cup of this beauteous body. When you are tired and satiated with this wine, you can go to work or play; and when I grow old I will accept humbly and gratefully whatever corner is left for me. Would it please your heroic soul if the playmate of the night aspired to be the helpmeet of the day, if the left arm learnt to share the burden of the proud right arm?

Arjuna   I never seem to know you aright. You seem to me like a goddess hidden within a golden image. I cannot touch you, I cannot pay you my dues in return for your priceless gifts. Thus my love is incomplete. Sometimes in the enigmatic depth of your sad look, in your playful words mocking at their own meaning, I gain glimpses of a being trying to rend asunder the languorous grace of her body, to emerge in a chaste fire of pain through a vaporous veil of smiles. Illusion is the first appearance of Truth. She advances towards her lover in disguise. But a time comes when she throws off her ornaments and veils and stands clothed in naked dignity. I grope for that ultimate you, that bare simplicity of truth.

Why these tears, my love? Why cover your face with your hands? Have I pained you, my darling? Forget what I said. I will be content with the present. Let each separate moment of beauty come to me like a bird of mystery from its unseen nest in the dark bearing a message of music. Let me for ever sit with my hope on the brink of its realization, and thus end my days.

Scene IX

Chitra *and* **Arjuna**.

Chitra (*cloaked*)   My lord, has the cup been drained to the last drop? Is this, indeed, the end? No, when all is done something still remains, and that is my last sacrifice at your feet.

I brought from the garden of heaven flowers of incomparable beauty with which to worship you, god of my heart. If the rites are over, if the flowers have faded, let me throw them out of the temple (*unveiling in her original male attire*). Now, look at your worshipper with gracious eyes.

I am not beautifully perfect as the flowers with which I worshipped. I have many flaws and blemishes. I am a traveller in the great world-path, my garments are dirty, and my feet are bleeding with thorns. Where should I achieve flower-beauty, the unsullied loveliness of a moment's life? The gift that I proudly bring you is the heart of a woman. Here have all pains and joys gathered, the hopes and fears and shames of a daughter of the dust; here love springs up struggling toward immortal life. Herein lies an imperfection which yet is noble and grand. If the flower-service is finished, my master, accept this as your servant for the days to come!

I am Chitra, the king's daughter. Perhaps you will remember the day when a woman came to you in the temple of Shiva, her body loaded with ornaments and finery. That shameless woman came to court you as though she were a man. You rejected her; you did well. My lord, I am that woman. She was my disguise. Then by the boon of gods I obtained for a year the most radiant form that a mortal ever wore, and wearied my hero's heart with the burden of that deceit. Most surely I am not that woman.

I am Chitra. No goddess to be worshipped, nor yet the object of common pity to be brushed aside like a moth with indifference. If you deign to keep me by your side in the path of danger and daring, if you allow me to share the great duties of your life, then you will know my true self. If your babe, whom I am nourishing in my womb be born a son, I shall myself teach him to be a second Arjuna, and send him to you when the time comes, and then at last you will truly know me. Today I can only offer you Chitra, the daughter of a king.

Arjuna Beloved, my life is full.

Behind the Veil: A One-Act Play (*Parde ke Peeche*) (1932)
Rashid Jahan

Translator unknown

Remembered for her remarkable contribution to Urdu drama and literature, **Rashid Jahan** (1905–52) was one of the founding members of the Progressive Writers' Association in the 1930s and a fierce spokesperson for women's rights. She trained as a medical doctor at Lady Hardinge College and joined the Provincial Medical Service of the United Provinces (the present-day state of Uttar Pradesh). Jahan commanded a brief but controversial literary career because of *Angare* (*Embers*, 1932), a creative writing collection, for which she wrote a short story and a play, and which was banned by the United Provinces government. Despite this controversial response, she wrote works such as *Aurat aur Deegar Afsane wa Drame* (*Woman and Other Stories and Plays*), and a collection of short stories *Shola-e-Jawwala* (*Sparks of a Volcano*). Jahan belonged to an upper-class Muslim family from Aligarh, United Provinces, where she received her early education, and continued her higher studies at Isabella Thoburn College in Lucknow. She wrote and directed plays for the radio and participated in the Indian People's Theatre Association, an activist all-India theatre organization that was formed in 1942. It is not surprising that as a medical doctor, a dominant theme in her works dealt with women and their bodies.

Published in 1932, *Behind the Veil* continues to generate interest today for presenting a radical intervention in Urdu literature and for addressing women's issues that often get overlooked. The action takes place in a room where issues about sexuality and patriarchy are raised through a conversation between two characters: Mohammadi Begum and Aftab Begum, upper-class Muslim women who discuss childbirths and pregnancies and their effects on women's bodies. The domestic space is important because it draws attention to the veiled spaces for women that both enable and limit their conversations. Nonetheless, the conversational tone that permeates the realistic frame of the room is strategic in highlighting a private space where women freely discuss subjects they would not otherwise bring up in public spaces, especially regarding women's reproductive health.

The conversation between the two women characters ends unexpectedly because of the call for evening prayers, and the play ends abruptly. Does this ending suggest that there is no immediate resolution to such problems? Or does it suggest that women's voices remain confined to domestic spaces, however defiant they may be? Or is it an attempt to shake the readers and audiences out of any kind of complacency and urge them to think about women's problems, their voices, and their choices?

Reference

Jahan, Rashid. *Behind the Veil*. https://archive.org/details/behindtheveilplayenglish/mode/2up (no translator listed).

A room with white flooring. A mattress is spread in the centre of the room. A woman, lying back on bolsters, is seated on the mattress. She looks sad and tired. Next to her is a surahi, containing water, which is placed upon a silver plate with its mouth covered with a small metal bowl. Seated in front of her is another woman who looks to be near forty. She is slicing betel nuts. On one side lies a round box and, on the other, a spittoon. The room has two doors in front. The walls around have many cupboards, shelves and ledges with different objects such as kitchen utensils, lids and covers. A cloth fan with a pink frill is hanging from the middle of the ceiling. A bedstead with a coverlet spread on it is visible in one corner of the room. At the other end is another mattress with a bolster and a spittoon next to it.

Mohammadi-begum   Aapa, who is bothered about us anyway? We have already lived most of our lives and Allah will see to the rest. I am so fed up and sick of this world that I would have poisoned myself if I was not concerned about these little children.

Aftab-begum   Have you gone mad, bua, my dear lady? This is hardly the age to talk of poison and of suicide. It is only now that spring has blossomed for you. The children, with God's grace, are grown up. How can the idea of poisoning yourself even come to you? Just look at me . . .

Mohammadi-begum   Why should I look at you? Do you think this has anything to do with age? Is it only the old who get weary of the world? The lust for life that I have seen in the old is hardly to be matched by the young. Death comes to so many people – God only knows where my death has gone and hidden itself. Everybody – including children – forgets everything after a while and life comes back on track soon after that . . .

Aftab-begum   Get a grip, my dear, get a grip! You are still too young to plead for death. You are a decade or so younger to me. They were talking about my marriage in the year that you were born. That was the year when the queen died. I remember it very well. May her soul find peace. Chachi amma was so happy. 'She's like a son for me' she used to say about you. You were born almost thirty years after chachi amma's marriage. What celebrations! There was eating and drinking; and the Dom women danced their special dance. Not just that, your marriage, too, was solemnized with such great fanfare. The whole city of Dilli went into raptures over it. Who could be as fortunate as you? Look at how unfortunate I am. Allah bless you, you have a husband, children, home, everything.

Mohammadi-begum   Yes, that's true. Husband, children, a home; I have it all. Youth? Who will call me young? I look like an old woman of seventy. This unending illness; the daily visits by hakims and doctors. And a child every year. Yes, of course, who can be more fortunate than I am? (*Her eyes fill with tears. She wipes her eyes with a handkerchief and, after spitting into the spittoon, she begins to speak once again.*) It just happened two months ago. It was decided that the lady doctor be called just before the miscarriage. Doctor Ghayas's diagnosis also pointed to the fact that my ongoing fever may be due to some internal disorder. He felt that it would be better to get an internal checkup done by the lady doctor. And as far as the ageing is concerned, you must listen to this. The lady doctor asked me my age. 'Thirty-two years', I said. She smiled in a way that gave me the impression that she did not believe me. I said, 'Miss sahib, why are you smiling? You should know that I got married when I was seventeen. And since then I have borne a child every year, except when my husband went abroad for a year. And the second time such a thing happened was when he and I had quarreled. These teeth that you see missing have been pulled out by Dr Ghayas. Some pyorrhea or something like that – God knows what disease it is – that's what has happened. The whole problem was that when my dear husband returned from his trip abroad, he began to complain that my mouth smelled bad. The poor lady doctor, what could she do? She just laughed.

Aftab-begum   You say such absurd things! What can people do but laugh?

Mohammadi-begum   Anyway, the lady doctor did check my stomach and my chest. Then when she did an internal check-up, she got really nervous and said, 'Begum sahiba. It looks like you are pregnant again. It has been two months.' My heart missed a beat! Another problem to confront now!

Just then, the sound of some children weeping and others shrieking and screaming is heard from the other room. **Begum-sahiba**, *who has been resting with her back on the bolster, straightens up and yells.*

Begum-sahiba   Arre, you ruffians! There isn't a moment of peace here. We keep so many haramzaadi maids but the children make a racket all the time. It would be better if God just ended my life and freed me of this world's problems.

The door opens. Two maids, dressed in clean clothes, enter with two weeping children. Some other, older, children are seen standing at the door. All the children are thin, pale and underweight. The inner courtyard is now visible through the open door.

First Maid   Begum-sahiba, Nahne-mian does not listen to me at all. Whenever he enters the room, he starts troubling all the other children. He doesn't let them play. Now he has run away with Nanhi-bi's doll and Chote-mian's ball. And he has run into the men's rooms.

Mohammadi-begum (*in anger*)   He's a butcher, the scoundrel, a butcher. He leaves nobody in peace in the house. Like father like son!

She picks up the child and comforts her. She then takes something out of the box and gives it to both the children to eat.

Go, for God's sake, leave now. All I get to hear from morning to evening is just shrieking and screaming.

Then, after a pause, seeing that the maid has left the door ajar, she says:

Arre! Shut the door at least. I have said the same thing so many times since morning! Whenever they go out of the room, they just leave the door open.

Aftab-begum   Bua, the wretched doctor attends to your family at all times. Even so, look at the children. They're so thin, pale, stunted and undernourished.

Mohammadi-begum How else can they be when they are deprived of their mother's milk? They bring home any kind of wet nurse they can find; the blind, the pock-marked, the fat, the thin. Whoever one stumbles upon is employed. My husband is the decision-maker. He says that I need not bother with all this when, with God's grace, we have the money. As far as he is concerned, all pleasure is limited to his own lust. His only worry is that he will be inconvenienced if a child stays with me. He is not concerned, be it night or day. All he wants is for his wife to be available to him at all times. And, of course, he does not stop at his wife. There is absolutely no holding him back from going to other places too.

Aftab-begum Mohammadi-begum, you blame your poor husband for everything. If he employs maids he becomes a villain and if he doesn't, he is a scoundrel. Bua, chant Allah's name.

Mohammadi-begum Aapa, you weren't here when Nasir died. The poor boy was just four months old. May Allah not let even our enemies suffer the way he did; even strangers could not bear to see his pain. His wet nurse looked quite hefty and tall but carried some disease which heated up her insides. Now how could anyone have known about that? As a result, the child exploded with sores. His whole body was covered with blisters. Raw flesh would squirt out when the blisters burst. All his joints were filled with pus. Doctor Ghayas used to drain out pots full of pus – I used to watch from behind the curtain. 'Don't even breathe', he'd say, 'just thank your stars.' After all this, the child festered for two months before he bid his final farewell. I have borne three children after that. I insisted so much upon feeding them myself but who cares? I am always terrorized by the threat, 'I will remarry if you breastfeed the children. I need a woman at all times. I don't have the patience to wait while you attend to the children.' And then you say . . .

Aftab-begum So, that's the problem! How was I to know all this? God save us from such men; even animals have some restraint. This behaviour is worse than that of animals. May one be saved from such men! Such things didn't happen earlier, bua. These days, all the men you see, wretched burly bullies, have the same problem. Now look at my husband, your own brother-in-law. He is old now but he avoided all excesses even as a young man. (*Smiling*.) I swear by God, I made him lick my feet for hours.

Mohammadi-begum (*sighing*) To each her own fate! What you just said has reminded me that the story of my conversation with the lady doctor is still not over. Words have a strange way of changing track. So then, after saying that I was two months pregnant, the lady doctor stared at me with surprise, 'Begum-sahiba, you were saying that you have been bedridden for the last four months and that you get fever every evening. And Dr Ghayas, too, said that you get hundred or a hundred- and-one fever every evening. So then, do you mean . . .?' I said, 'Aye, Miss sahib! You are fortunate. You earn money for yourself, you spend it the way you wish to, and sleep in peace. As far as I am concerned, who cares if I go to hell or to heaven! All that they care about is their pleasure and enjoyment. The wretched wife may live or die, all that men hunger after is their own lust. The lady doctor, poor thing, just heard me out and kept quiet. Then she said, 'You are so very ill', and bua, not just this doctor but all the other doctors also say that the children can't be healthy when I am so weak myself. And to make matters worse, the children keep coming so close to each other. Anyway, what can one do? It would have been better to have been born a Christian.

Aftab-begum   Tauba, tauba, don't utter such blasphemies! I have just one son and even he has kept a Christian woman. I had such dreams for his marriage. My brother, in frustration, has now gone and settled Waheeda's marriage somewhere else. Just imagine how my heart wrenches with anguish to know that the girl I had asked for since she was a child is now going to a stranger's home. It would have been better if he had never been born. He is as good as dead for me now.

Mohammadi-begum   How can you curse him so? He is the support of your old age, after all. He will certainly reform sooner or later.

Aftab-begum   What reform? He will never reform! It has been two years. I have yearned for him for so long, but haven't had the merest glimpse of him. He stays in this very city but has not stepped into the house even once. I hear he earns one hundred and fifty rupees now. And thank God, at least there is no child yet. I have only one prayer now. Even if I am left with no one to light a lamp on my grave, his wife, that haramzaadi, may she die in the bloom of her youth and never ever bear a child! Bua, who can we share our pain with? Each one of us is weighed down with our own misfortunes. Mohammadi- begum, did you hear this other news? Mirza Maqbool Ali Shah has just married again. Two wives have already died and even his granddaughters have children. And this latest wife of his is so young; with such an innocent face! She would hardly be twenty. The unlucky girl is doomed. She has six unmarried sisters. That's why the poor parents . . .

The twelve-year-old elder son, the lower ends of his pyjamas covered with grime, pushes the door open and runs in. He has a spool of thread in one hand and a pair of scissors in the other. Behind him enters a strong-looking girl wearing tight pyjamas.

Girl   Amma, Bade-mirza just won't listen. See how he has put cuts in my new pyjamas. (*Saying this, she lifts up her kurta and shows it to her mother.*) I was not even talking to him. I was just putting buttons on Abbajan's achkan. And look here, he has even torn my dupatta.

Frustrated, she leans against the wall and starts weeping.

The Boy (*imitating his sister*)   Ouh, ouh, ouh. You are not saying anything about what you were really doing. So, you were sewing? Were you? Should I tell Amma what vulgar books you were reading? Dildaar Yaar? Baanka Chhabila?

Girl (*turning towards him*)   For God's sake, don't lie! I swear by God, Amma, I was reading Moulvi Ashraf Ali Sahab's Bahishti Zevar. He started pestering me to show it to him. When I didn't, he just slashed my pyjamas. You never say anything to him.

Mohammadi-begum (*smacking her forehead*)   Shabash beti! Amma may live or die, but it never crosses your mind that you should help her. Instead, you end up quarrelling with your younger brothers. (*Then, turning towards her son.*) This rowdy creature keeps troubling someone or the other all the time. Get lost!

Aftab-begum   Come, mian, give me the scissors. Do you know of anybody else who troubles his sister like this? After all, she is with you only for a short time. She will get married and go away in a year or two. After that, however much you may yearn, you will not get even a small glimpse of her.

Sabira, *embarrassed with this talk, bends her head and quietly slips away.* **Bade Mirza** *rides on the bolster as if it were a horse and begins to jump up and down after a few moments.*

The Boy   So why did she not show me the book then?

Mohammadi-begum   Bade-mirza, have pity for God's sake! Don't shake me up like this. My whole body is trembling. My heart has begun to throb so hard. For God's sake, go out to your abba. Moulvi-sahib must be about to come. Have you finished your lessons?

The mere mention of studies makes **Bade Mirza** *feel that it would be better for him to go away.*

Aftab-begum   The house at least looks full when there are so many children. But the noise and the commotion can get on one's nerves. Bua, now I just stay at home all day, idle and twiddling my thumbs. My husband comes in only for namaaz. He sits for a moment or two and then goes back to the sitting room. May God never make anyone as lonely as me. What dreams I had!

The door opens and **Kolan**, *an old maid, enters, holding something in her hands.*

Kolan   Salaam, Begum-sahib. Salaam, Badi-begum. Here, take this. I was about to go to your house with your portion. So begum, how are you? How are the children?

Mohammadi-begum   Well, bua, I am surviving. I hope bhabhi is fine. And the kids, I hope they are fine too. My best wishes for the new grandson. This must be the panjiri. Rahiman, here, take this and empty the plate. (*She opens the small box.*) Aapa, please hand me a paan.

Aftab-begum   Rahiman, just take my share too. (*Saying this, she gets busy preparing paan.* **Mohammadi** *gives two annas to* **Kolan**.)

Mohammadi-begum   Convey my regards to everybody. I will come as soon as I feel a little better. Meeting you has renewed my desire to meet everybody once again. I really feel like seeing the baby. And bua, just ask bhabhi if she has sworn never to come here?

Aftab *hands the paan over and, taking out some money from her waistband, gives two annas to* **Kolan**.

Kolan   Begum-sahiba, my bibi, too, remembers you a lot but she hardly finds any spare time. These days, of course, the house is full. Everybody has come.

Aftab-begum   Convey my blessings to Sultan-dulhan. And my congratulations on the grandson. God willing, I will come on this Friday.

Kolan *takes the two plates, offers her salaam, and leaves.*

Mohammadi-begum Aapa, our bhabhi Sultan has her own special style. Her mian never earned more than forty rupees but she has such a talent that she has managed to do everything really well within her limited means. She got her sons and daughters married off. Now, with God's grace, her son has found a good job and earns something around a hundred and fifteen. There's also scope for promotion.

Aftab-begum The daughter-in-law is good, too. (*Sighs*.) It's fate. Look at us. Anyway, forget it. Is there any news of Razia? Your mamu got her engaged and married off in such haste that he hardly invited anybody.

Mohammadi-begum So what if he did not invite people? He got food and delicacies distributed twice or thrice amongst all the families. The poor girl got married under such circumstances . . . in the fear of disgrace. Still, may God bless them all.

Aftab-begum Was that it? I had no idea! So what happened?

Mohammadi-begum Really? You really don't know? Everybody seems to know about it now. The poor thing is so young. She's just about two years older than my Sabira. She was born after I got married.

When Chote-mamu came from Calcutta – he had come after many years – all of us were quite young at that time. Nani-amma, poor thing, even with her trembling limbs, was the happiest of all. I had brought Razia home with me for a few days. Then Choti-mami went to her parents' house. The girl stayed over with me for three or four months. Razia is so fond of her father's family that she can give her life for them. She is not so attached to her mother's side of the family. This is my house, her cousin sister's house but I had not the slightest inkling of what was happening. Razia went back when her mother returned from her parents' home.

One day a terse note from Razia arrived, saying, 'Aapa-jaan, for God's sake, hurry up and come here.' That's it, Aapa, what can I say? When I reached her house, then Choti-mami . . . you do know Choti-mami, don't you? You know how she can pretend to be very sweet. So, she welcomed me profusely. Razia handed me a letter in secret and said, 'Dulhe-bhai, your husband, comes here every day and Amma showers great attention and care on him in secret. They talk softly in secret'. Poor, young, unwed girl! What more could she have said? She had gathered all her courage to say even as much as she did. And the letter – it was my mian's letter to Razia.

A kind of love letter that is impossible to find even in romantic novels. I literally burnt up with anger. I talked to Razia and convinced her that her name will not be implicated. I came back home smouldering. I discussed them atter with my mian. Aye aapa, I swear by God, he was so shameless that he didn't even blink his eyes. 'So, what's the harm?' he said, 'I will marry Razia. Even if it means a talaq from you.' I said, 'Are you in your senses or have you bid goodbye to them? She is from a respectable family. Even if you as much as utter her name, her father, brothers and uncles will chop you to pieces. Don't even dream of anything as far as she is concerned.'

Aftab-begum So, your mumani had fixed everything on the sly.

Mohammadi-begum What else? She has nursed some deep grudge against Amma and me for long. Even when Amma was ill, she used to swear that she would not be at peace till she ruins my home. And it is not that she has this animosity only towards us. She has a similar grudge against elder mumani too. And since Razia was engaged to a boy in my chacha's family, she constantly fought about it, saying that she would never give away her daughter into the family of her enemies.

Aftab-begum (*laughing*) Andbua, what is attractive about your mian anyway? He has a wife and children; except, of course, that he has money. But then your elder mamun, too, is not poor. Do such things ever happen in respectable families? I have heard that in some places far off in the west, two sisters may wed their daughters to the same man but it doesn't happen in our families. But, of course, these are modern times. It seems that anything can happen now. So then, what happened next?

Mohammadi-begum When I lost my cool and said bitter things to him, he began to cajole me and said, 'Believe me, I am completely smitten with her. For God's sake, help me. It is your duty to help me'. He used to sit with the Quran Sharif and read out aayats about the kind of hell I will face after death if I don't help my husband. Anyway, which fire could have burnt me more than the one I carried within me, the one which scorched me all the time? In short, the same story that he would go mad was repeated endlessly. He confined himself to a room, lying all the time with his face buried in the bed and all he chanted was, 'Hai Razia, hai Razia'. And I had little choice but to quietly listen to this. I swear by God, Aapa, my heart is so deeply plagued by all this that all wealth and luxury have become a burden to me. I'd rather live poorly on dry roti if I could only get a little happiness. Aapa, just hand me a paan. My mouth has become parched from all the speaking.

She drinks water from the surahi. **Aftab** *takes out a paan for herself and hands one to* **Mohammadi**, *too.*

In short, this situation remained unchanged – He kept saying such vulgar and lustful things about that poor unmarried child I felt completely stifled but could hardly do anything besides listening quietly to all this. And as far as choti mumani is concerned, she continued to behave in the same way, greeting and welcoming him with the same warmth. 'Razia', she would say, 'your dulha bhai is here. Give him some paan and elaichi'.

Aftab-begum Achha! What is certain is that all this was hatched by your mumani.

Mohammadi-begum Of course! What else? That girl used to weep for hours. She expressed her agony and unburdened her heart to me whenever we met. I kept quiet for a month. Then both my mamus came to meet me. I then asked them, 'Mamu jaan, has Razia's engagement been called off?' Both the brothers were bewildered I was, of course, already full of all this to the brim and divulged everything to them.

After that, both of them must have considered and deliberated upon the matter and the result was that Razia was married off on the third day.

Aftab-be gum Allah, Allah, khair salla! All's well that ends well.

Mohammadi-begum But, bua, he did not enter the house for six months. He just spent all his time with those whores in Chaawadi. And I was happy. God knows, I sleep in peace on days when he goes there. Now the same story is repeated every day. He keeps saying, 'You keep ill. How long do you expect me to go through all this? I have decided to remarry.' And to top it all he also insists, 'You are the one who will have to arrange my marriage. When Islamic law allows four marriages, then why should I not remarry?' I said, 'Go ahead. Sabira will be married off after a year. Father and daughter can marry at the same time. On the one hand play with the grandson and with your new wife's child on the other.' That's it! He immediately starts quarrelling, 'What do women know about all this. God has not gifted them with passions that we have', I just say to him that, actually, he has within him the concentrated passions of all men put together . . .

Aftab-begum (*interrupting*) Mohammadi-begum, wherever you go, you will find the same problem. Men seem to have their way all along. They triumph in all situations – tails they win, heads we lose. Now tell me, isn't it bad enough to say, 'I will remarry', that he also insists that, 'my wife is the one who must arrange it!'

Mohammadi-begum That's the reason why I am in deep distress and pray for death to end my life. My own health is a big problem and the problems with the children make matters worse. The older children, God save them, are quite healthy but the younger ones are never well. All this has destroyed my desire to live. And the fear of his second marriage haunts me at all times. Khuda, bring death to me before he brings home another woman. And what all have I not done because of this fear of the other woman? I've undergone two surgeries.

Aftab-begum What we had heard was that you had got something done to put a stop to children from being born.

Mohammadi-begum Who told you all this? The real reason was that my uterus as well as my lower parts had begun to slide down. It needed to be corrected so that my mian could get the pleasure of a new wife from my body. Bua, how long can the body of a woman who produces children year after year remain fit? It slipped down again. Then once again I was slaughtered with force and threat. But despite all this, he is still unhappy.

The azaan is called from a mosque close by.

Aftab-begum Bua, it's time for the afternoon namaaz. I got so engrossed with chatting that I just forgot about everything else. (*She ties a cloth over her head and torso.*) Now I will go only after namaaz. Your brother, poor thing, will be waiting.

Mohammadi-begum Aapa, thank God you came today. I could at least unburden myself. Do keep coming more often. I am ill and just can't go out. (*She then calls out, 'Rahiman, Rahiman, Gulshaboo!'* **Rahiman** *appears.*)

Mohammadi-begum Go help Badi-begum with her wuzoo.

Curtain Drops

The Blind Age (*Andha Yug*) (1953, 1963)

Dharamvir Bharati

Translated by Tripurari Sharma

Bharati (1926–97) was a Hindi novelist, poet, journalist and playwright. He was born in Allahabad, Uttar Pradesh, and received his PhD in Hindi from Allahabad University in 1954. He published his first novel *Gunahon Ka Devata* (*The God of Sins*) in 1949 and his second *Suraj Ka Satvan Ghoda* (*The Seventh Horse of the Sun*) in 1952. Both are considered classics of Hindi literature. From 1960 to 1987, he was the chief editor of *Dharmayug*, during which time it became the most popular Hindi weekly magazine in India. Among his many awards are the Padma Shri for literature and education from the government of India in 1972 and, though he wrote only one play, the Sangeet Natak Akademi Award for Playwriting (Hindi) in 1988.

That play, *Andha Yug*, was written in 1953 for the radio because Bharati couldn't imagine it being produced on the stage. It was broadcast on All India Radio and didn't receive its first stage production until 1962 in Bombay (Mumbai). It has since been produced all over India in multiple languages. As the great Indian dramatist Girish Karnad wrote, 'The basic concern of the Indian theater in the post-independence period has been to try to define its "Indianness".' *The Blind Age* (*Andha Yug*), drawing on aspects of Sanskrit drama for its form and *The Mahabharata* for its story, was instrumental in helping launch modern Indian drama and the theatre of roots movement, which used historically Indian forms and source material.

The play's title references the four ages in Hindu cosmology, in which the world and humanity spiral downward. The first age, the purest, is Satya Yug, the second Treta, and the third Dvapara Yug in which the play is set. That age – a deceitful, competitive, jealous, pleasure-seeking but courageous age – ends when Krishna leaves the human realm late in the play. In the final movements of the piece, the characters grapple with how to live in the fourth age, the coming Kali Yug, The Dark Age, an age of vice, in which humans move away from God.

Like *The Shattered Thigh*, *The Blind Age* (*Andha Yug*) takes place at the end of the war between the Kauravas and the Pandavas, chronicling the last day from the perspective of the Kauravas. In the capital Hastinapur, Dhritarashtra, the blind king and his wife Gandhari, who has chosen to live blindfolded to be in the same state as her husband, await the arrival of Sanjay who will bring word of the battle. Their hopes of victory will be dashed, and the reactions on multiple levels throughout the community will be seen – the depths and limits of violence, revenge, hatred, and belief only in one's own right. The play raises a variety of questions. How can the cycle of revenge and violence be ended? Who bears responsibility for the defeat? For the breakdown of moral order? The Kauravas? The Pandavas? The gods? Are there any positive models, actors, in this world? Is there any possibility of redemption, of hope, in the play? In other words, is this a story of complete blindness or of the enlightenment that may come through blindness?

Though the narrative may be an ancient one, the play is a response to the violent upheaval that resulted from the end of British rule of India in 1947 when the British partitioned the subcontinent into India and Pakistan, along religious lines. Fifteen million people were displaced, Sikhs as well as Hindus and Muslims crossing the newly imposed borders attempting to maintain their communities. Millions were killed in the violence between the groups. What had been one Indian people under the British colonizers became warring clans, like the Kauravas and Pandavas. With beautiful language and horrifying emotions, the play portrays the devastation and asks, why do we continue to be divided, to make war against each other, even those within our own families? And, perhaps, to spur us to ponder how we may see ourselves and the world in non-destructive ways?

References

Bharati, Dharamvir. *The Blind Age (Andha Yug)*. Translated by Tripurari Sharma. New Delhi: National School of Drama, [2001?].

Bharati, Dharamvir. *Andha Yug*. Translated by Alok Bhalla. New Delhi: Oxford University Press, 2005.

The Cast

Sentry One
Sentry Two
Vidur
Dhritarashtra
Gandhari
The Old Mendicant
Sanjay
Kritvarma
Kripacharya
Ashwathama
Mute Soldier
Yuyutsu
Voice of Vyas
Voice of Krishna
Yuddhishtra

Time Period

From the evening of the Eighteenth (last) day of the battle to the moment of Lord Krishna's demise in a pilgrimage of light.

Prologue

The Blind Age

The Stage Comes into view, with the sound of conch shells. An actor makes the gesture of greeting and obeisance *(Namaskara)* and performs in accordance with the Holy Chant *(Manglacharan)* that is rendered in the opening. The announcement (unfolding the basis of the play) is made from off stage

Invocation

Narayanm Namaskritya Naram Chair Narottamam,
Devim Saraswatim Vyasm Tato Jayam Udiyaret

Announcement

The age that is described in this work,
Has been thus commented upon in the Vishnu Purana:

Tataschanudinam alpalpa Hras
Vyavachchhedad – dharm – arth – ayorjagatas – Samakshayo Bhavishyati

In that future –
Virtue and value shall degenerate
The entire earth shall slowly perish

'Tatascharth – evabhijan Hetu'

They,
Who control the wealth,
will wield power

Kapata Vesha dharanameva mahatva Hetu

Imposters alone
Shall command attention

Evem Chati lubdhak raja
Sahas-Sailanam – antaradronih praja samsriyashyanti

Rulers shall be greedy
And the people so oppressed
Shall hide in caves dark and obscure,
And thus abide their time.

(Obscure dark caves – real ones or the ones that lie deep within our frustrated selves?)
(The performer demonstrates a sequence of hiding himself and thus performing exits)

This blind age that has dawned,
Post war,

In which situations, attitudes and souls,
All are distorted.
There is an extremely slender thread of ethics.
But that itself is entangled midst the two sides.
Krishna alone has the courage
To resolve and redeem.
He is the Saviour of the future,
He is detatched.
But the rest mostly are blind
Misled, self destructive, decadent,
Inhabitants of the dark caves within themselves.
This tale is of those so blinded.
Or the legend of light comes through
The medium of the blind.

Act One

The Kaurav Kingdom

The trumpet blows thrice

Narrative Song
Torn and tattered, all codes scattered.
Hammered by both, the order shattered.
Some what less by Pandavas; and by Kauravas more.
This gory bloodshed – when does it now end.
A strange war indeed – for none is the victor.
The two are set to lose – and yet to lose more.
The throne of this age, adorned by the blind.
On both sides lost the discriminating mind.
On both sides it was blindness that won.
The blindness of fear; the blindness of love,
It was the blindness of claim that finally won.
All that was beautiful, benign and tender
Was lost – and so passes the era Dwapar.

The curtain rises.

This twilight of the last day of the great battle,
Everywhere sadness spreads its mantle.
In the forlorn corridor of the Kaurav palace,
Are two old Sentries that walk about and pace.

Sentry One   Weary are we,
But go on and on to keep vigil
In this forlorn corridor.

Sentry Two   In this forlorn deserted corridor,
On whose jewel studded floor,
Kaurav brides,
Would gently tread with lilting pace
And gracefully glide like delicate whittles of a scented breeze.
Today they are widows.

Sentry One   Weary are we,
Not because,
In the war we displayed
The power of our muscles.
Mere sentries were we.

Sentry Two   Seventeen days of this unnerving combat
During which –
These spears of ours,
These shields of ours,

Lay idle and meaningless.
A burden on the limbs.

Sentry One   We were only guards,
But nothing there was to guard.

Sentry Two   Nothing there was to guard here.
The culture of the old and blind,
Whose offspring had
Declared great wars.
In whose blindness the order,
Like a whore
With decay infested body,
Diseased even the subjects.
Of that blind culture,
Of that sick order,
We were the guards
Seventeen Days.

Sentry One   And this has now worn us out.
All our endeavour rendered meaningless.
Of faith,
Of courage,
Of Labour –
Of our entire existence.
There was no meaning.
No meaning at all.

Sentry Two   No meaning
No meaning at all.
In this meaningless
Empty corridor of life
We go to and fro,
To and fro,
Keeping vigil,
Now weary are we
Now worn out are we.

They become quiet – and move around. Suddenly the lights grow dim. Sound similar to that of a gale can be heard. One **Sentry** *strains his ear to listen – the other looks up – hand on eyebrows*

Sentry One   Did you hear –?
What's this sound –
So frightening?

Sentry Two   Suddenly – why is it darkening?
Try and see
Can you see anything?

Sentry One A blind king's subject – how far can he see!
Can't see a thing.
Yes. May be. It's a cloud.

*The **Second Sentry** comes closer to see, and is frightened.*

Sentry Two Not clouds.
These are Vultures.
Millions and billions,
Wings spread out.

Sentry One Look –
The entire sky
Of the Kaurav City
Has been surrounded
By vultures.

Sentry Two Bend low,
Bend low,
Beneath your shield
Hide!
They are man eaters.
These vultures are hungry.

Sentry One Look they've turned
In the direction of Kurukshetra.

Sentry Two As if death crossed and,
Went by, above.

Sentry One An omen –
It's terrifying this!
Who knows what will happen
By tomorrow,
In this Kingdom.

Vidur *enters from the left.*

Sentry One Who's there?

Vidur It's me
Vidur
Did Dhritarashtra see
See this terrifying spectacle?

Sentry How can he see.
He's blind.
Has he been able to see
Anything
So far?

Vidur I will meet him.

The signs are terrible.
Who knows Sanjay may bring
What tidings – today!

The **Sentries** *leave.* **Vidur** *stands thoughtful – in his place. The back curtain rises.*

Narrative Song
No tidings have come from Kurukshetra,
The remnant Kaurav clan has won or been vanquished?
On whose lump of flesh will descend
This man-eating hungry cloud of man eating vultures.
The inner chamber silent as a death yard.
Feeble Gandhari sits still, head lowered.
On the throne is Dhritarashtra – he too is quiet.
No tidings yet has Sanjay brought forth.

As the curtain lifts, the inner chamber is visible. A mat woven with dry grass is spread on a low stool which seats **Gandhari***. A small throne for* **Dhritarashtra***.* **Vidur** *moves to them.*

Dhritarashtra   Who – Sanjay?

Vidur   No!
It's Vidur.
My Lord.
Agitated is the whole city today.
Ten, twenty – the few who are left
In this Kingdom –
With unblinking eyes
Await,
Sanjay's arrival.

After having waited for the **King***'s response.*

My Lord.
So quiet –
Are you?
Mother Gandhari too is silent.

Dhritarashtra   Vidur!
For the first time in life.
I am gripped
By an apprehension, all pervasive.

Vidur   Apprehension?
That which strikes you today,
Had years ago, shaken us all.

Dhritarashtra   Earlier, but you had never said –

Vidur   Bhishm had said
Honourable Master Drona had said –

In this very inner chamber,
Had Krishna stood up and said,
Do not break the order,
An order fragmented, trampled upon,
Then, like, a crumpled python shall wrap the Kaurav
Clan in its coils, and crush it like a dry twig.

Dhritarashtra   You cannot understand –
Not you – Vidur.
I was born blind.
How could I
Ever grasp
The external truth or the social order?

Vidur   As you had absorbed the world.
Despite
Your
Blindness

Dhritarashtra   But that world
Had grown on its own from my darkness.
That which I had known from my individual senses,
Only that was the extent of the material world for me.
Like the myriad web born of hallucination,
In the opaque darkness,
From a blind spot –
My mind had developed all emotions.
All my traits and attitudes were propelled by it.
My love, my hatred, my polices, my righteousness, virtue
And duty,
All were shades of my personality.
The external parameters of ethics were not there at all.
Kauravs – who had grown from the layers of my flesh,
They were my ultimate truth.
My affections alone were my policy and politics –
The order. The ethics.

Vidur   But from the very first day –
Your ultimate truth.
The physical strength of the Kaurav army,
Began to prove itself, false and powerless.
Since seventeen days,
One by one,
The destruction of the entire dynasty,
Is all what you've been hearing yourself.

Dhritarashtra   For me that narration was totally meaningless.
Born blind,
I can only keep listening.

Sanjay gives me mere words.
But the pictures that these words paint
Is what I am still unfamiliar with,
Unable to visualize
How from the injured chest of Dushasan
Warm blood could have bubbled forth –
How cruel Bhim could have
Let it stream into his cupped palms
To drench his lips.

Gandhari   My Lord –
Do not repeat.
I am unable to bear it.

Dhritarashtra   Today I realize
That beyond my individual confines also
Does truth exist.
Today. I realize.
In a flash, it seems that a dam has collapsed
And a roaring ocean, unfathomable,
With its deafening screams thundering for miles,
Has flooded in –
And the small world of my calculations
Has been gorged by the lapping tongues of its poisonous tides
That have penetrated into my inner most depths.
Everything has been swept away –
All my individual values,
My confident, though ignorant beliefs.

Vidur   This, that has come with pain,
With defeat
This knowledge will
Also give you fortitude

Dhritarashtra   But this knowledge has
Brought only fear, Vidur.
For the first time in life.
I am gripped
By apprehension – all pervasive.

Vidur   If there is fear –
Then this knowledge is yet incomplete.
The lord had said,
Knowledge that does not submit,
Is incomplete.
Your mind and thought surrender
Unto me.
Freed of fear,

You will be attained by me.
Therein lies no doubt.

Gandhari (*with emotion*)   Therein lies the doubt.
No one else may suspect.
But I do.
Surrender unto me your thought and mind
He said this –
Who, when struck
By the arrows of the venerable great father Bhishm
Had lost his entire thought and mind?
He has said this –
Who has shredded this order again and again!

Dhritarashtra   Calm down.
Calm down.
Gandhari calm down.
Do not blame anyone.
Blind was I. . . .

Gandhari   But blind was not. . . .
Having seen this external material world well enough.
Virtue, ethics, order-all and all of it is sheer pompousness.
I had seen this again and again.
At the moment of decision, judgement and ethics,
Are proven worthless,
Rendered redundant always.
In the minds of all of us – there, lies somewhere,
A dark obscure cavity,
Wherein resides the barbaric beast, blind beast –
The savage lord of our judgement.
Ethics, order, self sacrifice, surrender to Krishna,
Are for the blind traits, splendid costumes
On which eyes of tattered cloth are sewn and patched.
This hypocrisy I could only detest.
And so of my own will, these – my eyes with a bandage
Have I kept bound.

Vidur   You've grown bitter –
Gandhari
The grief of your sons
Has made you
Feeble within.
It's you who had said
To Duryodhana –

Gandhari   I had said to Duryodhana
Where righteousness and virtue are, you fool,
There triumph shall be.

But virtue was nowhere there.
All were propelled by blind traits and considerations.
Him – whom you call god,
Whenever he so desired,
Altered the order to suit his own interest.
A depriver is he!

Dhritarashtra Calm down Gandhari.

Vidur Bitter Despair has led
To this defiant faithlessness.
Forgive, oh Lord!
Receive the bitter faithlessness,
As an offering at your feet!
You accept faith,
But who will receive faithlessness?
Forgive oh Lord.
Plaintive, with the sorrow of her sons,
A feeble mother is Gandhari.

Gandhari Do not call me mother.
He whom you call god
He too addresses me as mother –
The word that like a flaming rod of iron,
Stabs into my ribs
In these seventeen days,
All my sons, one by one, have been slain
With these hands of mine,
I have – from the wrists of their flower like brides,
Removed their bangles.
With this drape of mine
Smudged and wiped off their marks of vermilion.

From the curtain.

– Hail victory!
Victory to Duryodhana!
Victory to Gandhari!
May all be well,
For the ruler of all men – Dhritarashtra!
May all be well!

Dhritarashtra Look –
Vidur look. Sanjay comes.

Gandhari He has won.
My son Duryodhana
I had said.
He will win, surely this day.

Sentry *enters.*

Sentry It's a mendicant, my lord.

An old **Mendicant** *enters.*

Vidur A Mendicant who bears
An Upright forehead?
White haired
With long arms that denote noble lineage?

Mendicant I am that future
Which has been proven false
In the Kaurav capital today.
I had measured the movement of the stars,
Recorded it in numbers,
Calculated the unwritten alphabets
Of human destiny –
I was an astrologer of a distant land.

Dhritarashtra I do remember
You had said that conflict is inevitable,
For that would make the Kaurav's rule prevail.

Mendicant I am him.
Today my science reduced to a myth irrelevant.
Suddenly a man
Emerged
Stronger
Than the movement of galaxies.
Dominating the battlefield
To a dejected Arjuna, he said
I am omniscient.
Act, as I say, for
Truth shall prevail
Receive the truth from me. Do not fear

Vidur He was God.

Gandhari No. Never

Vidur In his movement alone
Is inherent
The divine pace of
All history, all planets.

Mendicant Can't say whether
God exists or not.
But that day it was proved,
That when any man,
Transcends himself and dares to challenge history,

That day the course of the stars is altered.
Redefined.
Destiny is not predestined.
It is made, and unmade,
Every moment by the decision of man.

Gandhari   Sentry give him a handful of coins.
You have said
Duryodhana will triumph.

Mendicant   I am a merely the false future
My words in this present,
Have no value
Like me
Umpteen – endless –
False futures,
Dilapidated dreams.
Decaying elements,
Are scattered in the Kaurav land,
Lurking in its lanes and alleys.
Gandhari is the mother,
Affectionately nurturing all!

Sentry *gives the coins.*

Victory to Duryodhana!
Victory to Gandhari! (*Goes.*)

Gandhari   Certainly,
Victory, will certainly come.
This, My hope,
Even if blind – let it be so
But he shall win. Duryodhana shall win.

Second Sentry *comes and lights the lamp.*

Vidur   The day has set . . .

Dhritarashtra   But
Sanjay has not come.
All warriors must have returned by now –
To their camps,
Who is the victor?
Who the vanquished?

Vidur   My lord,
Do not doubt,
The tidings that Sanjay brings shall be favourable.
Mother, go now and rest,
The city gates are open in relentless gaze,
Waiting for the arrival of Sanjay's chariot.

Vidur exits on one side; **Dhritarashtra** *and* **Gandhari** *on the other. The two* **Sentries** *move to and fro on the stage.*

Sentry One   Ethics! Order!

Sentry Two   Faithlessness.

Sentry One   Sorrow of sons!

Sentry Two   Futurist!

Sentry One   All these
Embellish the lives of kings.

Sentry Two   He, whom they all call God,
Takes it all in his stride.

Sentry One   But the lives of us two,
spent in this empty corridor –

Sentry Two   Who will,
Take that in his stride?

Sentry One   No ethical order have we violated,
For we had none of it.

Sentry Two   Faithlessness never shook us,
For we never had any deep faith
Neither belief – Nor disbelief.

Sentry One   We have been troubled by no sorrow.

Sentry Two   Known no pain.

Sentry One   Empty as this empty corridor, this life too is spent.

Sentry Two   Because we were the vassals.

Sentry One   Bearers of the commands of the blind King!

Sentry Two   We had no opinion of ours,
Nor any decision.

Sentry One   That's why in the forlorn corridor,
We go to and fro
To and fro.

Sentry Two   Even when dead,
In the corridor of Yama
Shall we go on and on always,
To and fro, To and fro . . .

They move about and exit. Darkness on stage as the curtain falls.

Narrative Song
Imminent now is defeat in this city deserted.

Where gradually all codes were corroded
This hazy dusk of defeat; of fear; of doubt.
In these corridors, darkness lingers about.
Where the future false with outstretched palms,
Jostles aimless like a beggar, seeking alms.
Within, only two diminishing lights remain.
The thinness of the King's blind vision.
Or the blind hope of Mother Gandhari.
Sanjay, who with a boon is blessed.
To be immortal, and impartial detached.
Know all and see all with vision divine.
Who shall to the blind King narrate all,
Who shall have no fear of weapons divine.
Who shall have no confusion nor doubt.
That Sanjay too,
Is way led in this night,
This night of entangled affections, lurking emotions
And thus he meanders pathless
In a known not thorny heath.

Curtain

Act Two

The Rise of the Beast

Narrative Song
Sanjay, is the detached onlooker; sculptor of words,
But he too is led astray in the woods of hesitation,
Indecision and doubt.
He has a responsibility massive, language incomplete, listeners blind
But truth must he impart in the hour of their crisis.
    That Sanjay too
    Way led by the night of emotions,
    Meanders pathless,
    In a known not thorny thicket,

When the curtain rises, the scenario of a forest pathway is visible. A warrior, keeping his weapons to a side, lies covered with a sheet, **Sanjay** *enters.*

Sanjay   I've gone astray
In a not known thorny thicket
Don't know how much further away.
Still is Hastinapur.
How will I reach?
And on reaching – what shall I say?
Even after this shameful defeat
Why do I still survive?
How can I say – though
Of words there's no dearth even today.
I myself have narrated to them,
Each and every event – as it happened.
But today, experiencing the finality of defeat,
Has – as if – altered the very nature of truth.
Now how will the same words,
Be the conveyors of this new sensibility?
This newly acquired perception?

The sleeping warrior wakes up and calls out — 'Sanjay'

Sanjay   Who calls me –
The sound of the ghosts
Or it's my own delusion?

Kritvarma   Fear not
I am Kritvarma.
Still alive are you Sanjay?
Pandava warriors left
You alive?

Sanjay Alive am I
Even Today.
When this earth, stretching for miles
Has been marked by Arjuna
With the headless torsos of the hacked Kauravs,
Dismembered, fragmented
Strewn and scattered all over its surface –
When none remains,
Not one valiant Kaurav survives,
Then Satyaki, so as to annihilate me,
Did lift up his weapon high!
Well would it be,
If I too
Had not been left alive, this day.
But Vyas had said – he will not die.
Sanjay cannot be killed.
What a curse did Vyas inflict on me.
Unknowingly.
Despite crisis, war, irreparable destruction,
Devastation, deluge and revolution,
Alive, you shall be Sanjay,
To say the truth,
Speak to the blind.
But how can I ever narrate, ah!,
The touch of the shinning cold iron
Of Satyaki's ready weapon –
To sense death so close!
For me it was
Quite a new vipration!
A new experience,
As a swift arrow
Rips right through and tears the delicate root of the lotus
So too in that sombre moment of extreme terror,
Someone ripped apart all my perceptions.
Now how will I ever give them this Entire Truth
With a perception so maimed, so distorted?

Kritvarma Bear with it Sanjay, be steady
You have to go and narrate to both
This episode of Duryodhana's defeat.

Sanjay How shall I tell . . .!
He who was the Monarch of Kings,
Stood
Empty handed,
Bare foot,
In blood stained

Tattered clothes,
Near the dismembered chariot,
Unarmed.
With moist eyes, he
Looked at me
And lowered his head
How can I describe,
All this to them – to both –
How will I?

Goes.

Kritvarma   There goes Sanjay too.
Many days ago,
Vidur had said –
This has to happen.
It has happened today.

Someone calls – Ashwathama-a-a-a . . . **Kritvarma** *listens.*

This is the voice of old Kripacharya.

The sound is repeated – **Kripacharya** *comes on stage. Sees* **Kritvarma**.

Kripacharya   That's Kritvarma!
You too are alive Kritvarma?

Kritvarma   Am alive.
Does Ashwathama also live?

Kripacharya   Live
Only us three.
This day
Getting off his chariot,
When king Duryodhana,
Bend his brow
To acknowledge subjugation,
Ashwathama
Saw it –
And immediately
Wrenched
His bow
And with a wounded cry,
Echoing in the elements.
Vanished towards the forest.
Ashwathama. . . . .

Calling out – goes. His voice is heard faintly in the background. Darkness – only a single spot of light on **Ashwathama**, *who sits with his broken bow.*

Ashwathama   This – my bow,
The bow of Ashwathama,

Whose string had been fixed by Drona himself.
Today when I
Saw Duryodhana,
Weaponless, vulnerable,
Eyes brimming with tears,
I wrenched,
This bow of mine.
Like a trampled snake crumpled,
Frightening, but –
Powerless is this, my bow –
As is my mind,
Convoluted, twisted.
On whose strength
Will I
Now avenge
My father's brutal slaughter?
Fearful in this forest, too
I am unable to forget
How on hearing
Yuddhishtras' proclamation,
That Ashwathama has been killed,
Honourable Drona,
Dropped his weapons on the battlefield.
He had an inviolable faith
In Yuddhishtra's speech.
Finding him unarmed,
Sinner Dhritdyumn
With his weapons hacked him to pieces.
I cannot forget,
My father was invincible.
With the half truth alone
Could Yuddhistra
Kill him.
Since that day
Within me too
All that was benign, bright and gentle
Was aborted
By the half truth
of Yuddhishtra, who
Being the acknowledged King of Righteousness and
Virtue, he said –
Man or beast –
He did not distinguish,
Did not segregate,
Man from beast.
Since that day am I,

A mere beast, a blind barbaric brute. Savage!
But today I too have gone astray –
In a blind cave.
This cave of subjugation. Defeat.
Duryodhana listen –
Listen Drona – listen –
I – this your Ashwathama
Coward Ashwathama,
Still Remains,
As in the mouth of
a diseased corpse
Remains
Filthy phlegm.
Stale sputum –
So do I remain – still.

Beats his chest.

Shall I stab myself –
Self annihilate?
Released of this
Impotent existence –
If I must
Boil in the melting fires of hell –
Even so perhaps –
Would not be so tormenting.
But no!
Alive I shall remain
As a blind barbaric beast
May the words of Righteous Yuddhishtra come true.
Under these ribs of mine
Two claws may sprout –
These pupils of my eyes,
Teethless may tear and chew
Whomsoever they find.
Kill and kill
Slaughter! Only slaughter! Only slaughter
Be the ultimate meaning
of my existence.

Sound of someone approaching.

Someone comes.
A Pandava warrior perhaps,
Alone. Unarmed.
Hide and from behind
Plunge upon and attack!
These hungry hands

Have wrenched the bow,
Now to wring the Neck.
Let me hide – behind the shrubs.

He hides. **Sanjay** *enters.*

Sanjay   Even so, shall I remain.
Even so, shall I remain.
Even so, shall I remain.
Howsoever bitter is truth,
Bitterer than bitter,
To the bitterest,
Even so shall I speak.
Only truth, Only truth. Only truth
is the ultimate meaning
of my . . . . . . aah!

Ashwathama *attacks him – holds his neck.*

Ashwathama   This is how,
This is how,
My hungry claws will clasp and slit,
That throat of Yuddhishtra,
Which poured out
Ashwathama no more

Kritvarma *and* **Kripacharya** *enter.*

Kritvarma (*yells*)   Leave him Ashwathama
He's Sanjay –
Not any Pandava

Ashwathama   Kill. Kill. Only Kill.

Kripacharya   Kritvarma, catch him from behind.
Tightly hold Ashwathama.
Kill – but only the enemy
What sort of a warrior are you Ashwathama?
Sanjay is indestructible.
Detached.

Ashwathama   Detached?
Uncle I am not a warrior.
Only a barbaric brute.
This word detached
Is for me meaningless.
Hear now the declaration –
of this blind barbaric beast
He, who does not stand by my side
Is an enemy.

Kritvarma Deranged are you?
Sanjay – go your way.

Sanjay Don't let me
I plead
Don't let me go.
Kill me
Give me death.
To face the blind and to them
Narrate the truth.
Ah the agonising pain of this,
Compared to which,
Death is more blissful.
Kill me
And free me
Ashwathama.

Ashwathama *looks helplessly at* **Kripacharya** *and rests his head on his shoulders.*

Ashwathama What am I to do – Uncle.
What am I to do?
To kill for me is not a principle, Nor ethics, Nor duty.
It is now for me a ganglion in the mind. An obsession.
Whom shall I seize?
Wrench slit.
What to do –
Uncle – what am I to do?

Kripacharya Do not despair yet.

Kritvarma There's a lot to be done.
Alive still is Duryodhana.
Let's all go and search for him

Kripacharya Sanjay,
Known to you
Are his whereabouts?

Sanjay (*slowly*)
He is in the lake.
Having controlled the flow of water,
By his yogic power,
He sits,
Motionless,
Inside.
Not known
To the Pandava clan

Kripacharya Be robust Ashwathama,
Come receive the instructions from Duryodhana.

Sanjay, take, us.
To the lake.

Kritvarma Who comes here –
an aged person?

Kripacharya Let's go
Before anyone
Can see us.

They go.

The stage is empty for a while. Then slowly the **Old Mendicant** *enters.*

Old Mendicant Far have I come –
Quite away
From Hastinapur.
Aged am I! Cannot see clearly.
Surely I had seen some people here.
Let me see whether the coins given
By Mother Gandhari
Are safe.
I had said –
This is inevitable
and that is inevitable,
This will happen and
That will happen on its own.
Today this hour of defeat
Proves
False all the inevitability of future.
Only action is truth.
The deed is the seed
How man acts –
What he does now this instant
In that is inherent the future
Of ages to come.
That is why he said,
Arjuna
Lift up your weapon,
With previous fervour and fight!
Not in *inertia,*
In Action alone lies
The meaning of man's existence.

Bends to see the bow of **Ashwathama**.

Who has left this bow here?
Has once more the mind of some Arjuna
Been gripped by dejection? Again?

Ashwathama (*enters*)
It's my bow –
this.

Mendicant   Who comes here?
Hail Ashwathama!
Victory to Ashwathama!

Ashwathama   Do not hail old man.
As your futurist science and all
Became worthless,
So too was my bow proven worthless.
I have just seen Duryodhana.
He, whose forehead dazzled
With the protective umbrella of jewel studded crowns,
Today on that forehead
Is a coating
of turbid water.
You had said,
Duryodhana will be victorious.

Mendicant   Victory to Duryodhana –
Still I say.
Though aged
and worn out,
I'll go and, explain.
This is not defeat Duryodhana.
Consider it to be the time for the New Truth to dawn.
I had foretold
The false future
Now I shall go and tell him.
Independent of the present – exists no future.
There still is time – Duryodhana.
Time there still is!
Each moment is the moment to transform history.

Begins to go slowly.

Ashwathama   What will I do –
Ah – what will I do?
Whose present consists of
Me and my counter violence.
A half truth of Yuddhishtra
Slaughtered my future.
But no,
Alive I shall remain.
But if in my favour,
The future is not determined before hand
If it is not predestined,

Then it is detached – objective – impartial,
And if so –
An enemy – if detached!

Moves towards the **Mendicant**.

Today he cannot escape
These hungry claws
Stop! Hey stop!
You – false future.
Decadent Depriver! Seize him

Compresses his teeth and runs behind the **Mendicant**. *Near the wings clasps him and drags him within.*

Kill – only kill – only to kill
Is my virtue.
Blood, only blood. Only blood is my virtue.

From the backstage – sounds of strangulation. The cruel laughter of **Ashwathama**. *Two spots of light move about on the stage.* **Kripacharya**, **Kritvarma** *hold and bring* **Ashwathama** *who breathes heavily – back on stage.*

Kripacharya   What's this you've done
Ashwathama
What's this?

Ashwathama   Don't know what I've done.
Uncle, what have I done!
Have I done something?

Kritvarma   Kripacharya
Afraid
Am I
Of this Ashwathama!

Kripacharya *makes* **Ashwathama** *sit, loosens his armour, belt etc. Wipes the sweat from his brow.*

Kripacharya   Sit.
Rest here.
You have not done anything.
Only been through a nightmare.

Ashwathama   What am I to do –
Uncle.
To kill is no longer a principle for me,
A ganglion.
It a ganglion, an obsession.
Having done this,
The tension that had seized the muscles
And held them tight

Has, as if, been released
Is this what is meant by
Being relieved of the self –
Transcending the self?

Kripacharya (*makes* **Aswathama** *lie down*)
Sleep, now
Duryodhana has said
go and rest.
Tomorrow we shall see what
the Pandava clan has in store.
Turn over
And sleep now.

(*To* **Kritvarma**.)
He has slept.

Kritvarma (*with sarcasm*)   Slept.
That's why we live.
To sleep.
In this war,
We, who were the chivalrous warriors,
Will now, on the sly
Kill
The old and the unarmed.

Kripacharya   Calm down, Kritvarma
Amongst all the well known warriors – the stalwarts –
Who has not done
What all
uptil now?
Drona was old, unarmed.
But
Did that prompt Drishtdumn –
Not to harm him?
Or did we for that matter –
Take pity on Abhimanyu –
Though he was totally unarmed,
Alone.
Seven stalwarts . . .

Ashwathama   I did not kill him.
I wanted to slay the future
I don't know how
That old man was found dead.
I did not kill him –
Uncle believe me.

Kripacharya   Sleep Now.

Sleep Kritvarma.
I'll be on guard – this whole long Night.

Curtain begins to fall.

Narrative Song
As after a flood the ebbing receding Ganges
On its banks does reject half-eaten crippled corpses,
So does Ashwathama lie on the sands rejected
By the changing tide of history surging ahead
This night of souls trailing behind
This night of soul entangled led astray.
This night of souls fragmented.
This night when triumph intoxicates the Pandava clan.
This night when helpless hides Duryodhana.
This night of brows.
Erect with pride
The night when hands fall
Limp on hands.

Curtain

Act Three

The Half Truth of Ashwathama

Narrative Song
As Sanjay's, chariot reached the city gates,
The night was dwindling
When does the vanquished Kaurav army come
Was being in whispers murmured,
Listening to Sanjay's war narration,
Soon was morning. Sadness so intense,
Still as stone was Gandhari, her pale face
Was bereft of all signs that reflect the living.
By noon the city was shaken of its slumber.
Fragmented chariots, broken carts were somehow laden
With returning Brahmins, women and surgeons,
Widows, dwarfs, the aged, injured and fragile.
The army that with colourful flags fluttering
Tearing through the earth, sky trembling,
Had gone to war eighteen days ago –
Is so ransacked at its homecoming.

The curtain rises. **Sentries** *at guard. Taking support from* **Vidur** – **Dhritarashtra** *enters.*

Dhritarashtra   Unable to see,
Yet by touching
The maimed and crippled soldiers
I've tried to see.
Close to the arm,
When the hand is, amputated
It seems so much like
The arm of my throne –

Vidur   My lord,
Steeped in such thoughts –
You Are?

Dhritarashtra   Nothing very extraordinary
Only from Sanjay's words
That which I had been hearing about,
Today, that war, I can touch
And experience with my own hands.

A maimed soldier, comes dragging himself on the ground, touches **Vidur**'s *feet to get his attention. Indicates that he wants water.*

Vidur   What is it? Oh –
Sentry, go – get some water.

Dhritarashtra   Who is it Vidur?

Vidur   A thirsty soldier my lord.

Dhritarashtra   What does he say?

Vidur   Says victory to Duryodhana.
The tongue is slashed –
He's mute.

Dhritarashtra   Except for the mute,
Who can hail my victory now!

Sentry *gives him water. Touches him.*

Sentry One   He's got fever.

Dhritarashtra   You've given him water?
Ask him to rest somewhere here.

The **Soldier** *goes behind and lies down.*

Get him some clothes
From Mother Gandhari.

Sentry   Mother Gandhari has not been at all
To the charity hall, today.

Vidur   Her eyes
Hold no tears.
Nor grief
Nor anger.
Still as stone, she sits
On the staircase.

Noise is heard.

Dhritarashtra   Sentry go and see
What this clamour is about.

Sentry *goes.*

Vidur   My lord,
Please come awhile
And console Mother Gandhari.

Dhritarashtra   I'll go
Even Sanjay is not with her.
Who knows what tidings he will bring
Of the last and ultimate combat
Between Bhim and Duryodhana

The noise increases.

Vidur My lord – come this way.

Dhritarashtra *goes with the* **Second Sentry**.

What's this? Ceaseless commotion?

Sentry *returns.*

Sentry There spreads
In the city
Sudden
Fear
And
Panic.

Vidur Why?

Sentry Along with
Our tired wounded army,
An opponent warrior,
Has also come
Into the Kingdom.
Braced with arms
Demon like –
What sort of a Warrior
Is he?
People say he's going to plunder the Kingdom

Vidur Sickening
This rumour is.
I'll go myself
and look at him.
Meanwhile, guard
The Royal Chamber

Goes.

Sentry Two Did you see
With your own eyes –
That warrior?

Sentry One He's a sorcerer.
Disguises himself.
Keeps altering his form
When the guards,
Closed the city gates,
He changed himself
Into a vulture.
High above

The closed city gates,
He flew and came in,
And started swallowing,
The children sleeping on the terrace.

Sentry Two Come – be quick.
Close the Western gates.

Sentry One (*with fear*) See there!

Sentry Two What's that –

Sentry One He comes.

Sentry Two Hide. Here –
Let's hide.

They hide. An ordinary **Soldier** *enters.*

Yuyutsu In fearing
Lies not so much agony
As in being that
Of whom others can only be terrified.
I am like that today.
These are the high mansions
Of my father and my mother,
But who knows
I may be welcomed here
With a poison edged spear

Sentry One This is Yuyutsu
Son of Dhritarashtra
Who in the war
Fought for Yuddhishtra

Yuyutsu My only crime is
That I was committed to the truth.
Drona, Bhishm
And all the stalwarts,
Could not oppose
Duryodhana.
Even so I did say –
I will not favour the untruth.
I too am a Kaurav.
But truth is higher than the Kaurav clan.

Sentry Two It certainly is Yuyutsu.
Seems he has returned
With the wounded army.

Yuyutsu Had I also
Borne with

The self willed impertinence of Duryodhana,
Then such contempt
Would I not receive
From my family.
Mother would have greeted me,
With arms wide open,
Though downcast and defeated my brow would be.

Vidur (*enters*)   I've been searching,
Long for you, Yuyutsu.
Child!
You've done well to come back.
Sentry go
Inform Mother Gandhari
Who, smitten with the grief of her sons.
May on finding you –
Forget her sorrow.

Yuyutsu   Don't know whether
She'll even look at me.
Or not.

Vidur   Don't say so
In this tale of tainted Kaurav sons,
You are the only one,
Whose brow is high with pride.

Yuyutsu   That's why, on seeing me come,
The doors were shut,
By the city dwellers.
Calling out names
Sorcerer!
Child eater,
Demon like,
Vulturius!

Vidur   Don't let this deject you, Yuyutsu,
From these ignorant, fear stricken simple folk,
This comes to the share always
Of those who move away.
Defy
The laid out track of fixed convention.
And define
Their path themselves.

Sentry Two *comes with* **Gandhari**.

Sentry Two   Mother Gandhari has arrived

Yuyutsu *touches her feet.*

Vidur   This is Yuyutsu,
Mother!
Touching your feet
Bless him.

Gandhari   Ask him Vidur
Is he well
Robust and happy?
Son,
These arms of yours,
So full of valour
Did they tire not
Slaying one by one
Your entire bretheren?

A pause.

After the grandeur of the Pandava forts,
This city of yours,
Must seem so devoid of lusture?
Why are you silent?
Weary must he be.
Vidur! Spread a bedstead of flowers for him.
No vanquished Duryodhana is he,
That he would sleep
In the slush
Of a pond!
So silent! Vidur! Why is he?
Because I am the mother
Of his enemies
Is that why!

Begins to go.

Come, guard
Let's go

Goes.

Vidur   Mother, this does not befit you.
Mother!

Yuyutsu   What's this –
That mother has done
Vidur?
Better would it have been
Had I
Compromised with the untruth.

Vidur   But
That was no solution at all

To the problem.
Had you
Compromised with the untruth,
From within you would have grown feeble.

Yuyutsu   As if now this bitterness of my mother,
Contempt of the people
Will strengthen me from within?
The ultimate predicament is
They both weaken you –
Make you fragile.
Whether you side with the truth
Or with untruth
What did I get Vidur –
What did I get?

Vidur   Calm down Yuyutsu
And endure it.
The deep pain is to be borne in the deep.

The sound of the mute **Soldier***'s hearing becomes louder.*

Vidur   What sound is this, Sentry –

Sentry   That mute soldier
Is perhaps passing away.

Sentry Two *brings the water.*

Vidur   Here Yuyutsu,
Give him water
And give him love,
Give life to the dying
And bear the bitter vicissitudes.

Yuyutsu (*goes to the mute* **Soldier**)
On my lap rest your head
Open your mouth,
Yes – like this
Open your eyes –

The mute **Soldier** *opens his mouth – the water touches his lips – suddenly he screams and runs out, stumbling and falling.*

Sentry   What's happened?

Yuyutsu   I am to blame
He – a rider in the Kaurav Cavalry
With my flaming arrow,
Were his knees scorched.
I destroyed his life
How can he now

Accept my pity?
My plight is such
Even love if I do give,
That too is not acceptable to others
Vyas had said
To me
Where Krishna will be –
Triumph too shall be there.
Such is the triumph of Krishna.
In which I am a murderer – a criminal,
Deprived of my mother, disdained, disowned,
A target of everyone's contempt.

Vidur Today in this hour of defeat,
I do not know
What has gone wrong where –
Fallen false where –
As if each and everyone –
All, have derailed from their axis today.
One by one,
From which all the wheels
Have Fallen apart,
That totally unfunctional useless axis
Is that you –
Is that you – God?

Suddenly there is a frightening cry from within.

Yuyutsu What could have happened Vidur

Vidur Sentry just go and see

Sentry *goes and returns immediately.*

Sentry Sanjay has brought the tidings.

Vidur
Yuyutsu } That?

Sentry One In the final duel
King . . .
. . . Duryodhana . . .
. . . is defeated.

Vidur *and* **Yuyutsu** *leave. The cries increase. The chorus announces 'King Duryodhana is defeated'. The back curtain rises. The triumphant noise of* **Pandava** *celebration can be heard. The scene of the forest road. Armed with their bows,* **Kritvarma** *and* **Kripacharya** *come in running.*

Kritvarma Hide somewhere here Kripacharya.

Blowing their conch shells,
Celebrating and, revelling,
The victorious Pandava clan
Is returning to their forts.

Kripacharya   Wait
Lift your bow.
Someone comes, who is it?

Kritvarma   No. No one. Only Ashwathama,
Who camouflaging himself
Had gone to see the combat of Duryodhana and Bhim.

Ashwathama *enters.*

Ashwathama   Uncle listen . . .
King Duryodhana has been slain
By unrighteousness.

Kripacharya (*indicates for him to be quiet*)
Hide.
Disassociating and moving away
from the Pandavas.
Angry Balram
comes this way.

Kritvarma   Krishna too
Is with him.

Kripacharya   Listen,
Carefully listen.

Balram (*from offstage*)
No
No
No
You may say anything Krishna.
Surely Bhim has done injustice today.
This treacherous attack
Was unrighteous. Immoral.

Kripacharya   Can't make out what Krishna is explaining

Balram   Pandavas are relatives –
Then were the Kauravas enemies?
I would have taught Bhim a lesson today.
But you withheld me.
I've known you since childhood –
Always been unethical,
Manouvering and replete with intrigue.

Kripacharya   They've turned away

Balram   Go to Hastinapur,
Counsel Gandhari
Do anything Krishna
But I say –
Despite your manouvering mind
and despite your godliness,
these Pandavas who bellowing their conch shells,
Go frenzied to their forts,
They too will surely be hit by unrighteousness.

Ashwathama (*repeats*)   They too will surely be hit by unrighteousness.

Kripacharya   Child,
What anxiety absorbs you?

Ashwathama   They too will surely be hit by unrighteousness.
Thought it,
Uncle, I've thought it all.
I, Ashwathama
Will slay those lowly treacherous Pandavas

Kritvarma (*mockingly*)   As you had slain
The aged mendicant.

Ashwathama (*put off*)   Yes. Exactly like that
Till I do not eradicate them –
Render them rootless.

Kritvarma   But Ashwathama
Pandava sons are not old
Nor unarmed
Nor alone
It's over now –
This dishonourable warfare,
Go and experiment
With your unholy luminous courage elsewhere –
You who are brimming with valour and chivalry.

Ashwathama   Prepared for that too am I Kritvarma
Don't mock with words –
Lift up your weapon,
For first I must slay you –
You who is a well-wisher of the Pandavas

Kripacharya (*scolds him*)
Ashwathama
Put down you weapon.
Deranged are you?
Not an iota of ethical considerations
Remains with you?

Ashwathama Are you Listening, father?
I in this counter violence
In this retaliation
Am absolutely alone.
You were killed by Dhristdumn with unrighteousness,
Bhim killed Duryodhana with unrighteousness,
Yet the world's entire burden of ethics and scruples,
Is imposed
Only on this sheer orphan Ashwathama

Kripacharya Come,
Sit here child
We all are with you
In the counter violence
But if – apart from concealed attack,
Some other path can be delineated.

Ashwathama Another path!
Have Pandavas left any other path?
An example of the Pandava ethics
I saw well displayed in today's duel.
How with an unholy attack
Duryodhana was flung on the ground by Bhim
With broken thighs, broken elbows, broken neck
Lay Duryodhana on whose forehead,
Placing his foot,
And crushing full weight,
Bhim with arms wide spread, let out a beast like roar!
How on both the temples of Duryodhana,
Two veins had swollen and suddenly burst.
How his lips pressed,
And once a tremor vibrated in the broken thigh.
With diminishing sight.
Duryodhana could gaze
At his subjects

Kripacharya Enough, Ashwathama, No more
May be your path
Is the only possible path.

Ashwathama Uncle,
Then you are under oath.
Do not delay
May be still alive is Duryodhana.
In his presence,
Have me proclaimed the general.
I'll find the path that wreaks vengeance.

Kripacharya Come along
Kritvarma, you too –

Kritvarma No let me be.
You go

They go.

They've gone both?
No coward am I.
And no doubt
Sorrowful because of Duryodhana's assassination.
But what horrendous
Pomposity is this
He whose bones are minced,
That vanquished Duryodhana,
Will appoint this eccentric the general
In whose army remain,
Only two –
Aged Kripacharya and coward Kritvarma.
Such is the plight –
Of the massive Kaurav army?
Let it be Kritvarma,
Be silent.
Having taken Duryodhana's side,
Then, until
Your last breath maintain it

Kripacharya *enters.*

You've come – Kripacharya?

Kripacharya Could not see any longer
That horrible sight
From the hollow of a tree were peeping two vultures.
Walking to and fro
Amidst the bushes.
Were roaming jackals and wolves,
Open mouthed, lapping tongues
Lapping tongues,
And with voracious eyes,
Unblinkingly staring
At King Duryodhana

Kritvarma Then how was general
Ashwathama anointed?

Kripacharya He said
Kripacharya,
you are the priest
There is no water here,
With the drops of sweat,

Anoint the forehead of courageous Ashwathama
How to lift my hand
To bless him?
The arms have swung away
From the shoulders.
I lifted his lifeless hand
In the stance of a blessing
But because of intense pain,
Instead of a blessing,
in a heart rendering voice he screamed.

Ashwathama (*enters*)   But alive shall he remain
He has said
Ashwathama
Until of our retaliation
Counter violence,
You do not bring tidings –
Till then shall I live,
Even if all my parts and limbs
Are chewed away,
By these wild beasts.
Did you hear that Kritvarma?
By tomorrow I will seek retaliation, wreak vengeance.
The army may desert,
Even so, I alone –

Kritvarma (*lying down*)
I am with you –
General (*Yawns.*)

Kripacharya   Now at least
Let us rest

Ashwathama   Sleep tonight
My soldiers
Tomorrow your general – Ashwathama,
Will tell you
What you are to do.

Kritvarma, **Kripacharya** *lie down*, **Ashwathama** *holding the bow, keeps vigil.*

How still and solitary is this forest.
Awake, only am I here.
Even the shadows of
Tamarind, Banyan and Peepal
Are steeped in slumber.

Slowly there is darkness on stage. The howling of jackals can be heard as if from the depths of the forest. The fearful sound increases. The stage is in pitch darkness, in which **Ashwathama** *paces. Suddenly the harsh sound of a crow can be heard and* *from the right enters an actor, clad in black clothes and a crow mask. He spreads his wings and circles the stage twice. Then folding his legs, placing chin on shoulders sits, taking on the posture of a sleeping bird. During this, there is no light on* **Ashwathama**. *Only a blue line of light is visible.*

Then the sound increases and from the left another actor enters dressed in white, with an owl mask and sharp claws. He sees the crow, grows alert, then with a sense of enjoyment sharpens his claws. Then demonstrates various postures of attack.

Now a spot of light falls on **Ashwathama**, *who wonder stuck watches the event.*

The crow turns over in his sleep – and despite seeing the owl, does not pay any attention to it. The owl is nervous. Then carefully checks out whether the crow is actually asleep or pretending to be. Assured of the former, he then plunges on the crow. Both remain entangled for a while in complete darkness. Then lights come on. The shredded feathers of the crow and the blood stained claws of the owl are visible. Owl lifts up the feathers and dances – the frenzied, dance of death and destruction.

Ashwathama *is in a spot of light. The expressions of his face change and he laughs. Scared, the owl stops. Sees* **Ashwathama** *coming towards it. He throws the shredded feathers at him and flies.* **Ashwathama** *holds the shredded feather in his hand and cries in excitement.*

Ashwathama   Got it!
Got it!
Uncle, I've got it!

The lights brighten. **Ashwathama** *is leaping with the feather in his hands. The other true warriors are startled and wake up. Perplexed,* **Kritvarma** *draws out his sword.*

Kripacharya   What have you found child?

Ashwathama   Uncle,
Truth has been discovered
By barbaric Ashwathama.

Kritvarma   This injured, tattered feather.

Ashwathama   As was the half truth of Yuddhishtra.
Injured and tattered.

Kripacharya   Where are you going!

Ashwathama   Towards the Pandava Camp.
Where Unarmed and unconscious
In sleep, lies the entire
Victorious Pandava clan!

Ties his belt.

Kripacharya   Now?

Ashwathama   Now. This instant.
They are alone.

Krishna is away to Hastinapur
Counselling Gandhari
A better chance than this
When will I ever get!

Kritvarma   This is the general's command?

Ashwathama (*does not hear*)
You had said
Man or beast is!
Beast like,
I only with the strides of my feet
Will pound and crush Dhristdumn.
As a deranged mad brute,
Trampling the lotus buds,
So too will I not spare Uttara
In whose womb is conceived.
Abhimanyu's son –
The future of the Pandava lineage

Kripacharya   No. No. No.
This I will not allow to happen.

Ashwathama   It will happen
You will not support?
Then.
alone will I go.
But will go.
will go!

With head lowered **Kritvarma** *follows him.*

Kripacharya   Wait!
But think Ashwathama . . .

Ashwathama *goes without listening.* **Kripacharya** *follows, calling out, 'Ashwathama . . . Ashwathama Ashwathama'! this sound is lost in the horizon. Only the sound of the wheels of three chariots and horses hooves remains.*

Curtain

Interlude: Feathers, Wheels and Bandages

*The **Old Mendicant** enters. The light spreads like the web of a spider creating a ghostly ambience.*

Mendicant Earlier I was the false future, an aged mendicant
Now I am a wandering spirit.
Ashwathama had slain me.
Life is an incessant flow and death held me by the arm
And pulled me to the shore.
And I, in detached form standing at the rim, can clearly
See that
This age is a blind ocean.
Surrounded on all sides by mountains.
And from the cracks and clefts,
And from the caves
Swirling terrible tornadoes surging from all sides
Are churning it.
And in that afflux, there is velocity, movement
Though not like a river – linear and regular.
But as in a dark cavity of the Serpent Kingdom
Countless, sloughs covered, blind Snakes,
Swaddled into each other,
Ahead – behind,
Above – beneath,
Crooked-convoluted
Crawl all over,
So do countless streams, sub-streams.
Like blind snakes, do restlessly whine –
Such is this blind ocean
That we can call the flow of existence today.
And some white sloughs now swim on the surface.
Like white bandages.
These bandages are on Gandhari's eyes,
On the wounds of soldiers.
I, with the power of my spirit,
Have bound
The entire flow,
The movement of the narrative
And all characters, in their spaces
Are caught motionless.
Because I, by ripping and dissecting,
Want to understand,
The intrinsic disjointedness of each.
These are those characters.
Compelled by my coded chants
To enter in the form of shadows

Yuyutsu, **Vidur**, **Sanjay**, *come on the stage – walking mechanically, and as if hypnotised – form a line behind the* **Old Mendicant***. One by one they come out to make their comments and then return to their positions.*

Yuyutsu   I am Yuyutsu,
I am like that wheel
Which during the war was attached to a chariot.
But now feels that it was fixed in the wrong axis
And I have fallen apart from that axis.

Sanjay   I am Sanjay
Outcast from the world of action.
I, stuck between two larger wheels,
Am a small decorative meaningless wheel
That with the larger wheels does rotate,
But does not propell the chariot forward
Nor is it able to touch the earth.
And the biggest misfortune of his life is,
That it cannot even break away its axis.

Vidur   I am Vidur,
Disciple of Krishna, worshipper and diplomat
But my diplomacy is of the simple ordinary kind.
And the age is full of situations, extraordinary.
And now my voice is afflicted by doubt.
Because it seems that my God,
Is like the unfunctional useless axis
Whose wheels have fallen apart
And it cannot rotate on its own.
But doubt is sin and I do not want to sin!

Sound of bells off stage and a Peacock feather falls on the stage. The **Mendicant** *picks it up.*

What's this?
A peacock feather?
After assuring Gandhari,
Returning from Hastinapur,
The feather has fallen,
It seems from Krishna's crown.

Listens.

Yes. These bells are of his chariot.
Shall I block its way –
As I have blocked the flow of the Narrative?

His attempt at hypnosis fail.

No, in him the flow of entire time, ethics and order is bound.
I cannot bind him.

And of course, this the other chariot,
Whose velocity, let alone me, even Krishna is unable to obstruct.

This chariot is of my assassin, Ashwathama.
Black, as the tattered feather of a crow.
His blood stained hatred fearsome
Is unyielding.
Will the peacock feather conquer it or lose to it?
This New Kaliya Serpent of Hatred,
Who has risen,
Is its destruction now possible for Krishna?

The sound of the chariots increases.

The chariots move forward
I am powerless.
The movement of the Narrative, is no longer –
Bound by my binding.
Krishna's chariot trails behind in the darkness.
Look there! Ashwathama's chariot
Reaches the Pandava fort.
Ah but – here comes – who –
Gigantic Demon like man
In the Darkness Looming large –
Facing Ashwathama
As would the massive opaque cliffs obstruct!

Rubs his hands as if witnessing something terrible. A frightening roar offstage.

Curtain

Act Four

The Curse of Gandhari

Narrative Song
He was Shankar
In Furious Form Formidable
God of Doom
At the fort gate seen
By Ashwathama
Countless venomous vipers
On arms
entangled,
Countless Destructions
In each pore
Of his,
At the fort gate
Seen by Ashwathama
He spoke in a tone thunderous Devastating.
'Conquer me first then go within?'
Fiercely did Ashwathama fight.
Who else can withstand weapons divine
Darts, iron bows, clubs, maces lethal lances,
All that infuriated Ashwathama hurled,
In one pore of his,
Were absorbed
All.
Defeated he bounced low
In salutation
Then.

Ashwathama (*chants*)   Jata Kataha Sambhrman – nilimpa Nirjhari Sama
Vilol Veechi Vallari Viajman murdhani
Dhagad-dhagad-dhagaj Jwalal – lalata-pattapavke
Kishora Chandra Shekhare rati Prati Kshana Mama

Narrative Song
Simple is Shankar,
The generous giver.
Raising his hands in blessing,
He said to him
'Ashwathama you will be victorious for sure,
The virtues of Pandavas now begin to wane,
For the tender regard of Krishna,
I have given them protection so far,
Bestowed triumph on them.

Energised them anew with valour,
But by unholy slaughter.
They have themselves opened the gates of death'
Simple is Shankar,
The generous giver.

When the crutain rises, **Gandhari** *is seen sitting,* **Vidur** *and* **Sanjay** *stand close by in positions indicating that a conversation has been going on for some time.*

Gandhari   Then what happened?

Sanjay – what happened next?

Sanjay (*as if reading aloud*)
Receiving Shankar's divine blessing Ashwathama
Swiftly reached Warrior Dhrishtdumn's bedstead
Like lightning, pounced and dragged him down.
With ire unleashed, kneaded and crushed him with his knees
And clasped his neck in claws.
From the bowls of his eyes, dugout the pupils round
That burst like unripe mango seeds
And from the cavities bubbled dark black blood.

Gandhari   Blinded him at the start,
How merciful is Ashwathama.

Sanjay   With great difficulty, piercing together words,
He mumbled, 'kill if you must –
But slay with weapons'
'You don't deserve it – beast like man Dhrishtdumn.
Drona weaponless was killed cowardly by you
Now this is revenge!' then in wrathful vengeance
Bounded to a pulp
His vital organs with the strokes of his heel.

Vidur   Stop. No more.

Gandhari   Then what happened?

Sanjay   Clamour resounding the scattered warriors awoke,
Rubbing their eyes came out,
And within moments where lying about.
Pierced by arrows, sharp and lethal
Not finding anything around, with a wheel
Did Shatanik aim.
Ashwathama hacked off his knees.
At a distance slept Shikhandi Going close,
He aimed an arrow that through the forehead
Ripping the brain and slitting the cot of Sandalwood
Buried itself in the earth.

Gandhari   Then what happened, Sanjay?

Vidur   Your heart is of stone, Gandhari.

Gandhari   From the mines of stones, jewels are extracted.
Do not obstruct Vidur
Sanjay, then

Vidur   Not Sanjay, but from me hear
How heinous was that
Counter violence.
The retaliation.
Kripacharya, Kritvarma waited out.
As the aged, children and attendants rushed outwards
Kritvarma pierced them with arrows,
Trumpeting terrified elephants
Transgressed the fortress,
And running amuck caused havoc.
On the bedsteads the sleeping women were
Trampled where they lay.
And at that instant, these two gallant men
Set the Pandava fort ablaze.

Gandhari   I wish that my own eyes,
Could see this.
What splendid light
Must have surrounded Ashwathama then.

Sanjay   Smoke, flames, littered flesh, injured horses and Ransacked chariots die about.
Amidst, blood, marrow, serum and skulls,
And Dismembered torsos,
Does morbid Ashwathama stroll,
Roaring like a leopard.
With the clotted human blood, that sword of his
Is glued to his hands like an organ,
That had grown, as if,
Out of his own armpits.

Gandhari   Wait
Sanjay wait.
With your vision divine, let me once see
Brave Ashwathama.

Sanjay   Mother he is odious,
Terrorising

Gandhari   Yet he is brave.
He has achieved
What my hundred sons could not

Drona could not.
Bhishma could not.

Sanjay   Mother
Vyas has given me this divine vision,
Only for the duration of the war.
And may be taken away anytime,

Gandhari   That is why I say
After all this, unjust Krishna will not allow
Ashwathama to live.
Let me see him once.

Sanjay   I will try.
May the power of all my virtuous actions accumulate
And collectively reveal to you a sight of Ashwathama

Meditates.

Walls, move aside –
Barriers in the way that obstruct the vision
May they by this power contract and diminish.
Distance may by obliterated,
And across the horizon
All that is concealed to the vision,
May those scenes slide close –
Into my view.

The back curtain rises and lights from the front begin to dim.

It is dark
This is the space
Where almost dead, Duryodhana lay till yesterday.
Braced with arms,
Who are the two warriors who come?
They are Kripacharya and Kritvarma.

They call out far away in the dark – 'Lord Duryodhana, Lord Duryodhana'.

Kripacharya   Kritvarma
Shoot the light Dart
So the darkness may reduce.

Kritvarma (*looks into the wings*)
There lies our King.
Certainly has half dead Duryodhana,
Been dragged by violent beasts into those shrubs.

Kripacharya   Yet alive.
See – his lips seem to move.

Kritvarma   Blood oozing from the mouth has congealed

Forming dark clots all around.
The wind pipe too must be clogged,

Kripacharya (*haltingly and loud*)
My lord,
General Ashwathama
Has razed to ruins the entire Pandava fort
Not one soldier remains.

Kritvarma   The King's face brightens,
A gleam of satisfaction is visible!

Kripacharya   His eyes open.

Kritvarma   Searching for someone –
Perhaps Ashwathama?

Kripacharya   My lord,
Ashwathama's gone to collect the Brahmastra.
The ultimate weapon supreme of Brahma and his jewel.
Taking that along, the three of us shall
Go into the thick forest.

Kritvarma   From the King's eyes flow tears.

Light falls on **Gandhari** *and* **Sanjay**.

Sanjay   What's this mother.
The bandage still not removed?
See! There comes Ashwathama.

Gandhari   No. No. No.
No way,
Will I be able to see.
Duryodhana facing death
Leave it, Sanjay,
This bandage is bound. Let it be bound.
Just keep telling me – all that is happening there.

Vidur   Nothing is visible to me.

Sanjay   Ashwathama has come
But head lowered
Completely silent

Lights fade out from the front.

Kripacharya   My lord,
Your Ashwathama is here.
Unable to lift your hand –
Lift your gaze once and bless him!

Ashwathama   No lord no

I still am undeserving
I have settled score with Dhristdumn
To avenge my father's sinful murder
But, yet, unable to seek vengeance on your behalf.
That still remains.
Unharmed is Uttara,
Who will give birth to Pandava heir and descendant.
But, lord,
This task of mine, I will accomplish
When in the Kingdom of Sun, you meet Drona.
Tell him –

Kritvarma   With whom do you converse
With whom do you converse Ashwathama
The King is no more.

Plaintive music. **Kripacharya**, *overwhelmed covers his face. In the front portion,* **Gandhari** *lets out a cry and faints.*

Ashwathama   Whose cry is this? Who laments?
Mother Gandhari
I plead, have patience.
As Krishna has rendered your womb barren,
So too will I, render Uttara barren
Alive will I not let her be.
Though Krishna may defend her with all his
Power of science and magic sorcery – Yogmaya!

The back curtain begins to fall.

Gandhari   Sanjay
Sanjay remove my bandage
I will see Ashwathama
Steel his body.
Make it Vajra. Impenetrable.
Sanjay –
Here, I've thrown off this bandage
Where is Ashwathama?

Sanjay   What's this, mother?
All that with the divine vision I could see till now,
Suddenly as if a curtain has fallen over it.

Gandhari   Hurry –
Lest tears may drip!

Sanjay   Walls move aside!
Walls move aside!
Mother – Mother –
What has happened to my divine vision today?

Walls!
Walls!
Barriers –
These eyes no longer see
In revealing the truth to the blind,
Must I also go blind?

Vidur   Sanjay,
What can you not see.
The forest, or Duryodhana or –

Sanjay   No Vidur Nothing.
Only walls!
Barriers arid Barriers!

Vidur   As if the hour has come
For all to end

Sanjay   Vyas, why did you bestow the divine vision.
Only for such a small duration?
Now onwards never will this limited visual world
Grant me contentment.
To break boundaries and dissolve into the eternal
This thirst of my soul shall remain unquenched always

Vidur   Get up, mother
Leave Hastinapur
Perform the last rites of your kin.
Sanjay
Inform all relatives, friends, kith and kin.
This day itself shall we depart for the battlefield.

Sanjay (*while going*)   Eighteen days of this unnerving battle
Gave and took away my vision on its way out

Yuyutsu *enters*.

Vidur   Come, mother,
Let's call the King.
Yuyutsu you too come

Yuyutsu   He who himself has killed
Who will accept the offering of his hands
The water to the deceased from his palms?
They are my brethren,
My kith and kin.
But tell me Krishna –
With what face can I offer the oblation of my hands?

Narrative Song
They leave behind the Kaurav Kingdom deserted,

They leave behind the jewel studded throne,
Which had been disputed in battle so long.
Empty roads and squares, forlorn courtyards,
The glittering golden chamber of Duryodhana
Where fierce beasts now freely stroll about.
They leave behind the Kaurav Kingdom deserted.
For the last rites of a hundred sons all gone.
In chariots ahead are Kaurav Widows,
Moving along with the remnant army
Walking behind with heads lowered, come
Dhritarashtra, Yuyutsu, Vidur, Sanjay and Gandhari

In, this order the characters come on stage – walking slowly. **Dhritarashtra** *stumbles once.*

Dhritarashtra   Old is the body
And feeble,
Unable to walk.

Vidur   Sanjay – wait a moment.

Dhritarashtra *sits. Others stop.*

Yuyutsu   Whose chariots are those?
Concealed behind the shrubs – stealthily moving?

Sanjay   He is of course Kripacharya

Vidur   And here comes, Kritvarma.

Gandhari   Sanjay! Is Ashwathama –

Sanjay   Yes Mother
There that is Ashwathama

Dhritarashtra   Let him be.

Gandhari   Stop him.

Sanjay   Stop
Hey stop, Ashwathama.
It's us Sanjay
Mother Gandhari, our King
Vidur and Yuyu –

Dhritarashtra   Sanjay
Do not mention Yuyutsu
Wrathful Ashwathama may not let him live.
I have only one – remaining son
If he too is snatched away – how will I live?

Gandhari   Specially when that son is so valiant and renowned?
Sanjay come,

Let Yuyutsu be here.
Son hide somewhere
Save yourself
For you are the sole support
of your blind father and aged mother.

She goes with **Sanjay**.

Yuyutsu   All this will I hear
And continue to live
But for whom?
But for whom?

Dhritarashtra   Born of my blindness were you son.
That was your circumference,
Trespassing which
you desired to be in a halo of effulgence.

Yuyutsu   Was that a crime?

Gandhari *and* **Sanjay** *return.*

Dhritarashtra   You've returned, Sanjay!

Sanjay   Ashwathama is
So completely changed
Not gallant and brave,
But as if he is a replica of fear
Every now and then trembles and shivers
And the reins of the chariot slip out of his hands.

In the distance conch shells are heard.

Gandhari   He's senseless – lost his mind.
Says he'll adorn a bark
And take refuge in the sacred forest.
He's scared of Krishna.

Sanjay   Along with the Pandavas,
Krishna is coming
In his search.

Gandhari   Krishna cannot hit him.
I have seen him
And armoured his body,
Made it metallic.
Inviolable

In the distance – an explosion.

Vidur   It appears
God has traced him

Dhritarashtra Sanjay, try and see.

Sanjay My divine vision has been withdrawn by Vyas.

Yuyutsu This light is of Arjuna's fire arrows.

Vidur Scorched and charred
The vegetation crumbles!

Few burnt out fire arrows fall on stage.

Dhritarashtra Sanjay, let's move further away from this area.

Gandhari But Krishna if you dare touch
Ashwathama

More arrows fall on stage.

Vidur Mother come
It's not safe here
Burning arrows fall all around.

*They go. The stage is empty for a while. Offstage are heard conch shells. Continuous explosions. Sharp light. Suddenly **Aswathama** comes running. An arrow is stuck in his neck. He pulls it out and blood flows. Another arrow comes flying at him, but he escapes. Then stands erect – his face seething with anger.*

Ashwathama Defend
Yourself now you Arjuna
Yourself now you Arjuna
I had thought
Adorning a bark would remain in the sacred grove
But perhaps till all the Pandavas
Are rendered rootless,
Krishna's lust of war.
Will not be content.
So then – have it.
This is Brahma's weapon –
The ultimate weapon supreme
More potent than all weapons divine.
Arjuna, now the time has come
For you to remember.
All your past deeds.
For its impact
Not one, but even a million Krishnas
Cannot nullify.
Hear, all of you, Gods of the sky,
Ascended on your celestial chariots,
Who are seeing this battle,
You will be witness
That compelled have I been by Arjuna,

Here it comes.
The weapon ultimate!

Throws an imaginary object. Sound like that of volcanoes errupting. Bright flash of light. Then darkness.

The voice of **Vyas** *is heard.*

Vyas What have you done
Ashwathama! Ignoble!
What have you done!

Ashwathama Who invites his death
By obstructing my vengeful ire
This my retaliation!

Vyas I am Vyas
Are you aware of the consequence.
If this weapon ultimate
Fulfils its target. Oh human beast
For centuries to come
The earth will not bear any sweet or edible vegetation
Infants will be born deformed or leprosy afflicted.
The entire human race dwarfed.
All the knowledge accumulated and crystallized by man
Through the ages of Truth, Treta and Dwapar,
Will vanish forever
In the ears of corn, vipers will slither
Rivers will carry in their tide, molten fire.

Ashwathama Let there be ashes.
Let the Doom come Vyas!
I'll see the power of Krishna's protection

Vyas Then look thither
At Krishna's word, already
Arjuna has shot in the sky
His weapon ultimate
But ignoble
Now the two will collide in the sky
The sun will extinguish
And the earth
Will be barren

Sound of collision. Bright light then darkness.

Ashwathama What am I to do.
Having been compelled by Arjuna.
I was alone and unjust Krishna along with Pandavas
Was eager to destroy me.

Frightening sounds.

Vyas Listen Arjuna
I am Vyas
Retrieve your weapon ultimate
Ashwathama, do not let your cowardice
Devastate humanity.
Withdraw your weapon and return the jewel,
Retreat into the forest.

Ashwathama Vyas. I am powerless.
Bearing familiar with the modus of attack alone
To withdraw is not what I or my arms
Have learnt from my father.

Vyas The sun will extinguish
And the earth
Will be barren.

Ashwathama Well then hear, you, Vyas.
Hear Krishna.
This unerring aim of Ashwathama
May surely target
The womb of Uttara.
It shall not be retrieved.

Vyas A brute you are
A brute you are
A brute you are

Ashwathama *laughs.*

Ashwathama I was not
But have become one
Because of Yuddhishtra.

He laughs in a cruel, distorted manner.

The curtain falls. The scene in the forest begins. The wailing of the Pandava women can be heard. **Gandhari** *and* **Sanjay** *enter.*

Gandhari Keep moving, Sanjay.
What is this wailing –
You hear?

Sanjay Ashwathama's weapon ultimate
Has crashed on Uttara's womb.

Gandhari He shall –
He shall fulfil his vow.

Sanjay Mother, but Krishna will not forgive him.

Gandhari Keep walking, Sanjay
He cannot be killed by Krishna.

The disk of Krishna may
Splinter me into bits,
But even so,
This instant will I go
Where
In the deep slumber of death sleeps Duryodhana
Keep on walking, Sanjay.

They go, **Dhritarashtra** *and* **Yuyutsu** *enter.*

Dhritarashtra   Child take my years too
And live on.
If Ashwathama's weapon supreme
Has fallen on Uttara.
Then who knows one day Yuddhishtra
May entrust the governance of the Kingdom to you.

Yuyutsu (*with a bitter laugh*)
And in this way
The beastliness of Ashwathama
Will restore my lost fortune.
No father No.
Is this much insight not enough for this unfortunate being!

Triumphant noises from the **Pandava** *side.* **Vidur** *enters.*

Dhritarashtra   Who hails this victory!

Vidur   My lord,
Uttara is protected by my God!

Dhritarashtra   How so Vidur?

Vidur   He said, even if
This Weapon Supreme does fall on its target, let it
But the dead infant who will be born,
I will give it life, by infusing mine.

Dhritarashtra   And Ashwathama –
Has been let off by Krishna?

Vidur   Let off!
With only the curse of womb destruction
Inflicted on him and
his jewel disarmed
Returning the jewel, receiving the curse,
Sore and melancholy Ashwathama
Retreated with head bowed.

Yuyutsu (*who appears to be unmoved*)
I apprehend
That Mother Gandhari

Hearing about the defeat of her Ashwathama
May do something – I know not what.

Dhritarashtra Come Vidur
She has gone ahead.
I too will catch up slowly.

They go in the direction of **Sanjay** *and* **Gandhari**. *The back curtain rises.* **Sanjay**, **Gandhari** *and* **Vidur** *are present.*

Sanjay This is that space –
Somewhere here had King Duryodhana fallen on the earth
This his golden helmet,
This his mace.
and this – his armour, amulet and lamina

Gandhari *takes off her bandage. She holds and feels each object. As she holds the armour she breaks down.*

Vidur Mother forbear, endure
This armour was a delusion
Only the deeds of the self,
Scrupulous and ethical demeanour.
Is the armour
That protects a person.
Mother.

Gandhari (*suddenly looks into the wings*)
Who is he.
Sitting by the shrubs, so still, so silent,
A person alive?

Vidur Mother
Don't look there.

Gandhari Appears as if Ashwathama

Sanjay No, No
Not so hideous and grotesque
Each pore rotting with leprosy.
Emitting a stink like diseased dogs.

Gandhari He turns to go.
Who is he, Vidur.
Stop him.

Vidur Mother let him go
He is Ashwathama
Chastised by Krishna for the destruction of the womb.
Cursed –
That he will be alive
But always the wound will be raw.

On his body the Lord's disk
Drenched in blood will rotate.
In dense forests for ages endless.
With ulcers errupting in his organs.
Blister and boils on his limbs,
Bandages stuck on decaying wounds,
Wallowing in puss, spit and mucous will he live.
God will not let him die, but the agony of a thousand hells
Shall remain kindled in each pore of his!

Gandhari Sanjay stop him.
Today I will deal with Krishna on his behalf

Vidur He has gone.
Perhaps had come to bid farewell
To the ultimate remains of Duryodhana.

Gandhari Ultimate remains?
So is that what lies –
The skeleton of my son?

Vidur Forbear, Mother.

Gandhari So there lies the skeleton of my son.
All of it brought about by Krishna –
You who have done it all.
Listen
Today you too listen.
I, pious Gandhari
Deriving power
From the virtues of my whole life,
And the virtues of all my past lives,
And thus empowered, I speak –
Krishna listen –
If you had wanted, this war could be prevented.
I did not give birth to that skeleton – there.
Instigated by you alone could Bhim be so unscrupulous.
Why did you not inflict that curse on Bhim,
That you have thrust on irreproachable Ashwathama
You have misused your godliness.
If there is strength in my service,
Virtue in accumulated austerity.
Then listen Krishna.
God or almighty
whoever you are
Whatever you may be
Your entire clan
Like this – like deranged senseless dogs shall
Tear apart and chew each other.

You yourself will annihilate them
And then after some years
In a thick forest
You will be killed by the hands of an ordinary hunter.
God you are,
But shall be slain like the beasts.

Flute. Shadow of **Krishna**.

Krishna Mother.
God or almighty
But a son unto you am I. You are the mother.
I said to Arjuna
The entire account of your deeds, the sin. The virtue
Will I carry on my shoulders.
In these eighteen days of horrific warfare
No one, but I alone died a million deaths.
As many times as a soldier touched ground,
It was no one
But I myself
Who fell wounded on the battlefield
From Ashwathama's limbs,
Will I bleed and trickle incessantly
As blood, mucous, sweat.
For ages endless
If I am life,
Then death too am I mother.
This curse of yours I do accept.

Gandhari What's this you have done, (*cries*)
Never did I weep
For my hundred sons.
But Krishna for you –
My affection in unfathomable.
Had you refused this curse of mine
Would I have been pained?
I was in despair – disconsolate and bitter.
A woman sonless.

Krishna Do not say so
Mother.
Till I live
Sonless you are not.
God or almighty,
But a son unto you am I.
You are the Mother.

Gandhari (*weeps*) What have I done Vidur –
What have I!

Narrative Song
The moment Krishna accepted the curse
That moment the light of the stars diminished.
Lifeless were the ethics crystallized through ages.
Benefit of poesy were the verses of poets
All heard this curse, stricken by awe.
None would say a word to Mother Gandhari.
But like the twilight of the age –
A blemish like shadow.
The curse did loom on every mind.

Curtain

Act Five

Victory: a successive suicide

Narrative Song
Days, weeks, months and years passed. The earth
Scorched by weapons divine
Though somehow was green and fertile,
The crowning of Yuddhishtra being long over.
Yet its lost glory again,
Could not the Kaurav Kingdom attain
All were victors, but with beliefs shattered
Master of ceremonies was Krishna himself
Though curse afflicted.
Thus the Pandava rule began, devoid of virtue,
Disoriented and dishevelled.
Was Bhim mild in mind, by nature proud.
Arjuna aged before time, and Nakul ignorant
Sahdev semi developed since his childhood
Only one Yuddishtra
Whose thoughtful brow was burdened
With dreams of the incoming age – deformed.
Was he alone able to grasp the gravity of events
When curse afflicted god
Would cast away the body's abode.
This age that we have sown together in the field of battle.
Its shoots will bloom and shroud entire knowledge
Seated on the staircase, head pressed to knees.
Often lost in fruitless contemplation.
Would he look out with vacant eyes.
At the spread out darkness, still and dense

The curtain rises. The two old guards – behind. In front is **Yuddhishtra**.

Yuddhishtra Such an immense war, grim and gruesome
With half-truths, bloodshed and violence has been won,
Yet defeated and drained do I feel within
This too is agony.
Those for whom I fought,
They, all my kith and kin I accept are ignorant
Inanimate like – uncivil or fragile,
This throne that I have acquired
I accept that it brings with it,
The inviolable solid tradition of blindness
These, the subjects,
I accept, are also cast

In the deformed mould of the previous reign.
And
Outside the window in the darkness deep
To hear the sound of the incoming age – sinister
The very notion of which makes me shiver.
Even so
To be alive, adorning the jewel as on the forehead
Of assassin Ashwathama;
This is that agony.
Seeing which, Brother Duryodhana!
You were so fortunate
That you went away earlier.
Left am I
In the darkness, to see and stare fixedly
At the incoming sinister footsteps.
But whom can I tell?
These my brethren are ignorant; rash and arrogant.
Or fragile

Sound from offstage.

This my
Decadent clan –
Which in a few years will be gorged
By the darkness outside
But is engrossed in Bhim's
Debased, dehumanising waggery!

Sound of collective laughter from within. Enter **Vidur**.

Vidur My lord
Now its getting intolerable
How will it ever stop
This permissiveness of Bhim?

Yuddhishtra What happened now?

Vidur The same
Like everyday
Today also, Yuyutsu has been
Humiliated by Bhim.

Kripacharya And each one of them
Enjoyed his muteness

Yuddhishtra Who knows what has happened
To Yuyutsu's voice
Now he is almost completely mute.

Vidur For the past many years,
He has got only contempt from his family

and people
He had an inviolable faith in Krishna,
But he too is curse afflicted.

Kripacharya   Dependent on you was he.
But hurt by the stinging and curt remarks of Bhim
When Blind Dhritarashtra and Gandhari
Left for the forest –
That day onwards, his voice
Slowly grew muffled.

Vidur   He alone has suffered agony –
To stake life
Against your own brethren
But in the end for the belief to crumble,
To bear the tarnish and reproach
And be unable to do even as much
As could the human brute Ashwathama

Kripacharya   My lord
Do come and yourself
Give solace to Yuyutsu

They exit. The **Sentries** *come forward and begin to talk.*

Sentry one   Somebody's deranged, incoherent

Sentry Two   Someone curse afflicted.

Sentry One   We are

Sentry Two   As we were.

Sentry One   Rulers changed

Sentry Two   Situations remain unchanged.

Sentry One   In comparison the previous rulers were better.

Sentry Two   They were blind.

Sentry One   But at least they used to govern
These are saints wise and brilliant

Sentry Two   They'll govern – how!

Sentry One   Unaware of nature of their subjects.

Sentry Two   Knowledge and all ethics!

Sentry One   What shall one do with them

Sentry Two   Can we what – grind them?

Sentry One   Or what – swallow them?

Sentry Two   Or wear them?

Sentry One   Or spread them –?

Sentry Two   We need to get grain

Sentry One   Clear and definite orders.

Sentry Two   A vigorous efficient leader who can perform

Sentry One   Blind instruction

Sentry Two   Labelled either as war or peace.

Sentry One   They are unaware of the nature of their subjects!

Seeing **Yuyutsu** *enter from within – they become quiet and return to their earlier positions.* **Yuyutsu** *enters and seems to make incoherent attempts that appear pitiable, and – exits on the other side.* **Vidur** *and* **Kripacharya** *enter.*

Vidur   Have you seen Yuyutsu? (**Sentry** *indicates towards the wings.*)

Kripacharya   He is unfortunate
Wanders aimless

Vidur   Is he humiliated less
In the palaces in
That he goes out
To be further insulted by people

Kripacharya   Look there –
Beggars, the lame and the maimed;
Rough urchins
A motley crowd taunting and mocking
trails behind him.

Vidur   Ah there – someone has hit a stone.

Worried, goes out.

Kripacharya   In Yuddhishtra's rule,
That is the fate of Yuyutsu,
Who stood by virtue.

Vidur *brings* **Yuyutsu**. *His face bleeds.* **Vidur** *wipes it with his shawl. Behind is the mute soldier – now a beggar. He hits a stone at* **Yuyutsu** *and laughs cruelly.*

Vidur   Sentry who has allowed
This pauper to enter here?
Yuyutsu – come with me.

The beggar indicates that **Yuyutsu** *has broken his feet.*

Kripacharya   Your feet alone have been smashed
By Yuyutsu
But today, I will not leave you alive!

Takes the spear from the **Sentry**'s *hand and rushes out.* **Yuyutsu** *comes forward to stop* **Kripacharya** – *and takes the spear to pierce his own chest. As he exits, a cry from the wings.* **Vidur** *runs within.*

Vidur (*from within*)
My lord,
He's killed himself. Yuyutsu has.
Make haste, Kripacharya!

Kripacharya *goes. The* **Sentries** *come forward.*

Sentry One   Whether it's war or peace.

Sentry Two   There is bloodshed.

Sentry One   If arms exist –

Sentry Two   They are bound to be used

Sentry One   Till now these weapons

Sentry Two   Were geared against others.

Sentry One   Now they will be used against ourselves.

Sentry Two   These our weapons – that till now were meaningless

Sentry One   At least they have been

Sentry Two   Put to some use today.

Laughter within. **Kripacharya** *enters.*

Kripacharya   Even this they mock at,
All of them ignorant, idiotic – uncivil and arrogant,
These brothers of Yuddhishtra.
What the blood of Yuyutsu
Has inscribed on this land of assault,
They do not realize today.
This suicide will echo
In this entire civilization,
In its philosophy, religion and arts,
In politics and governance,
Self annihilation will be the ultimate aim of man

Vidur *comes.*

Vidur   Salvation is achieved by all, sooner or late,
Even by him, who annihilates his brethren,
Slays his own mother, beloved and dear ones,
Children and women.
But he who annihilates the self
Dwells distraught in the darker regions of the deep abyss,
As a spirit haunted for ever and ever.

Kripacharya   Such was the predicament of Yuyutsu
Vidur! In these high mansions of Yuddhishtra
I suddenly can hear,
Footsteps of the inauspicious and sinister.
Till now, while staying here,
I imparted education, training of arms to Parikshit.
But now that this
Self destructive, impotent and decadent traits have come
To the fore,
I now ought to leave Hastinapur
In that lies the well being.
Suicide flies and clings
Like a disease, fatal.

Vidur   But –

Kripacharya   I've been a warrior all along
In this
Civilization of Yuddhishtra.
Where suicide abides,
I will be unable to live

Goes.

Vidur   In the Kingdom of Yuddhishtra
Suicide will flourish.
Wise intellectuals will retire.
What is this peace
You've given us god?
What will the almosphere be in the forest,
When Dhritarashtra hears
Of such a death of Yuyutsu!

Yuddhishtra *enters.*

Yuddhishtra   There is life yet –
Still in Yuyutsu

Vidur   If he is alive
Then please have him sent,
To my hutment.
I'll protect him, tend to him.
He has suffered till now.
For the sake of Krishna.
A retribution to that, as far as possible,
I shall try and make –

Vidur *and* **Yuddhishtra** *exit conversing.*

Sentry One   What's this untimely darkness!

Sentry Two Encircling clouds form over the forest area.

Sentry One Seems there's a conflagration ablaze!

The back curtain rises.

In a burning forest are **Dhritar-ashtra** *and* **Sanjay**.

Dhritarashtra Leave it, Sanjay
You will not be able to save me now.
Too feeble and fragile –
How much can I run away from fire!

Sanjay At a short distance is a protected place.
My lord, let's keep going, (*turns behind*)
Ah Mother Gandhari
She's stopped there –
Mother – Oh Mother!

Dhritarashtra Now all effort is futile.
Leave me here itself
All my life
I've meandered in the darkness of blindness
This is not a fire – but a sphere of effulgence
Seeing the truth yet would I not absorb it,
So today.
On my aged ashes,
Will I adorn the truth
Almost as a garland of cinders!

Sanjay The conflagration spreads and comes close
Ah there. Mother Gandhari is engulfed by flames,
Whom shall I save –

Gandhari (*enters, almost half burnt*)
Sanjay go ahead
This is my own curse.
That I had pronounced on Sri Krishna
Now in the form of fire, suicide, family feuds and strife
Has grown hundred fold and scattered over Kingdoms
And forests.
Sanjay tell him that
Of my curse
I am the first offering of fuel.

Voice offstage 'Gandhari.'

Dhritarashtra Ah.
Aged Kunti is left behind in the forest
Return Gandhari.

Sanjay My Lord,

My lord,
The massive conflagaration,
With its innumerable tongue like flames
May have devoured Mother Kunti!
My lord
This space is safe
Do not go!

Gandhari Sanjay,
All their life
Who were led astray by darkness,
Let them die
In this fatal all consuming light.

Taking **Dhritarashtra**, *goes.*

Sanjay Today
Today an entire, massive blazing Banyan
Has collapsed on both.
Shedding its embers
Even so, I remain yet.
Even so, I remain yet.
But why?
Why?
Who else would be as meaningless as me?
Aah!

A burning branch falls on his foot. He holds it The curtain falls.

Narrative Song
Thus passed the days of Pandava rule,
Yuddhishtra grew more distressed and agitated
The victory emerged hollower day by day
All beliefs lost in overwhelming darkness.

The two **Sentries** *enter. On one of their spears, dangles the crown of* **Yuddhishtra**.

Sentry One This the crown
Of the emperor of the world!

Sentry Two Who has stopped
Adorning it.

Sentry One Since
Ominous events began to occur in Hastinapur.

Sentry Two Keep it away
As here comes my lord.

Yuddhishtra *and* **Vidur** *enter.*

Vidur My lord certainly this

Omen is related –

Yuddhishtra   To the demise of Krishna.
I know it.
Messengers have brought
Me the tidings
Strife has increased
In the Yadav clan.

Vidur   Please send Arjuna soon
To Dwarikapuri

Yuddhishtra   Vidur –
What will I do?
Mother Kunti, Gandhari
And King Honourable
Have been reduced to ashes by the flaming conflagaration.
At the time of the last ritual,
Offering water to the deceased,
The wounds of Yuyutsu flared up again.
And after so many days
This attempt at self annihilation
Has borne result.
Unable to save his life,
Even so, will I continue to live
To see the crumbling of god
With these eyes?
No.
Let me go.
Let me perish – decay on the forsaken
Peaks of the Himalayas.

Vidur   My lord
That too is self annihilation?
The height of the peaks
Does not abate
The lowliness of the act

Yuddhishtra   And what is triumph –
A long and tedious process,
That slowly steadily infecting each pore, succeeds
In self annihilation.
No other path remains
Now for me.

They exit conversing. The **Sentries** *come forward.*

Sentry One   Foreboding certainly are the events that take place.
Here each day.

Sentry Two The gale burst forth yesterday
Raining pebbles and stones.

Sentry One In the sun headless
Dark moving torsos
Are to be seen.

Sentry Two And he, whom they all
Call their God,
It is heard
That his destruction
Is now close at hand.

Sentry One They say
In Dwarika
At midnight – clad in black
And yellow colours.
Strolls Yama – forboding death

Sentry Two Skilled archers
Rain their arrows at him,
But transforming into a dark cloud
He suddenly drifts away.

Sentry One He whom they all
Call their god

Sentry Two He who on his shoulders
Was to raft across
Their welfare –

Sentry One He is the one who now –
Pathless and aimless as they are,
Abandons them here below.

Sentry Two And prepares to depart for his Kingdom.

Sentry One And now these helpless folks –
What are they going to do?

Sentry Two Compared to them all
We are much better off.

Sentry One We have not borne grief.

Sentry Two Known no pain.

Sentry One As we were before

Sentry Two So are we now!

Curtain

Epilogue

The Demise of the Lord

Invocation
You, the creator of sound, of all meanings the meaning supreme.
Sheltered by whose shadow, no voice rings futile.
Obeisance to you and to them salutation,
Who with pure and simple mind.
Sing of your colourful acts for centuries immemorial.
Of Lords mysterious life,
Is this somewhat different,
The solitary path of my faith.
Give me words, give succulence, give rhetoric ornate declamatory
So may I portray your death.
Full of compassion and mystery.

Narrative Song
There was a lustrous patch of forest by the ocean shore
The sea foam melting in the whirling oscillation.
There blows a gale, blasting and swirling the palms,
The scent of wild basil, shade of the pipal pure,
On the earth beneath is God in calm and restful repose.
Seeming somewhat exhausted.
That blue cloud like body tawny.
In the largest lotus of the garland was left a single petal.
The shadow of two playful leaves of pipal
Would time to time sway on his golden forehead.
Those eyelids both were drowsy and would half open.
As would softly bloom the petals of a blue lotus.
On his right thigh he placed
His left foot that seemed shaped like a deer's face,
And sighed 'how strange was this age.'

The curtain rises. **Ashwathama** *enters in a form that is horrifying.*

Ashwathama   False is this invocation; these words of praise
Krishna has done exactly
What I had done in the Pandava fort.
A person asleep or drowned in drunkenness
Is in similar state.
He has massacred his drunken brethren,
A murder all pervasive.
I have seen –
On the bright sands of the ocean shore,
Drenched in thick black blood,
Are scattered the countless corpses of Yadav warriors,
Slain by Krishna himself.

He has done exactly
What I had done that night.
The only difference being
That I had killed the enemy
But his own clan has he destroyed.

There beneath the Ashwatha tree he sits,
Devoid of power, splendour, and is tired
Him will I question –
This torment of a million infernal regions
That grows in my flesh.
Why do these wounds not burst
On that lotus body of this?

He exits towards the back. From another side **Sanjay** *enters, dragging himself.*

Sanjay   I had said once.
Do not give me arms, even so will I embrace you.
Do not give me eyes, even so will I continue to see you,
Do not give me feet, but till you –
Will I reach, god!
Today that pride of mine is shattered.
All my life was I impartial truth.
Never got down to action.
Slowly deprived of the divine vision.
That day in the hazardous fire episode
These knees too were scorched!

Near the back wings, a hunter comes and sits and aims a target with his arrow.

Narrative Song
At a distance in a thorny thicket.
Sat a hunter, half concealed,
Mistaking the lords feet for a deer,
Pulled his bow, aiming it there.

Sanjay   Stop! Hey stop.
Ah – he does not listen
The light diminishes.
How shall I reach – beneath the Ashwatha tree.
I've come dragging these knees for many miles –

The **Hunter** *shoots his arrow. A light flickers and extinguishes. The strand of music breaks thrice – like a hiccup.* **Ashwathama** *laughs with a cry,* **Sanjay** *falls down unconscious. Darkness.*

Narrative Song
The stars extinguished – all around was darkness deep.
It seemed more fearful – that fearsome forest
The moment that god departed.

Dwapar age did pass away.
On this godless earth, devoid of faith,
The Dark age placed its first step.
It seemed more fearful that fearsome forest.

Ashwathama *enters.*

Ashwathama   Only I am witness,
Hiding behind the grove of palms, I have seen his death
Sharp and painted like the edge of a sword,
Shaking and swinging palm leaves
Were piercing my wounds,
Heavy with purulent matter
But holding my breath I stood still

In an aggressive tone.

But ah – what is that I saw –
As the arrow pricked the sole of the foot
Mucous filled stinking blue blood
Came flowing out
Like the one that oozes
Often from these wounds of mine
In his feet burst forth similar wounds
Listen, my enemy Krishna, listen.
At the time of death
Did you cast this Human Brute Ashwathama
In your feet?
In your crimson blood was I manifest?
As with the extraction of putrefied blood
Relieves the pain of the blister
So do I experience past grief.
This cleansing that I perceive.
Is that faith?

Yuyutsu (*voice as if coming from a distance*)
Whose voice do I hear in these blind regions?
Who has found new faith?
The Human brute Ashwathama?

Laughs.

A worn out coin named faith.
Has been discovered now by Ashwathama,
Which I on finding it counterfeit and adulterated
Had discarded in the litter years ago.

Sanjay   This is the voice of Yuyutsu
Who drifts pathless as a blind spirit in the universe

Yuyutsu I received the commandment
You are a self annihilator.
And so will drift pathless in these blind regions.
Blinder than the earth – where lies a darker abyss?
I was born of blindness
And led astray by the luminous sphere
Of false faith in Krishna
But committing suicide, through the cliffs
I opened a door
And have returned
To the dark blind caves,
I too had come to see
This exalted and grandiose death of Krishna.
When alive he was unable to conquer faithlessness.
Now by staging a pageant of death,
He wants to have us bound.
But I say.
He was a depriver, coward powerless.
He could not save Parikshit or even me.
And has returned to his Kingdom.
In this age whenever infant future is
Destroyed by weapon supreme,
Serpent Takshak shall bite Parikshit,
Or many more Yuyutsu like,
May commit suicide,
Then who will come to save them?
Will you Ashwathama –
You who are immortal!

Ashwathama But I am dehumanised half truth
Whose logic is hatred and status that of a beast

Yuyutsu You, Sanjay –
You who are the faithful one?

Sanjay But I am inactive. Inert.
Impartial truth
Cannot destroy
Cannot save.
Separated from action,
I successively lose,
The meaning of my existence

Yuyutsu That is why I say with courage,
Our destiny is not bound to the death of God,
But with the future of man!
The life of Parikshit
How will he be saved?

How will he be saved?
This is my question.
His question.
Who all his life, for the sake of God,
Suffered contempt.
Is there no faithful – who remains
To answer?

The **Old Mendicant** *enters, carrying a bow.*

Mendicant   I am there yet to answer.

Yuyutsu   Who are you –
I cannot see!

Mendicant   Now I am an old hunter,
Of the name Jara.
The arrow of my bow, It was
That became the death of Krishna.
Earlier I was the aged astrologer,
Slain by Ashwathama.
And so a lurking spirit am I
Untouched by salvation –
To free me from the spirit world and form
Krishna did say –
The term of Mother Gandhari's curse is complete
Lift the bow
Shoot the arrow.
I was terrified, but he said.
Ashwathama had slain you –
The sin was his; the chastisement will I take
My death will free you from the present shackles.

Ashwathama   Mine was the sin.
I had slain
But these hands were not mine
That heart was not mine.
The blind age had penetrated deep
Into each vein
And becoming blind counter violence,
Possessed and maddened by which
What else could I do?
Only unfathomed a counter-violence. Once
Whom you call God,
He was my enemy.
But my suffering too –
He has absorbed.
Wounds there are on this body of mine.
But the pain has been fully pacified.

I am condemned
Yet I am free!

Yuyutsu   May be murderers attain freedom
By the death of God.
But how?
Will the future of man be saved.
In the blind age.
After this cowardly demise of God?

Ashwathama   Cowardly demise
My enemy he was
Yet will I say
Divine peace was visible
On his golden brow.

Mendicant   At the moment of dissolution thus spoke God.
Not death is this aged hunter
Mere transformation
I had borne the liability of all on myself,
Now I entrust my obligation to all.
Till now I vitalized the future of man
But in this blind age a portion of me
Shall remain inert, remain self destructive.
And continue to melt and dissipate,
Like Sanjay, Yuyutsu, Ashwathama.
Because their onus is on me.
And he said –
But the remainder of my onus
Shall be on the rest
This onus will reside,
In that sphere of every human mind
Under whose guidance,
Overcoming all circumstances
Will he build anew on the debris of the past
By ethical demeanour,
By constant new creation
In moments
Of fearlessness,
Of courage
Of love
Of joy
Will I stir alive and rejuvenate again and again.

Ashwathama   In this his new meaning
Will every small and petty being,
Deformed, half barbaric, self destructive

And replete in faithlessness
Be able to attain meaningfulness in his life?

Mendicant   Certainly
He is the future.
But held in your hands.
The moment you want you can destroy him
The moment you want you can give him life,
Take in life.

Sanjay   But inert and maimed am I.

Ashwathama   I, inhuman

Yuyutsu   And I self annihilator – blind.

Mendicant *comes forward. The others go behind. The curtain falls on them. Only the* **Mendicant** *remains.*

They are disappointed
In despair –
And blind
And inert
And semi brute
And the darkness grows deeper and deeper.
Will someone listen –
Who is not blind, not deformed,
And will save the future of man?
I am the hunter named Jara
And this transformation happened through me.
I have heard the last phrase pronounced
By god facing death
And raising both my arms
I repeat them
Someone hear!
Will someone hear

Narrative Song
That day the Blind age descended on the earth,
It does not terminate but recurs again and again
As a tide that repeats itself in refrain.
In each instant God somewhere meets his death
In each instant does darkness deepen and deepen
In each of our minds there is the cloud of the age.
There is darkness, and Ashwathama and Sanjay
The servile traits of the sentries two do creep in.
Blind is the doubt and shameful defeat
But one element there is; a seed in every mind
In courage, in freedom, in new creation

It is impartial but comes to us in life.
In commitment, ethical and free demeanour.
That little part of our mind does protect us
From half truth, weapons supreme and fear,
To save the future of mankind
From blind doubt slavery and defeat.

Curtain

One Day in the Season of Rain (*Ashadh ka ek din*) (1958)

Mohan Rakesh

**Translated from the Hindi by Aparna Dharwadker
and Vinay Dharwadker**

Rakesh (1925–72) was a writer of plays, short stories, novels, essays and a translator of works from Sanskrit and English into Hindi, including Kalidasa's *Shakuntala*. He was born in Armritsar, Punjab, Madan Mohan Guglani, later adopting the pen name Mohan Rakesh. He received his bachelor's in English literature and master's in Sanskrit literature from Punjab University, Lahore, and later a master's in Hindi literature from Punjab University, Jalandhar. He taught at various universities and colleges before devoting himself full time to writing.

One Day in the Season of Rain was published in 1958 with productions later that year and early in 1959. There was initial antagonism in reaction to Rakesh's depiction of Kalidasa (called Kalidas in the play), India's most revered Sanskrit writer. However, at a January 1959 theatre festival, it won best production, and later was given the prestigious Sangeet Natak Akademi award for best Hindi play of 1958.

Little is known of the historical Kalidasa. Thus, the trajectory Rakesh creates for him in the play, though possible given what scholars surmise, is almost wholly invented. What is clear is the impact of Kalidasa's writings on the play. Several of his poems are mentioned, and one, *A Gathering of Seasons* (*Ritusamharam*), seems pivotal to the play's title and setting. Is the fact that there is some disagreement if this poem is actually by Kalidasa a provocative choice by Rakesh? His attempt as a Sanskrit scholar to make a claim? A subtle indication that the character in the play is not to be literally taken as the revered poet? That the inferior quality of the poem may be the result of it being by a young writer? That the poet, Rakesh's character as well as the historical man, may not be all we imagine him to be?

A Gathering of Seasons tracks love and lovers through the six Indian seasons. Rakesh shows us the lovers meeting only during the rainy season (monsoon). The sounds of thunder and rain are heard before we see anyone. When Mallika, Kalidas' lover enters, she's exhilarated and soaked. Her mother Ambika is clearly upset. Is it because she fears Mallika may take ill? Or because she suspects that her daughter is returning from a tryst with the young poet who will never marry her? And what is the image the audience has? The young woman flush from the sexual encounter, her clothes sticking to her body from the rain, the sensuousness of the moment, reminiscent of the initial lovers' scene in another Kalidasa work?

When Kalidas enters a short time later, the link to *Shakuntala* becomes direct: he carries a fawn, bleeding from the wound of an arrow shot by someone from the court. Kalidas would seem not to be Dushyanta; and yet, we must wait to see how he will treat the woman he claims to love. Mallika perhaps seems more akin to Shakuntala, the trusting, enamoured lover of nature. What will she do if her lover goes off and refuses to acknowledge her? Then again, Mallika cares not that Kalidas has vowed never to marry and, on a certain level, what she wants is not marriage or a child but for him to create his wondrous art.

Rakesh's play may be an inverted or warped version of Kalidasa's play. Though Kalidas may be crucial, he is not the central character of *One Day in the Season of Rain*. Mallika is. It is her journey. A journey in terms of him, similar perhaps to the way in which *Shakuntala* is Dushyanta's journey in terms of her. The literal Sanskrit title, *The Recognition of Shakuntala*, points to who needs to make the dramatic change. Does the fact that Rakesh's play, unlike Kalidasa's, stays in one season presage something about the possibility of change? If we are forever in the rain, does it mean the drying heat of summer, the bracing awakening of winter, the blossoming of new life of the spring will never come to be?

One minor note important to prevent English language readers from misinterpreting one of Rakesh's first stage directions: 'Hindu swastika symbols are painted here and there in vermilion.' The swastika is an ancient Indian religious symbol, the name derived from a Sanskrit word meaning 'well-being'; it has no connection to German Nazism in the play. It may be meant to resonate through the play, however, as the wall decorations fade throughout until they're barely visible. Are we meant to intuit how health and good fortune disappear?

The devolution of the walls, the entirety of Mallika's home in fact, are only one of the many changes that occur in the play. The season may stay the same; other things do not. What does the play want to ponder about this? About love? About art? About the past and our present? About our choices, why we make them and how we and others see them over time? The title says 'One Day'. Which day? What does that mean for us?

Reference

Mohan Rakesh. *One Day in the Season of Rain*. Translated from the Hindi with an Introduction, an Afterword, and Notes by Aparna Dharwadker and Vinay Dharwadker. Gurgaon: Penguin Books, 2015

Dramatis Personae

Ambika	*an old woman in the village*
Mallika	*her daughter*
Kalidas	*a poet*
Dantul	*a courtier*
Matul	*the poet's uncle*
Nikshep	*a man from the village*
Vilom	*a man from the village*
Rangini	*a woman from the city*
Sangini	*a woman from the city*
Anusvar	*an official*
Anunasik	*an official*
Priyangumanjari	*a princess – the poet's wife*

Act One

Before the curtain rises, soft sounds of thunder and rain, which continue for a few moments after, then gradually fade away.

The curtain rises slowly.

An ordinary room. The walls are made of wood, but their lower portion is plastered with smooth clay. Hindu swastika symbols are painted here and there in vermilion. The front door opens into a dark entranceway. On either side of the doorway are small niches containing little unlit clay lamps. A door upstage left leads to a second room. When this door is open, only one corner of a simple bed is visible. Both doors are also plastered with clay, and are decorated with outlines of lotuses and conch shells in vermilion and deep yellow. Upstage right is a large lattice window through which lightning is occasionally visible.

On one side of the room is a small wood-burning clay stove. Clay and brass pots and pans are arranged neatly around it. On the other side, at some distance from the lattice window, are three or four large clay jars discoloured by soot and moss. Their mouths are covered with reed mats kept in place with stone weights. Next to the lattice window is a wooden seat with a tiger skin draped over it. Near the stove are two low square stools.

Ambika *sits on one of the square stools, husking grain in a reed winnowing pan. She looks towards the window once, sighs deeply, and again busies herself with the winnowing.*

The front door opens and **Mallika** *enters, shivering and hugging herself in wet clothes.* **Ambika** *remains busy, with her eyes lowered.* **Mallika** *pauses for a moment, then approaches her.*

Mallika   The first day of the season of rain, and such rain, Ma.

Such torrents of rain. Even the most distant foothills were drenched. And me, too. See how wet I am, Ma!

Ambika *looks her up and down once, and gets busy again.* **Mallika** *kneels down and rests her head on* **Ambika***'s shoulder.*

I went out thinking I'd watch the flight of cranes coming in from the south, and now, look, all my clothes are soaking wet.

She kisses her mother's hair and stands up, shivering with cold.

Where are my dry clothes, Ma? If I stand here like this, I'll freeze. . . . Why aren't you saying anything?

Ambika *looks at her angrily.*

Ambika   The dry clothes are on the bed inside.

Mallika   You've already put them out?

She goes towards the inner room.

You knew I'd get wet. And I knew you'd be worried. But, Ma . . .

Near the door she turns and looks at **Ambika**.

. . . I'm not at all sorry about getting wet. If I hadn't gotten wet, I'd have been deprived of something today.

She leans against the door frame.

Smoky clouds had gathered all around. I knew it was going to rain. Yet I kept going down and down the trail, into the valley. At one point, the wind even blew away my wrap. Then it began to drizzle.

Her gaze meets **Ambika***'s.*

Let me change, then I'll come and tell you. That was an amazing experience, Ma – really amazing.

Mallika *goes inside.* **Ambika** *gets up and puts the winnowed grain into one of the large jars, and takes out fresh grain from another.* **Mallika***'s words continue to be heard from the inner room. The audience also catches a glimpse of her every now and then.*

Tender and moist like the blue lotus, gentle as a breeze, and picturesque as a dream! I wanted to fill myself with the experience, and close my eyes. . . . Even my body's being wrung out, Ma! How much water have my clothes soaked in! Oh! After the bite of cold, this touch of warmth!

She begins to hum.

[*Song*] The water lily that is blue,
   Blue without a blemish,
     Is vain about its eminence . . .
Where shall I put the wet clothes, Ma? Shall I leave them here?

[*Song*] The mildest movements stir,
   Stir the gentle breeze,
     In all its gentleness . . .

Travellers, in distress
   Without their homely women,
     Are vexed and perplexed . . .

She returns to the front room.

I'll never forget those moments today, Ma. I've never witnessed such beauty before. As though that beauty were intangible – yet substantial. I could touch it see it drink it in. In that instant I understood what turns feeling into poetry. For the first time in my life I understood why someone would get lost in a train of clouds caressing the mountain peaks, why someone would be so enchanted by images appearing and disappearing in the sky, instead of being absorbed in his own body and mind . . . What's the matter, Ma? Why are you so quiet?

Ambika You can see I'm working.

Mallika Well, you're working all the while. But you aren't quiet like this all the time.

She comes and sits near **Ambika**, *who continues to winnow the grain in silence.* **Mallika** *takes the winnowing pan from her hand.*

I won't let you work. . . . Talk to me.

Ambika What do you want me to say?

Mallika Say anything. Scold me for coming back soaked. Or tell me that you're tired, so I should husk the rest of the grain. Or say that you were home alone and didn't like it.

Ambika I like everything.

Ambika *takes the winnowing pan from* **Mallika**.

And when am I not alone at home? Am I not alone even when you're here?

Mallika I'm not going to let you work any more.

She takes back the winnowing pan from **Ambika**'s *hand, and puts it down near the large jars.*

You're alone even when I'm home? . . . Sometimes you reproach me for getting in the way of your work when I stay at home. And sometimes you say . . .

She puts her arms around **Ambika**'s *neck from behind.*

Tell me, why are you so sombre?

Ambika I've boiled the milk. Add some sugar and drink it.

Mallika No, answer me first.

Ambika And go rest on the bed for a little while. I still have to . . .

Mallika No, Ma, I don't want to rest. Why should I rest when I'm not tired? Within me, I can still feel the thrilling sensation of the raindrops falling on my skin. Every fibre of my being is still tingling. Why don't you answer me? If you keep doing this, I won't talk to you, either.

Saying nothing, **Ambika** *wipes her eyes with the end of her sari. She then pushes* **Mallika** *away from behind herself, and makes her sit down on one of the nearer square stools.* **Mallika** *looks at* **Ambika** *silently for a moment.*

What's happened, Ma? Why are you crying?

Ambika Nothing, Mallika! Sometimes one feels sad for no reason.

Mallika   One feels sad for no reason. But one doesn't just sit and cry. . . . If you don't tell me what's wrong, Ma, you'll be forsworn.

Some noises and the sound of horses' hooves are heard in the distance. **Ambika** *rises and goes to the window.* **Mallika** *remains seated for a moment, then she, too, walks to the window and looks out. The sound of hooves approaches and then recedes.*

Who are these people, Ma?

Ambika   They're probably royal court officials.

Mallika   What are they doing here?

Ambika   Who knows what they're doing! . . . Every few years these characters turn up in our village. And, whenever they appear, there's some calamity or other. Sometimes they bring news of a war, sometimes of an epidemic.

She takes a deep breath.

When your father died in the last plague, I'd seen the same figures here.

Mallika *shudders from head to toe.*

Mallika   But why have these people come here today?

Ambika   Who knows why they've come.

Ambika *tries to pick up the winnowing pan again, but* **Mallika** *grabs her arm and stops her.*

Mallika   Ma, you haven't told me what's wrong.

Ambika *stares at her for a moment.* **Mallika** *lowers her eyes.*

Ambika   Agnimitra has come back today.

Ambika *picks up the winnowing pan and goes back to her stool.* **Mallika** *remains standing at the window.*

Mallika   He has come back? From where?

Ambika   From where I sent him.

Mallika   You sent him?

Her lips begin to quiver. She advances towards **Ambika**.

But I'd told you there was no need to send Agnimitra anywhere.

Gradually her voice grows more agitated.

You know I don't want to get married, then why do you keep trying? Do you think I just rant and rave pointlessly?

Ambika *takes up fistfuls of grain, rubs it between her palms, and lets it drop into the winnowing pan.*

Ambika   I can see that things are turning out exactly as you wanted. Agnimitra has brought back the message that the people to whom I'd sent him aren't interested in this match. They say . . .

Mallika What do they say? What right do they have to say anything at all? Mallika's life is her own property. If she wants to destroy it, then who has the right to criticize her?

Ambika When have I said that I have the right?

Mallika *turns her head sharply and tries to suppress her agitation.*

Mallika I'm not talking about your rights.

Ambika You may not say it, but I'm saying it. Today your life is your own property. I have no rights over you.

Mallika *sits down on the other square stool and places her hand on* **Ambika**'s *shoulder.*

Mallika Why do you talk like this? . . . Why don't you try to understand me?

Ambika *removes* **Mallika**'s *hand from her shoulder.*

Ambika I know that, today, even you don't have any rights over yourself. But I can't bear such a huge transgression.

Mallika *crosses her arms over her knees and rests her head on them.*

Mallika Ma, I know there's unpleasant talk. I also understand your unhappiness. And yet I don't feel guilty. I've followed an impulse and chosen one emotion out of many. For me, that one bond is greater than all other bonds. I'm really in love with my emotion – which is pure, tender, eternal.

Ambika's *face becomes distorted.*

Ambika And I feel repelled by such an emotion. 'Pure, tender, eternal!' *Hunh!*

Mallika Ma, why don't you trust me?

Ambika What you call emotion is only duplicity and self-deception. 'I've followed an impulse and chosen one emotion!' . . . I ask you, what does it mean to choose emotion on an impulse? How does that fulfil the necessities of life? . . . 'Chosen one emotion on an impulse!' *Hunh!*

Mallika *stares at the ceiling for a moment.*

Mallika The gross necessities of life aren't everything, Ma. There's so much else besides them.

Ambika *begins to winnow the grain again.*

Ambika Maybe there is – I don't know.

Mallika *looks at* **Ambika** *for a few moments.*

Mallika The truth is, Ma, like other people in the village, you too look at him with suspicion and revulsion.

Ambika The other people in the village don't know him as well as I do.

For a moment they stare at each other.

I detest him.

Mallika's *face becomes marked with anguish, helplessness, and strong emotion.*

Mallika Ma!

Ambika What do other people have to do with him? But I do. His influence is destroying my home.

Kalidas's *voice can be heard from the direction of the entranceway. The lines on* **Ambika**'s *brow deepen. She stands up with the winnowing pan. She looks towards the entrance for a moment, then walks towards the inner room.*

Mallika Wait, Ma, why're you leaving?

Ambika A mother's life is action, not emotion. She has a lot to do around the house.

Ambika *leaves.* **Kalidas** *enters, carrying a fawn in his arms and soothing it. Blood drips from the fawn's body.*

Kalidas We'll live, little fawn, won't we? We won't give up our life just for being wounded by an arrow. So what if our body's tender. We can endure pain. If an arrow can take life, then a hand's gentle touch can also give life. We'll find new life. We'll rest on some soft blankets. Our limbs will be massaged with oil. Tomorrow we'll roam in the forest again. Feed on succulent grass. Won't we?

Mallika *gathers herself and goes towards the door.*

Mallika This wounded fawn . . . what kind of person here would have wounded it? Is it that, as in the south, here too . . .?

Kalidas I've noticed many new presences in our rural province today.

He moves towards the window seat and sits down on it.

Some officials from the royal court have come to the village.

He hugs the fawn to his chest and starts soothing it.

Kalidas Will we go to sleep now? Yes, if we sleep for a little while, our pain will go away. But, before that, we've to drink some milk. . . . Mallika, if you have some milk, get it in a bowl.

Mallika Ma has boiled the milk. I'll go see.

She goes to the clay stove and starts looking among the pots and pans around it.

Just a little while ago we saw two or three royal officials passing by on horseback. Ma says that whenever these people appear, there's some calamity or other. After the exhilaration of the rain . . . I found all this very strange.

She picks up the pot of milk and begins to pour some into a bowl.

Ma's very upset today.

Kalidas *begins to rock the fawn in his arms.*

Kalidas We're happier than before. Our pain's slowly receding. We're getting better. . . . I don't understand how he could shoot an arrow at this body that's soft as cotton. It came bounding into my lap. I said, 'I'll take you where you'll find eyes like your mother's, and love like hers, too.'

He looks at **Mallika**. *She comes up to him with the milk.*

Mallika Really, Ma's very upset today. She must have realized that I was with you in the rain – otherwise I wouldn't have come back soaking wet. Ma's always so worried about scandal.

Kalidas Let me hold the milk, and you take the fawn in your arms.

He takes the bowl from **Mallika***'s hand. She takes the fawn in her arms and brings its mouth close to the milk.* **Kalidas** *brings the bowl even closer.*

Kalidas We won't drink the milk? No – we aren't going to be so obstinate! We'll certainly drink the milk.

The courtier **Dantul** *enters and pauses near the door. He watches them for a moment.* **Kalidas** *holds the milk to the fawn's mouth.*

Yes, like this . . . like this.

Dantul *advances into the room and draws close to them.*

Dantul You want to give it milk and make its flesh even more tender?

Kalidas *and* **Mallika** *look at him, startled.* **Mallika** *retreats a little with the fawn.* **Kalidas** *places the bowl of milk on the seat next to himself*

Kalidas So far as I know, we aren't acquainted – how did you dare to enter a home where you're a stranger?

Dantul *looks once at* **Mallika**, *then at* **Kalidas**.

Dantul What a coincidence – I wanted to ask you exactly the same kind of question! We've never been acquainted, but you had no scruples about carrying away a deer brought down by my arrow. Luckily, there's a trail of blood leading to this door – otherwise, would I have been able to track you down on this dark, overcast day?

Kalidas I can see that you're not a native of this region.

Dantul *laughs sarcastically.*

Dantul I applaud your insight! My appearance itself is an indication that I don't belong to this place.

Kalidas I'm not saying this because of your appearance.

Dantul After looking at the lines on my brow, then? It seems that, besides robbery, you also practise clairvoyance.

Mallika *advances a little, looking as though she is hurt.*

Mallika Don't you feel any shame in casting such aspersions?

Dantul Forgive me, lady. But this fawn you're carrying in your arms has been wounded by my arrow. So it's my property. You'll return my property to me, won't you?

Kalidas In this province, there's no hunting of deer, sir. You're an outsider, so it's enough that we don't treat you as a criminal for this act.

Dantul So villagers will sit in judgement on a courtier for a crime! My rustic friend, do you even know the meaning of crime and justice?

Kalidas It's surprising to learn that words and meanings are the property of courtiers.

Dantul You seem to be a smart fellow. Yet you don't know that the rights of courtiers extend far and wide. I'm getting late. Give me this fawn.

Kalidas This fawn is the property of this mountain region, sir. And we, the inhabitants of this region, are its kinsmen. You're making a mistake if you think that we'll hand it over to you. . . . Mallika, take it inside and lay it down on the bed or on a blanket . . . .

Ambika *emerges suddenly from the interior.*

Ambika The beds and blankets in this house aren't meant for fawns.

Mallika You can see, Ma . . .!

Ambika Yes, I can see. That's why I'm speaking out. The beds and blankets are for people, not for animals.

Kalidas Give me the fawn, Mallika!

He puts the bowl of milk down on the floor and advances to take the fawn in his arms.

The cushion of my arms will be enough for it. I'll take it home with me.

He walks towards the door.

Dantul And Dantul the courtier will simply watch you taking it away!

Kalidas That depends on the courtier's preference.

He walks to the entrance without glancing at **Dantul***.*

Dantul Perhaps it will be necessary to acquaint you with what the likes and dislikes of a courtier are.

Kalidas *leaves. Only his response is heard offstage.*

Kalidas Perhaps.

Dantul Perhaps?

He wants to go after **Kalidas***, with his hand on his sword.* **Mallika** *moves quickly to stand between* **Dantul** *and the door.*

Mallika Stop, sir! Don't insist on taking the fawn. For you it's a question of your right, for him it's a question of compassion – though unarmed, Kalidas won't think twice about your weapon.

Dantul Kalidas? . . . You mean to say that the man with whom I was arguing about the fawn is the poet Kalidas?

Mallika Yes – yes. But how do you know that Kalidas is a poet?

Dantul How do I know! Every member of Ujjayini's royal court knows of the poet Kalidas, the author of the poem *A Gathering of Seasons*.

Mallika Every member of Ujjayini's royal court knows of him?

Dantul The emperor himself has read *A Gathering of Seasons* and praised it. That's why the court now wants to honour its author, and offer him the position of court poet. That's precisely why Acharya Vararuchi has come here from Ujjayini.

On hearing this, **Mallika** *seems to freeze with astonishment.*

Mallika The court wants to honour him? Offer him the position of court poet . . .?

Dantul I regret that my conduct with him was uncivil. I should go and apologize to him.

He leaves. **Mallika** *remains standing like that for a few moments. Then suddenly she seems to become conscious again. In the meantime,* **Ambika** *picks up the bowl of milk and puts it in a corner. She looks at the pot of milk, pours the rest of the milk into a smaller tumbler, adds some sugar, and stirs it. Her hands are trembling, as though she is deeply agitated. Biting her lower lip,* **Mallika** *runs up to her.*

Mallika Did you hear, Ma? The royal court wants to offer him the position of court poet.

Ambika *somehow holds on to the tumbler of milk about to fall from her hands.*

Ambika I've spread the wet clothes out to dry. There's a little milk left, and I've added sugar to it.

Mallika Ma, didn't you hear what the courtier was saying?

Ambika Drink your milk. I hope nobody else needs to be welcomed here now.

Mallika Welcomed? . . . I'd like to be able to welcome the whole world into this home today.

She takes the tumbler from **Ambika**'s *hand.*

Shall I bathe you in this milk, Ma?

She raises the tumbler. **Ambika** *snatches it from her hand.*

Ambika I've done enough bathing in milk already.

Mallika How heartless you are, Ma! Didn't you hear that the court's honouring him? Even then, you . . .

Ambika Drink your milk. And if you aren't tempted to get wet in the rain again, I'll prepare your bed for the night . . . Let me remain heartless, as I am.

Mallika *puts her arms around* **Ambika***'s neck.*

Mallika No, you aren't heartless. When did I say you're heartless?

Ambika No, you didn't say it. Drink your milk.

Mallika *takes the tumbler from her hand, finishes the milk in a single gulp, and puts it down in a corner. Then she pulls* **Ambika** *by the hand, makes her sit down, and lies down with her head in* **Ambika***'s lap.*

Mallika Ma, can you imagine how happy I am today?

Ambika I don't have the strength to think about anything. Now let me get up, I have lots of work to do.

She tries to get up, but **Mallika** *holds her down.*

Mallika No, don't get up. Just sit like this. . . . The court's honouring him, Ma! He'll hold the position of court poet . . .

Suddenly she leaves **Ambika***'s lap and sits up.*

. . . he, whom the people close to him have never tried to understand, to this day. Who has only been attacked and disgraced inside and outside his home . . . Surely, you can now believe, Ma, that my emotion isn't baseless.

Ambika *stands up.*

Ambika I've already told you that my power to think and understand is gone.

Mallika Why, Ma? Why are you so prejudiced? Why can't you think of him with generosity?

Ambika I'm past the stage at which one can live with one's eyes shut to reality.

She moves towards the interior. **Mallika** *stands up.*

Mallika And your realistic vision can see nothing but flaws?

Ambika *turns and stares at her for a moment.*

Ambika Where there's a flaw, my vision certainly sees a flaw.

Mallika What flaw do you see in him?

Ambika That man is completely self-centred. He has no attachments to anyone other than himself in the whole world.

Mallika Only because he doesn't tend to his uncle Matul's cows, and remains lost in the clouds?

Ambika I'm not concerned with Matul and his cows. I'm looking only at my own home when I say this.

Mallika Sit down, Ma!

She grabs **Ambika** *by the hand and takes her to the window seat.*

I want to understand what you're saying.

Ambika   I, too, want you to understand this today. . . . You say your bond with him is one of emotion. What's that emotion?

Mallika   I don't give it any name.

She sits down at **Ambika**'*s feet.*

Ambika   But people do give it a name. . . . If he really has an emotional bond with you, then why doesn't he want to marry you?

Mallika   You've always been ungenerous towards him, Ma.

You know the ironies of circumstance in which his life has been spent. What his condition has been in Matul's home. In that life of deprivation, without resources, how could marriage even be imagined?

Ambika   And now, when his life will no longer be deprived and lacking in resources?

Mallika *falls silent for a few moments and stares at her feet.*

However great a reason deprivation is for avoiding commitment, the end of deprivation becomes an even greater reason for refusing to commit.

Mallika   This is Vilom's language, not yours.

Ambika   I understand his kind of man very well. His only connection with you is that you're a receptacle and a refuge through which he can love himself, be proud of himself. But aren't you a flesh-and-blood person? Don't you – and doesn't he – have any obligation towards you? Tomorrow, when your mother will no longer be physically present, and there will be no arrangement in the house for even one proper meal a day, how will you answer the question confronting you? Will your emotion be able to resolve that question? Tell me again that this is Vilom's language, not mine.

Mallika *sits silently for a few moments, with her head bowed. Then she looks at* **Ambika**.

Mallika   Ma, life has somehow managed to pass so far. What's yet to come will also pass. But today, when his life's taking a new direction, I don't want to stand before him proclaiming my self-interest.

Matul'*s voice is heard offstage.*

Matul   Ambika! . . . Ambika! Are you home, or aren't you?

Ambika *and* **Mallika** *look towards the entranceway.* **Matul** *enters in a dishevelled state.*

Indeed, you're home! I'm going to announce to the entire village that I have no connection whatever with this creature who bears the name of Kalidas.

Mallika   What has happened, Arya Matul?

Matul   I raised him, I nurtured him. All for this day – so that he could betray his clan like this?

Mallika   But what we've heard is that he's being honoured by the royal court. Some senior scholar has come from Ujjayini.

Matul   That's exactly what I'm saying. Some scholar has come from Ujjayini.

Mallika   But you were just saying . . . .

Matul   I'm saying it right. The scholar wants to take Kalidas with him to Ujjayini right away, tomorrow.

Mallika   But . . .

Matul   He has come with two chariots, two charioteers, and four mounted guards. Didn't I always tell you, Ambika, that the son of the son of the daughter of the founding father of our clan fought for the Gupta empire against the Shaka invaders?

Ambika   You were talking about your sister's son.

Matul   I'm still talking about him. You should understand that, in one respect, the court's honouring our entire clan. And this glorious descendent of our clan says, 'I don't want this honour . . .'

Mallika *stands up abruptly.*

'I'm not here to be bought and sold with royal coin,' he says.

Matul *begins to pace up and down the room excitedly.* **Mallika** *stands oblivious for a few moments.*

Mallika   He doesn't want to accept the court's honour?

Matul   I can't understand how buying and selling comes into this business. If you're given an honour, accept it. Otherwise, what's poetry worth?

Mallika   Poetry has some value, Arya Matul, that's why the honour also has value. . . . I can understand where this honour pricks his conscience.

Lost in thought, **Ambika** *begins to twist the end of her sari in her fingers.*

Ambika   I assure you, Matul, that he'll definitely go to Ujjayini.

Matul *continues to pace.*

Matul   He'll definitely go! These people of course are his devotees who'll sing his praises and carry him away!

Ambika   When a person receives an honour, the indifference he expresses towards it increases his importance. You should be happy that your sister's son is well versed in public relations, too.

Matul *stops suddenly.*

Matul If this is public relations, then I'll have to say that public relations and pinhead relations amount to the same thing.

He resumes pacing.

When a person offers something – whether wealth or honour – he can also change his mind – and when the mind changes, it changes.

He stops again.

You think about it – the emperor can even take offence that an ordinary poet has turned down his honour.

Nikshep *enters.*

Nikshep Matul, you're still here, while the Acharya's waiting for you over there.

Matul And what are you doing here, Nikshep? Didn't I tell you to stay with the Acharya until I got back?

Nikshep But you also told me to inform you as soon as the Acharya had finished resting.

Matul Yes, I said this. But I also said that. This you could understand, but that you couldn't?

Nikshep But, Matul . . .

Matul But what? Is Matul a fool? Tell me, do you think I'm a fool?

Nikshep No, Matul . . .

Matul If I'm not a fool, then you're a fool, for sure. . . . What has the Acharya said?

Nikshep He has said that he wants to tour this entire village region with you . . .

An expression of pride appears on **Matul**'s *face.*

. . . the region that gave birth to Kalidas's poetry.

Matul's *expression changes to one of revulsion.*

Matul Kalidas's poetry!

He starts pacing again.

God knows what special qualities such a great scholar sees in his poetry!

He pauses and looks at Ambika.

This man has no sense of even ordinary conduct with people, and you talk about his public relations. . . . His lordship was coming home with a fawn in his arms. Luckily, I spotted him just outside the house. I pleaded with him: 'O master of the tribe of poets, this is not the time to enter our home in such a state. A great scholar has come for you from Ujjayini, and is waiting for you.' As soon as he heard this, his lordship turned away. As though he'd seen a snake in his path.

Mallika *sits down near* **Ambika** *on the window seat.*

Matul *resumes pacing.*

Ambika Mallika, bring Matul a seat from the inner room.

Mallika *begins to rise, but* **Matul** *stops her.*

Matul No, I don't want a seat. The Acharya's waiting for me.

Nikshep *looks at* **Ambika** *and smiles.* **Matul** *walks up to the end of the room and turns back.*

I said to him, 'O poet supreme, the Acharya's here to take you back to Ujjayini with him. You'll be honoured by the royal court.'

Matul *stops again.*

Hearing this, his lordship paused. Pausing, he looked at me with fire in his eyes. 'I'm not here to be bought and sold with royal coin.' He said this as though the coins of the royal treasury were consumed by longing for him, and then he left. . . . I fell into a moral predicament: should I pursue his lordship, begging and pleading, or should I look after my guests? Then I came here, after telling this Nikshep to stay with the Acharya – and now, like a wheel that has spun off its axle, he has come careening after me.

Nikshep But, Matul, I've just come to inform you that . . .

Matul And I thank you for keeping me informed. Well done! The guests are sitting over there without a host, and you've come all the way here to inform me! . . . And, now, just do me this one favour – wherever that crown jewel of the tribe of poets may be, please find him and bring him back.

Matul *moves towards the exit.*

My sense of duty tells me that I should find whatever way I can to present him before the Acharya. . . . And my brain tells me that, wherever I find him, I should seize him then and there by the tuft of his poetic hair, and . . .

Matul *exits.*

Nikshep Matul's third eye is always open.

Mallika But where's Kalidas right now?

Nikshep Kalidas is at the temple of the goddess Jagdamba at this moment.

Mallika Have you seen him?

Nikshep I've seen him.

Mallika But you didn't tell Matul?

Nikshep I didn't want Matul to go there straight away.

Mallika Why? You, too, don't want Kalidas to . . . ?

Nikshep I definitely want Kalidas to go to Ujjayini. That's why I didn't think it would be appropriate for Matul to go to him at this time . . . Matul gets so much pleasure from listening to the words coming out of his mouth that he just goes on talking, and doesn't want to understand the situation around him. . . . Kalidas is insisting that until the guests from Ujjayini have left, he'll stay on in Jagdamba's temple and not return home.

Ambika   What far-sightedness!

Nikshep   Far-sightedness?

Ambika   Of course, it's far-sightedness.

Nikshep   Where's the far-sightedness in this, Ambika!

Ambika *gives* **Nikshep** *a sharp look.*

Ambika   The court wants to honour the poet. Indifferent to the honour, the poet's lost in meditation at Jagdamba's temple. The court's representatives come to the temple and supplicate the poet. The poet opens his eyes very slowly . . . Isn't it far-sighted to create such a big drama?

Nikshep   Kalidas isn't creating a drama, Ambika! I'm convinced that courtly honours don't hold any attraction for him. He really doesn't want to leave this mountain region.

Ambika *rises from her seat and goes towards the pots and pans near the stove.*

Ambika   Doesn't want to leave! . . . *Hunh!*

She takes a platter to one of the jars and begins to take out fistfuls of rice grain.

Nikshep   No one's persuasion – neither Matul's nor anyone else's – can overcome his obstinacy.

He gives **Mallika** *a meaningful look. She lowers her eyes.*

There's only one person at whose request he could possibly give up his stubbornness.

Ambika *sizes up* **Nikshep***'s meaningful look and then looks at* **Mallika***.*

Ambika   No one in our house is concerned at all whether he gives up his obstinacy or not.

Ambika *takes the platter to the stove and, with her back to the other two, tries to busy herself.*

Nikshep   In his sensitivity, Kalidas is forgetting that he'll lose a great deal by disregarding this opportunity. Ability moulds only one quarter of one's personality – fame and recognition complete the rest. Kalidas should definitely go to the royal capital.

Ambika *tries to appear busy but fails.*

Ambika   So what's impeding him?

Nikshep   I've sensed that somewhere, at the root of his obstinacy, there's a streak of profound bitterness.

Mallika I know where that streak lies. . . . He's had a confrontation with a courtier a little while ago.

Nikshep Only you can dispel that bitterness, Mallika! Opportunity doesn't wait for anybody. If Kalidas doesn't leave this place, the court won't lose anything. The office of court poet won't remain vacant. But, for the rest of his life, Kalidas will remain what he is today – a local poet! Even the people who're praising *A Gathering of Seasons* today will forget him in a short while.

Mallika, *seemingly lost in thought, stands up abruptly.*

Mallika No, he mustn't disparage this honour. This is a tribute to his poetic self. He shouldn't deprive that self of its rights. Come, I'll go with you to Jagdamba's temple.

Ambika *gets up suddenly.*

Ambika Mallika!

Mallika *gives* **Ambika** *a steady look.*

Mallika Ma!

Ambika Will I have to say in front of an outsider that I'm not in favour of your going there at this time?

Nikshep Nikshep is not an outsider, Ambika!

Mallika This is a crucial moment, Ma! I really must go there right now. Come, Arya Nikshep.

Mallika *exits, without glancing at* **Ambika**. *A wave of anger crosses* **Ambika***'s face, and changes into an expression of defeat.* **Nikshep** *stands still for a moment, observing* **Ambika***'s emotions.*

Nikshep Please forgive me, Ambika.

He follows **Mallika**. **Ambika** *remains standing for a few moments with her eyes closed. Then she stares at the household objects around her one by one, and, as though broken, sits down on a stool and begins to rub the rice grains lying on the platter between her palms. Her eyes brim over with tears, which she wipes with the end of her sari. The lights dim. A choked sound escapes her lips.*

Ambika Emotion! . . . Oh!

She covers her face with the end of her sari. The lights dim further. Just then the glow of a wooden torch appears in the darkness of the entranceway. **Vilom** *enters with a torch in his hands. At the sight of* **Ambika** *sitting like this, he pauses momentarily. Then he draws close to her.*

Vilom The gathered clouds have cast an untimely darkness today, Ambika – or did you lose track of time?

Ambika *raises her head from her sari. In the torchlight, her face looks furrowed and her eyes appear sunken.*

Vilom I'm surprised that you haven't lit the lamps as yet.

Ambika   Vilom! . . . Why have you come here?

Vilom *moves towards the lamp in the niche on the left of the front door.*

Vilom   Shall I light the lamp?

He lights the lamp with his torch.

Vilom's visit isn't such a surprising thing.

He begins to light the lamps set along the stage front. **Ambika** *rises.*

Ambika   Go away, Vilom! You know very well that your coming here . . .

Vilom   . . . is unbearable to Mallika.

He lights more lamps and looks at **Ambika**.

I know, Ambika! Mallika's very innocent. She doesn't know anything about the world and about life.

He props up the torch in the bracket on the wall.

She doesn't want me to enter this house because Kalidas doesn't want me to.

He turns around and approaches **Ambika**.

And why doesn't Kalidas want me to come here? Because he sees the truth of his own heart staring back at him from my eyes. He feels bewildered. . . . But you know very well, Ambika – my only flaw is that I bluntly say exactly what I feel.

Ambika   I don't want to discuss your faults and virtues right now.

Vilom   I can see that you're very unhappy right now. . . . And when have you not been unhappy Ambika? Your very life is a chronicle of pain. Are you a little thinner than before? . . . I've heard that Kalidas is going to Ujjayini.

Ambika   I don't know.

As though he hadn't heard her, **Vilom** *goes to the window.*

Vilom   The royal court will honour Kalidas. He'll live in Ujjayini as the court poet. I think that he and Mallika should get married before he leaves. You've surely thought about this.

Ambika   I don't want to think about anything right now.

Vilom   You – Mallika's mother – don't wish to think about it? That's astonishing.

Ambika   I've told you, Vilom, you should leave.

Vilom   Kalidas will go away to Ujjayini, and Mallika – whose name has become the subject of malicious gossip all over this province because of him – will be left behind here? Right, Ambika?

Saying nothing, **Ambika** *sits down on the window seat.* **Vilom** *turns around to face her.*

Right? Have you endured all that pain for so many years only for this outcome? Even a distant observer can tell what you've had to go through all these years. Time has destroyed the unity of your mind, body, and soul. You've let yourself be consumed atom by atom, so that Mallika wouldn't experience any deprivation. And today when deprivation for the rest of her life is the issue before you, you don't want to think at all?

Ambika You aren't lessening my pain by saying all this, Vilom! I'm requesting you to leave me alone right now.

Vilom I think it's essential for me to be with you in this situation, Ambika. I've come to say all these things – not to you, but to him. I'm hoping that he'll come here soon with Mallika. I saw Mallika going towards Jagdamba's temple. I want to wait here for her.

Kalidas *appears in the entranceway, with* **Mallika** *behind him.*

Kalidas You won't have to wait very long, Vilom.

On seeing **Vilom**, **Mallika**'s *eyes fill with anger and revulsion, and she moves to the window.* **Kalidas** *draws close to* **Vilom**.

I know where, when, and why you eagerly look for face-to-face encounters with me. . . . Tell me, what new poetic metre are you studying these days?

Vilom The study of poetic metres is not my inclination.

Kalidas Yes, I know you have a different inclination.

He looks at **Vilom** *for a moment.*

That inclination has probably separated you forever from the study of poetic metres.

Vilom Today you can undoubtedly take pride in your study of poetic metres.

He approaches the wall and begins to fiddle with the torch in its bracket. His face glows in the torchlight.

I've heard that an invitation has come from the capital.

Kalidas I've heard, too. Were you unhappy?

Vilom Unhappy? Yes, yes, very. Who isn't sorry to lose a friend? . . . Will you leave at the first auspicious opportunity tomorrow, at the crack of dawn?

Kalidas I don't know.

Vilom I know perfectly well. The Acharya certainly wants to leave at the auspicious moment of dawn tomorrow. Living in luxury in the capital, you won't forget this provincial village, will you?

He glances at **Mallika**, *then looks again at* **Kalidas**.

I've heard that once a person reaches the city, he becomes a very busy man. Life there has so many kinds of attractions – entertainment halls, wine houses, all sorts of pleasure chambers!

Mallika's *expression hardens visibly.*

Mallika Arya Vilom, this isn't the time or place for such talk. I didn't expect to see you here now.

Vilom I know you aren't pleased to see me. But I came to see Ambika. We hadn't met for a long time. This isn't such an unexpected thing.

Kalidas Nothing that Vilom does is unexpected. What would be unexpected is his not doing a great many things.

Vilom It's really a matter of great joy, Kalidas, that we understand each other so well. There's certainly nothing in my nature that's hidden from you.

He gazes at **Kalidas** *for a moment.*

What's Vilom? An unsuccessful Kalidas. And Kalidas? A successful Vilom. In some ways, we come very close to each other.

He moves away from the torch and approaches **Kalidas**.

Kalidas Undoubtedly. All opposites come very close to each other.

Vilom It's good that you accept this truth. Because of the prerogative that intimacy grants me, can I ask you a question? . . . It's possible that I may never have another opportunity to talk to you. Just a day's interval will take you very far from us, won't it?

Kalidas Even the interval of years doesn't separate opposites from each other. . . . I'm eager to hear your question.

Vilom *draws very close and places his hand on* **Kalidas***'s shoulder.*

Vilom I want to know that you're still the same Kalidas – aren't you?

He gives **Ambika** *a meaningful look.*

Kalidas I don't understand what you're trying to say.

He removes **Vilom***'s hand from his shoulder.*

Vilom What I mean is – you're still the same person that you were until yesterday, aren't you?

Mallika *leaves the window and advances towards them.*

Mallika Arya Vilom, I don't find this kind of presumption forgivable.

Vilom Presumption?

Vilom *draws close to* **Ambika**. **Kalidas** *moves a couple of paces in the other direction.*

What's presumptuous about this? I'm asking a very meaningful question. Well, Kalidas? Isn't my question meaningful? . . . What do you think, Ambika?

Ambika *gets up in an agitated state.*

Ambika I don't know anything about this – nor do I want to know.

She begins walking towards the inner room.

Vilom Stop, Ambika!

Ambika *stops and looks at him.*

A whole lot has been said all this while, all over this village region, about Kalidas's relationship with Mallika.

Mallika *takes another step forward.*

Mallika   Arya Vilom, you . . . !

Vilom   In view of that, wouldn't it be appropriate for Kalidas to say clearly whether he's going to Ujjayini alone, or . . .

Mallika   Kalidas has no obligation to answer any question you ask.

Vilom   When did I say that he's obliged to answer me? But it's possible that Kalidas's conscience will compel him. Well, Kalidas?

Kalidas *turns around. The two come face-to-face with each other.*

Kalidas   I certainly feel obliged to praise you. You enter not only people's homes, but also their lives, without any right to do so.

Vilom   Enter without any right? . . . I? Well, Ambika, to what extent do you agree with Kalidas's claim that I, Vilom, intrude upon people's lives without any right to do so?

Ambika   I've already said that I don't have anything to say about all this.

She goes into the inner room.

Vilom   That's it – she's walking away? All right, Kalidas, you tell me – to what extent do you find your own claim appropriate? Whose life have I invaded? Come, let's go to the village and ask anybody . . . .

He gives **Kalidas** *a malevolent look. Then he goes to the torch, pulls it out of the bracket, and holds it in his hand.*

So, you aren't compelled even by your conscience to answer my question! Perhaps the question itself is such . . .

Kalidas   You're free to speculate as you wish. All I know is that I don't have the slightest desire to leave this rural province and go to Ujjayini.

Vilom *brings the torch close to* **Kalidas**'s *face.*

Vilom   Undoubtedly! Why would you have such a desire? An ordinary person may have it, but why would you have it? But I only want to know that, if it so happens – let's assume for a moment that you decide to go – then, in such a situation, isn't it appropriate that . . .

Mallika *positions herself between* **Vilom** *and* **Kalidas**.

The torchlight falls on her face.

Mallika   Arya Vilom, you're crossing the limit with the way you're talking today. I'm not a child – I understand what's in my best interest. . . . Maybe you're not aware that your presence here right now is like that of an unwelcome guest.

Vilom I didn't think it was necessary to be aware of that. I know that you despise me. But I don't despise you. That's reason enough for me to be here.

He throws the torchlight again on **Kalidas**'s *face.*

There was one other thing, too, that I wanted to say to Kalidas.

Looking meaningfully at **Kalidas**, *he turns again to* **Mallika**.

You're very close to Kalidas, but I know Kalidas much better than you.

He looks again at both of them, one by one, and moves towards the entrance-way. From there, he turns around and looks once more at **Kalidas**.

May your journey be auspicious, Kalidas! You know that Vilom's just your well-wisher.

Kalidas Who can know that better than me?

A contemptuous sound escapes from **Vilom**'s *lips, and he looks at* **Mallika**.

Vilom It's possible that this unwanted guest may intrude again sometime. Asking your forgiveness in advance for that, too . . .

He smiles sardonically and leaves. **Kalidas** *looks at* **Mallika** *for a moment. Then he goes to the window.*

Mallika You're sad again?

Kalidas *continues to look out of the window.*

Look, you've given me your word.

Kalidas *turns back and draws close to her.*

Kalidas Think again, Mallika. The question isn't merely one of accepting an honour and court patronage. There's a much larger question before me.

Mallika And I'm that question . . . am I not?

She takes him by the arms and draws him to the window seat.

Sit down here. You know me. Don't you?

Kalidas *continues to gaze at her.*

Do you think I'd be happy if you spurned this opportunity, and continued to live here?

Trying to suppress her tears, she blinks and turns her gaze upwards.

I know that your departure will fill my being with emptiness. The outside world will perhaps feel very desolate, too. In spite of that, I'm not deceiving myself.

She tries to smile.

I'm saying from my heart that you should go.

Kalidas I wish you could see your eyes right now.

Mallika My eyes are tearful because you don't understand what I'm saying.

She sits down on the floor near him and places her elbows on his knees.

Do you think you can be very far from me, even if you leave? If you stay on in this rural province, how will your talent have the opportunity to develop? The people here don't understand you. They want to test you by the standard of mediocrity.

She rests her chin on her forearm.

You believe, don't you, that I know you? I know that if any limit encircles you, you'll become confined. I don't want to confine you. That's why I say – go.

Kalidas   You're not grasping this fully, Mallika. The question isn't one of your confining me.

Stung by these words, **Mallika** *still tries to retain her composure.* **Kalidas** *gets up as though lost in thought, and begins pacing.*

I feel that this village region is my true ground. I'm connected to this land by many links. Among these links are – you, this sky and these clouds, the greenery here, the young deer, the herdsmen.

He pauses and looks at **Mallika**.

If I leave this place, I'll be uprooted from my land.

Mallika *rests her elbows on the seat and leans on it.*

Mallika   Why don't you consider the possibility that you'll find the new soil richer and more fertile than the soil here? You've already absorbed whatever you could from this landscape. At this stage, you need new soil that will make your self more complete.

Kalidas   A new land could also dry me up.

He begins pacing again.

Mallika   There's no soil that doesn't contain a measure of freshness. Your imagination will certainly find a way to be touched by that freshness.

Kalidas   And that life will also come with its own expectations . . . .

Rising and drawing close to him, **Mallika** *takes his hands in her own.*

Mallika   Why is it necessary for you to fulfil those expectations? You can create your own new expectations in others.

Kalidas   Even so, a lot of doubts and apprehensions keep cropping up. I don't feel any enthusiasm in my heart.

Mallika   Look at me.

Kalidas *gazes into her eyes for several moments.*

You still don't feel any enthusiasm . . .? Believe me, you won't be separated from this place even after you've gone away. The wind, the clouds, the deer of this landscape –

you'll take them all with you. . . . And I, too, won't be far from you – I'll be gathered up in the clouds that come floating by.

Lightning flashes and the sound of thunder can be heard. **Kalidas** *continues to hold her hands.* **Mallika** *tries to control her tears by blinking.*

It looks like rain, again. As it is, it has grown very dark. The Acharya must be waiting for you.

Kalidas Are you asking me to leave?

Mallika Yes! You'll see – after you've left, I'll be cheerful, I'll wander about a lot, and every evening I'll go to Jagdamba's temple, to watch the sunset . . . .

Kalidas This means that I should take my leave of you.

Mallika No! I'm not going to give you leave. Because you're going, I'll only pray that your passage may be praiseworthy.

She lets go of his hands.
Go.

Kalidas *keeps his eyes closed for a few moments. Then he turns abruptly and leaves. Hiding her face in her hands,* **Mallika** *goes to the window seat and sits down. Loud thunder is heard in the background and, with that, the sounds of rain beginning.* **Mallika** *tries to control herself but begins to sob.* **Ambika** *emerges from the interior and puts her hand on* **Mallika***'s head. Then she raises* **Mallika***'s face.*

Ambika Mallika!

Mallika *rises from the seat and, moving to the window, leans her head against its frame.*

You're not well, Mallika. Come inside and rest.

Mallika *remains standing in that posture, trying to control her sobs.*

Mallika Let me stay here, Ma. I'm not unwell. Look, Ma, what dense clouds have gathered all around us! Tomorrow, these clouds will travel towards Ujjayini . . . .

She sobs again with her face in her hands. **Ambika** *goes to her and holds her close.*

Ambika Don't weep, Mallika.

Mallika I'm not weeping, Ma. What's pouring from my eyes isn't grief. It's happiness, Ma, happiness . . . .

She hides her face on **Ambika***'s breast. The sound of thunder again, and the noise of rain growing louder.*

End of Act One

Act Two

Some years later.

The same room. The condition of the room has changed perceptibly. The plaster is peeling in several places. The swastikas, conch shells, and lotuses painted in vermilion are now faded. There are far fewer pots and pans around the stove. There are only two clay jars, and they are now covered completely with moss. A few pages of bark manuscript are scattered on the seat near the window, and some more pages are wrapped in silk. There is a broken round cane stool near the seat, on which lies a blank book made of bark sheets sewn together. In a corner near the stove is a clothes line, on which a few clothes are spread out to dry. Most of the clothes are torn, and covered all over with patches.

Another broken round cane stool is placed near the entranceway. There is only one square stool left, on which **Mallika** *sits, grinding medicinal herbs in a stone mortar. The corner of the bed in the inner room is visible as before.* **Ambika** *is lying on the bed. Every now and then, she turns on her side.* **Nikshep** *enters.* **Mallika** *adjusts her wrap.*

Nikshep How's Ambika's health now?

Mallika She still runs a fever, as before.

Nikshep There's no difference, compared to earlier?

Mallika Doesn't look like it.

Nikshep The same recurring illness, for two years running!

Mallika *sighs with resignation, and begins to pour the powdered medicine from the mortar into a bowl.* **Nikshep** *drags the second cane stool and sits down near her.*

Ambika really worries too much.

Mallika She also doesn't take her medicine properly.

She adds milk and honey to the medicine and stirs it. **Nikshep** *sits with his fingers intertwined, gazing at her.*

Nikshep How's your health?

Mallika It's okay.

Nikshep You're getting thinner. . . . No one has come from the capital for a long time.

Mallika *averts her eyes and keeps stirring the medicine busily.*

I sometimes think that I should go to Ujjayini and meet him.

Mallika Why?

Nikshep I want to talk to him about a lot of things. I often feel that it's all my fault.

Mallika *looks at him gravely.*

Mallika What's your fault?

Nikshep *sighs deeply.*

Nikshep You know what it is. . . . I didn't expect Kalidas to go to Ujjayini and just lose himself there like this.

Mallika And I'm very happy that he's so busy with his life there. Here he wrote only *A Gathering of Seasons*. There he has composed several new long poems. The merchants who came this way two years ago brought me copies of *The Origin of the Young God* and *The Cloud-Messenger*. They said there was a lot of talk about another long poem of his, but they couldn't get a copy of it.

Nikshep For that matter, I've heard that he has also written some plays that have been performed in Ujjayini's entertainment halls. Even so . . .

Mallika Even so, what?

Nikshep It pains me to say this. We also heard so many other things from the lips of the same travelling merchants . . .

Mallika When a man prospers, gossip of all sorts gets attached to his name.

Nikshep I'm not talking about mere gossip.

He gets up and starts pacing.

We also heard, didn't we, that he was married to a princess of the Gupta dynasty.

Mallika So, what's wrong with that?

Nikshep From one angle, there's nothing wrong. But what about his insistence while he was here – that he'd never get married?

He pauses and looks at **Mallika**.

What happened to that assertion? Didn't he realize that it was to honour his vow that you . . . ?

Mallika In relation to him, I don't figure anywhere. I'm one among countless ordinary people. He's extraordinary. He needed someone extraordinary as his companion in life. . . . I hear that the princess is very learned.

Nikshep Yes, I've heard. She has studied many philosophies and disciplines. I said, didn't I, that from one angle, there's nothing wrong with this situation. But, looking at it from another angle, one feels a great deal of remorse.

Mallika On the contrary, I feel an aversion to myself – because, being what I am, I could have become an obstacle to his success. If I hadn't encouraged him to leave at your urging, what a great loss it would have been!

Nikshep That's exactly why I'm sad – if you hadn't done this at my urging, your life wouldn't have acquired this shape today.

Mallika How's my life different from what it was? Earlier, Ma used to do the work. Now she's unwell, and I do the work.

Nikshep That's all the difference one can see on the outside.

Mallika That's all the difference.

She stands up with the medicine.

Let me give Ma her medicine. I'll be right back.

She goes in and, helping **Ambika** *to sit up, feeds her the medicine.* **Ambika** *swallows, then shakes her head.* **Nikshep** *strolls over to the lattice window. Outside, the sound of horses' hooves approaches, then recedes.* **Nikshep** *continues to watch from the window. Having taken her medicine,* **Ambika** *lies down.* **Mallika** *emerges from the inner room, and turns in the doorway to look at* **Ambika**.

Mallika Ma, if you're cold, shall I shut the door?

Ambika *nods.* **Mallika** *shuts the door.* **Nikshep** *steps away from the window.*

Nikshep Looks like some outsiders are visiting us again today.

Mallika Who?

Nikshep They're probably royal court officials. I noticed a couple of figures like the ones we'd seen when the Acharya came to fetch Kalidas.

A shiver runs through **Mallika**.

Mallika The same kind of figures?

Suppressing her mood, she tries to laugh.

Do you know what Ma says about this? She says that whenever these figures appear, some calamity or other strikes us. Sometimes a war, sometimes an epidemic! . . . But nothing of the sort happened last time.

Nikshep Didn't happen?

Averting her eyes again, **Mallika** *busies herself with checking the damp clothes on the line.*

Mallika What happened? . . . And whatever happened was for the best.

She removes one or two garments from the clothes line, then spreads them out on the line again.

It's so humid these days that clothes don't dry for hours.

The sound of hooves is heard once more. **Nikshep** *goes to the window once more. Suddenly, he exclaims in surprise.*

Nikshep What . . . what? . . . No? . . . But how not?

The sound of hooves recedes into the distance. **Nikshep** *steps away from the window in agitation.*

Mallika Why are you suddenly agitated, Arya Nikshep?

Nikshep I've just seen another figure passing by on horseback.

Mallika So what? Like Ma, are you also dreading a disaster?

Nikshep That's a very familiar figure, Mallika!

Mallika A familiar figure?

Nikshep I'm sure it's Kalidas himself.

Mallika *freezes, still clutching the clothes in her hand.*

Mallika Kalidas? . . . How's that possible?

Nikshep I saw him with my own eyes. He has gone galloping towards the mountain peak. Others may not be able to recognize him in his royal garb, but Nikshep's eyes can't be mistaken. . . . I'll go and look right away. The court officials must have come with him.

Nikshep *leaves in the same state of agitation.*

Mallika He's here, and he has gone towards the mountain peak?

She bites her finger, and, experiencing pain, walks mechanically towards the window, as though in a daze. **Rangini** *and* **Sangini** *appear in the entranceway.* **Mallika** *looks at them in surprise.* **Rangini** *pushes* **Sangini** *forward.*

Rangini Ask her, can we come in?

Sangini *pushes* **Rangini** *forward, and steps back herself.*

Sangini You ask.

Mallika *approaches them.*

Rangini Okay, I'll ask. . . . Look here, is this your home?

Mallika Yes, yes. Please come in. . . . Have you come to visit me?

Rangini *and* **Sangini** *enter the room, and look around with searching eyes.*

Rangini We haven't come to visit anyone in particular. Just think of it this way – we're here for no reason at all, we're just wandering about the countryside.

Sangini We want to see the homes around here.

Rangini And we want to study the life here.

Sangini Let me perform the introductions first. This is Rangini. She's a student of dance at the theatre academy in Ujjayini. She's also interested in writing plays.

Rangini And this is Sangini – she's learning how to play the *mṛdanga* and the *veena* at the same academy. She writes very beautiful love songs. Now she's inclining towards prose. And how do you introduce yourself?

Mallika *does not answer, and continues to stare at them in astonishment.*

Sangini   You haven't introduced yourself.

Mallika   I have nothing to introduce. Please come, take this seat here.

Sangini   We've come here to study, not to sit down. What do you people call this kind of space?

Mallika   Which space?

Rangini   She means this entire space where we are at this moment. In Ujjayini we call this a room. What do you people call it here?

Mallika   A room.

Rangini   You people also call a room a room? And . . .

Going up to the large clay jars, she touches one of them.

. . . this?

Mallika   A jar.

Rangini   A jar. You call a room a room, and a jar a jar?

She shrugs her shoulders in disappointment.

Sangini   Look, don't you have any local words here?

Mallika *continues to stare at them in bewilderment.*

Mallika   Local words?

Sangini   Yes. Regional dialect words. Don't you know – the great Sanskrit grammarian, Patanjali, has noted that some people say *yenn* for *when*, and *zenn* for *then*. As he states, '*Yenn* is *yenn* and *zenn* is *zenn*.'

Mallika   I don't possess such great learning.

Sangini *sits down on the window seat with a somewhat disappointed look.* **Rangini** *walks around the room, inspecting each and every object closely.* **Mallika** *goes up to* **Sangini**.

Sangini   Look, we want to learn a few things that are connected to life in this place, and this place only. Your homes and clothing are almost like ours. What's truly special about life here?

Mallika   Truly special about life here?

For a moment she looks towards the window.

I don't know. From every angle, our life's very ordinary.

Sangini   I can't accept that. This region has given birth to an extraordinary talent like Kalidas. Each and every thing here ought to be extraordinary.

After examining all the objects around the stove carefully, and after peeking into the inner room, **Rangini** *rejoins* **Sangini**.

Rangini Look, let me explain to you. The thing is that, by royal order, we're both doing research on the background of poet Kalidas's life. You can understand what a big and important task this is. But, after wandering about this place, we're almost in despair, because there's no material here at all.

Sangini Okay, tell us the names of some of the local plants.

Mallika What kinds of plants?

Rangini What kinds of plants?

She begins to ponder.

As Kalidas has written in his poem *The Origin of the Young God*, 'great healing herbs are radiant jewels'. What are these medicinal herbs that emit light?

Mallika Medicinal herbs don't emit light.

Sangini *rises abruptly.*

Sangini Medicinal herbs don't emit light? Do you mean to say that what Kalidas has written is false?

Mallika He hasn't written anything that's false. What he has actually written is that . . .

Rangini Let it be, Sangini! She doesn't really know much about this place.

Sangini *also rises, with a grimace of disappointment.*

Sangini Okay, we've wasted a lot of your time. Forgive us. Let's go, Rangini!

Both leave. **Mallika** *shuts the front door. She sits down on the floor near the window seat, and rests her head on the scattered pages of bark manuscript. She closes her eyes.*

Mallika You've come back today after so many years. I used to think that, on the day of your return, the clouds would be gathered in the same way, the day would be dark in the same way, I'd get drenched in the rain again in the same way, and I'd say to you – look, I've read all your poems . . .

She picks up a few pages.

How often have I begged the merchants travelling to Ujjayini to bring back copies of your poems for me! . . . I used to think that I'd sing verses from *The Cloud-Messenger* to you. That the temple bells would ring out from the mountain peak, and I'd place this gift from me in your hands . . .

She picks up the blank book lying on the round stool.

That I'd say – look, this is for your next work. I've prepared these blank bark pages and stitched them together with my own hands. Whenever and whatever you write on them, I'll feel that I, too, am present somewhere, that I, too, have something.

She heaves a sigh, and puts down the book.

But now that you're here today, the whole atmosphere's quite different. And . . . and I'm unable to understand if you yourself are the same, or . . .?

Someone knocks on the door. She gets up quickly, straightening her clothes, and opens the door. **Anusvar** *and* **Anunasik** *appear in the entranceway, standing together.* **Mallika** *looks at them with incomprehension.*

Anusvar I'm certain I'm standing before the lady Mallika at this moment.

Mallika Yes – go ahead.

Anusvar Please accept greetings from the servants of Lord Matrugupta.

They both greet her with a deep bow. **Mallika** *continues to gape at them.*

Mallika Lord Matrugupta? Who's this Lord Matrugupta?

Anusvar The lord of poets, the creator of *A Gathering of Seasons, The Origin of the Young God, The Cloud-Messenger,* and *Raghu's Dynasty,* the scholar who's a master of politics and the future governor of Kashmir. Lord Matrugupta's royal consort, a daughter of the Gupta dynasty, the supremely accomplished lady Priyangumanjari, is eager to be in your august presence, and desires to arrive here shortly. We, her minions, are here to give you advance notice of her arrival.

Mallika The author of *A Gathering of Seasons, The Cloud-Messenger,* and so forth, is Kalidas, but you're saying that . . .

Anusvar He's on his way to take up the governorship of Kashmir, on behalf of the Gupta dynasty. His new name's Matrugupta.

Mallika He's going to be the governor of Kashmir? And and . . . his royal consort's coming to meet me?

Anusvar I'm sure that, on this proud occasion, you'll consider it essential to carry out a few changes in the arrangement of objects in the room where you receive your guests. Taking this as your command, we'll accomplish the task with our own hands right away. Come, Anunasik.

Entering the room, the two of them begin to examine all the objects with an eye to managing the change. **Mallika** *moves aside, to be out of their way.* **Anunasik** *goes up to the window seat.*

Anunasik In my opinion, this seat should be near the front door.

Anusvar The princess will enter through the door, and the seat will be right next to it?

Anunasik In that case, this seat should be moved from its present position seven finger-widths to the south.

Anusvar To the south?

He shakes his head in disagreement.

In my opinion, its position should be five finger-widths to the north. The sun's rays fall directly upon it through the window.

Anunasik I don't concur with you.

Anusvar I don't concur with you.

Anunasik So?

Anusvar So, because the issue is contentious, the seat should be left where it is.

Anunasik Okay, then. Let it remain where it is. And these jars?

He goes up to the jars.

Anusvar In my opinion, one jar should be in this corner, and the other in that corner.

Anunasik But, in my opinion, the jars shouldn't be here at all.

Anusvar Why?

Anunasik There's no answer to 'why'.

Anusvar I don't concur with you.

Anunasik I don't concur with you.

Anusvar So?

Anunasik So, the jars should also be left where they are.

They both go towards the area where clothes have been spread out to dry on a line. **Mallika** *gathers up the manuscript pages scattered near the window seat, places them on the round stool, and goes quietly into the inner room.* **Anusvar** *touches the damp clothes.*

Anusvar These clothes?

Anunasik The clothes are still damp, so they shouldn't be removed.

Anusvar Why?

Anunasik That's the standard procedure, according to the canonical books.

Anusvar What standard procedure is that?

Anunasik That I don't remember.

Anusvar But you do remember that such a standard procedure exists?

Anunasik Yes.

Anusvar So?

Anunasik So, this is an obscure and dubious topic.

Anusvar Yes, it's certainly an obscure and dubious topic.

Anunasik Since the whole subject is so dubious, the clothes, too, should be left where they are.

Anusvar Okay, then. The clothes, too, should be left where they are.

Anunasik But this stove must definitely be moved from its present position.

Anusvar Moving the stove would mean that all the objects around it would also have to be moved. That would take a lot of time.

Anunasik In addition to time, it would take a lot of patience.

Anusvar In addition to patience, it would take a lot of physical labour.

Anunasik In my opinion, handling pots and pans is not appropriate for people of our rank and station.

Anusvar I have exactly the same opinion.

Anunasik So, do we both concur that the stove shouldn't be moved from its present position?

Anusvar In my opinion, we both concur.

Anunasik *looks all around the room.*

Anunasik There's nothing else left to be done, is there?

Anusvar *also looks all around the room.*

Anusvar In my opinion, there's nothing else left to be done.

Anunasik No – there's something left.

Anusvar What?

Anunasik This square stool's lying in the way here. It should be removed from its present position.

Anusvar I concur.

Anunasik So

Anusvar So?

Anunasik So, it should be removed.

Anusvar Yes, it should definitely be removed.

Anunasik So?

Anusvar So?

Anunasik Remove it.

Anusvar Who – me?

Anunasik Yes.

Anusvar Not you?

Anunasik No.

Anusvar Why?

Anunasik There's no answer to 'why'.

Anusvar Even so!

Anunasik   I asked you first.

Anusvar   But you noticed the stool first.

Anunasik   So?

Anusvar   So?

Anunasik   Move it.

Anusvar   You move it.

Anunasik   Then let it be.

Anusvar   Let it be.

Anunasik   What now?

Anusvar   Yes, what now?

Anunasik   Let's review everything once more.

Anusvar   Yes, let's review everything once more.

Matul *enters in an agitated state.*

Matul   Members of the official class, has your work here been duly completed?

Anunasik   What say you, Anusvar?

Anusvar   Yes, it has been duly completed. It has, hasn't it? What say you, Anunasik?

Anunasik   Yes, it's all done. All that's left is to review everything once more.

Anusvar   Yes, all that's left is to review everything once more.

Matul   Then let that review be, for now. Princess Priyangumanjari has arrived outside.

Anunasik   The princess has arrived outside! Then let's go, Anusvar.

Anusvar   Let's go.

Both walk out together. **Matul** *also follows them, and returns in a few moments, showing* **Priyangumanjari** *the way.*

Matul   She's the most virtuous, most humble, and most innocent girl in the whole region . . . .

Mallika *emerges from the inner room.*

Come, come, Mallika! I was just singing your praises to the princess.

He laughs obsequiously.

From the moment she arrived, the princess has been asking only about you. . . . So this is our Mallika, the royal swan of this province. Um . . . um . . . Mallika, which seat has been chosen for the princess?

Mallika *ceremonially greets* **Priyangumanjari***, who smiles and acknowledges the greeting.*

Priyangumanjari   Arya Matul, you should go and rest now. The attendants will wait outside until I'm ready to return.

Matul   But a seat for you . . .?

Priyangumanjari   Please don't worry about that. I won't be inconvenienced.

Matul   Of course, you'll be inconvenienced. It's quite another thing if you choose not to consider an inconvenience an inconvenience. And this, in fact, is what's called nobility. The mark of a noble family is precisely that . . .

Priyangumanjari   Please go and rest. I've already tired you out a great deal.

Matul   Tired me out? You have?

He laughs obsequiously again.

Would I be tired out by you? Even if you were to tell me to go up and down between the bottom of a gorge and the top of a mountain all day long, I still wouldn't get tired. Matul's body is made of iron – solid iron. I won't indulge in self-praise, but, in addition to intellectual brilliance, our clan also possesses a great deal of physical strength. I've often covered ten leagues in a day while tending to my herds. I say that the hardest work in the world is raising a herd. If even one animal strays from the path, then . . .

Priyangumanjari   Look, your animals must be wandering off today as well. Please go and check on them at least once.

Matul   Do you think I still look after animals? A connection with the Gupta dynasty – and the tending of animals? I sold off all my animals years ago. And, truth be told, even that turned out to be profitable for me, because . . .

Priyangumanjari*'s gaze meets* **Mallika***'s. She advances and takes* **Mallika***'s hands in her own.*

Priyangumanjari   You're really just the way I'd imagined you.

Somewhat perturbed, **Mallika** *continues to stare at her.*

Matul   Because . . . oh . . . oh . . . okay. Then please give me leave. There are a lot of things scattered around in my house. I have to make a lot of different arrangements. So the attendants will wait for you. . . . Even so, if you have any orders for me, please send me word. . . . Mallika, do make some arrangement for the princess to sit down. Otherwise, she'll remain standing like this. Okay, I'm leaving. If you have any orders, please let me know.

Priyangumanjari   You should go. There's no need to worry about anything here.

Matul   Okay . . . okay . . . !

He starts on the way out.

Why do I need to worry? Mallika's here to do the worrying – and Ambika too. . . .
Even so, if you have any task for me, please let me know . . . .

He exits. **Priyangumanjari** *gazes at* **Mallika** *for a moment, and then reaches out and touches her chin.*

Priyangumanjari You're really very beautiful. Do you know, even though we're not acquainted, you don't seem unfamiliar to me.

Mallika Please sit down, won't you?

Priyangumanjari No, I don't want to sit down. I want to look at you and your home. He has talked about you and this house numerous times. He'd recall this place very often while composing *The Cloud-Messenger.*

Her gaze circles around the room, and settles again on **Mallika***'s face.*

Today, it's precisely the attraction of this land that has brought us here. Otherwise, it would have been more convenient for us to travel by a different route.

Mallika I can't figure out what I should do to welcome you as a guest. If you'll take a seat, I'll . . .

Priyangumanjari Don't worry about hospitality. I haven't come to your home as a guest. . . . It was quite possible that he wouldn't have come here, but I've brought him back with a lot of special pleading. I wanted to see this region for myself at least once. Besides . . .

A sound of suppressed anguish escapes her lips.

. . . besides, there was another reason. I wanted to carry away some of the atmosphere of this place with me.

Mallika The atmosphere of this place?

Priyangumanjari *looks at her with a smile, and then strolls to the window.*

Priyangumanjari One can see even very distant mountain ranges from here. . . . What unsullied beauty! Ever since I arrived here, I've been feeling envious of you.

Mallika *advances a couple of steps towards her.*

Mallika It would be our good fortune if you'd stay in this region for a few days. Of course, you'll face inconveniences here, but . . .

Priyangumanjari *looks at her again with a pained expression.*

Priyangumanjari All of life's conveniences seem trivial before this beauty. Even a whole lifetime isn't enough to drink it in with one's eyes.

She moves away from the window.

But where are the time and leisure to do so? The politics of Kashmir is so unstable that our staying away from it for a single day can create a host of problems. . . . The governorship of an entire province is an enormous responsibility. Our responsibility's even greater, because the situation in Kashmir is extremely dangerous at the moment. In a way there's just as much talk about the beauty of Kashmir, but where will we have the leisure to view it?

She sits down on the window seat, and leans back on her arms.

That's why I'm envious of you. This easy enjoyment of beauty is a mere dream for us. . . . Sit down.

She gestures to **Mallika** *to sit beside her on the window seat. When* **Mallika** *moves to sit on the floor,* **Priyangumanjari** *stops her.*

Sit here – next to me.

Mallika Let me get another seat.

She picks up a stool from the corner, places it next to the window seat, and sits down, gathering into her lap the bark manuscript pages that were lying on it.

Priyangumanjari It seems that, even though you live in this rural province, you have an attachment to literature.

Mallika *lowers her eyes.*

Whose works are these?

Mallika Kalidas's.

Priyangumanjari's *eyebrows contract slightly.*

Priyangumanjari Now he's known as Matrugupta. Are his works available even here?

Mallika I've obtained these copies from merchants travelling from Ujjayini.

A slightly sarcastic smile appears on **Priyangumanjari**'s *lips.*

Priyangumanjari I can understand that. I've learnt from him that you've been his companion since childhood. Your attraction towards his works is natural.

She begins to look at the ceiling, as though lost in thought.

Whenever he talks about this place, he becomes totally self-absorbed. That's why his mind often begins to lose interest in political matters.

Her eyes settle on **Mallika**'s *face again.*

On such occasions, one has to make a great effort to keep his mind on an even keel. Politics isn't literature. In politics, each and every moment is vital. If ever there's even a momentary lapse, it can result in great harm. To keep his groove in political life, a person needs to be extremely vigilant. . . . Literature was the first phase of his life. Now he has entered the second phase. Most of my time's spent in an effort to ensure that this step forward doesn't become a step back. . . . This involves a lot of hard work.

She tries to smile.

Don't you think that's right?

Mallika I don't know anything about life in politics.

Priyangumanjari Because you've always lived in a rural region.

She stands up abruptly. When **Mallika** *also begins to get up,* **Priyangumanjari** *stops her by placing a hand on her shoulder, and makes her sit down again.*

Keep sitting.

She walks around, biting her lower lip.

I told you I want to carry away some of the atmosphere of this place with me. That's because I don't want him to feel he's missing something. Such a feeling often causes a lot of damage. He unnecessarily loses his composure, which wastes both time and energy. His time's very valuable. I don't want his time to be wasted in that way.

She pauses before **Mallika**.

That's why I'm taking a lot of things from here with me. We'll take some fawns, which we'll rear in our garden. The medicinal herbs from here will be planted in the garden pavilion and the surrounding areas. We'll also have some houses in the style of this region constructed there. Matul and his family, too, will accompany us. We'll take some orphans from here and educate them there. I think all this will make a difference.

She strolls over to the other side of the room.

I see that your home's in a pretty dilapidated state. Its restoration is essential. If you want, I'll issue orders for this task before I leave. Two skilled builders have come with us from Ujjayini. What do you say?

Mallika *rises and approaches her.*

Mallika You're very generous. But we're used to living in a home like this, so we don't find it inconvenient.

Priyangumanjari Even so, I'd like to have this house restored. The early years of his life had a connection with this home as well. I've already ordered the construction of a new mansion in place of Matul's house. I've told the builders to get stone of the finest quality from Ujjayini and start the work. Regrettably, I won't be able to stay back and supervise the work in person. We'll have to begin the rest of our journey tomorrow. . . . Why don't you come along with us?

Mallika *stares at her incomprehendingly.*

Mallika Me?

Priyangumanjari *draws near and places a hand on her shoulder.*

Priyangumanjari Yes! What's standing in the way? You're not really bound to this place with any such thread that . . .

Mallika My mother's here.

Priyangumanjari That's no obstacle. Arrangements can be made to take your mother along as well. Our builders will work on the renovation of this house, and you'll live there with me as my companion.

An expression of hurt pride appears on **Mallika***'s face. But she continues to keep herself in check.*

Mallika I beg your pardon. I don't consider myself worthy of such an honour.

Priyangumanjari But I believe you're worthy of much more than this. . . . Before I arrived, two court officials had come here.

A twisted smile appears again on her lips.

I didn't send them as a mere formality. Have you seen both of them?

Trying to figure out her meaning, **Mallika** *looks at her uncertainly.*

Mallika I've seen them.

Priyangumanjari We can arrange for your marriage to whichever one of them you find suitable. They are both capable officials.

Mallika Your Highness!

Clutching the bark manuscript pages to her chest, she retreats a few steps towards the window seat. Giving her a level look, **Priyangumanjari** *walks slowly towards her.*

Priyangumanjari It's possible that you find neither of them suitable. But these aren't the only two officials in the kingdom – there are many others. Come with me. Anyone you wish to marry . . .

Mallika *sits down on the window seat and, with suppressed agitation, bites her lip.*

Mallika Please stop discussing this subject.

Because her voice has become hoarse, the words are not clearly audible. The door to the inner room opens and **Ambika** *appears, weak and trembling with illness and rage; then she stops, as though to gather herself.*

Priyangumanjari Why? Don't you have a vision of a home and a family of your own?

Ambika *advances slowly towards them.*

Ambika No. She has no such vision.

Priyangumanjari *turns around to look at* **Ambika**. **Mallika** *rises in a state of agitation.*

Mallika Ma!

Ambika She has no such vision in her head because she lives at the level of pure emotion. For her, in life . . .

She becomes breathless, and the words catch in her throat. **Mallika** *puts down the manuscript pages on the window seat and, going up to* **Ambika**, *supports her by the back.*

Mallika Why did you get up and come out, Ma? You're not keeping well. Come, lie down inside.

Mallika *wants to take* **Ambika** *back into the inner room, but* **Ambika** *pushes* **Mallika***'s arm off her back.*

Ambika Can't I even talk to a visitor? I've been suffocating here for days, months, years. For me this home isn't a home, but a cave of death in which I'm locked up all the time. And you don't even want me to talk to anybody?

In an effort to walk, she stumbles. **Mallika** *holds her up.*

Mallika But, Ma, you're not well.

Ambika I'm in better health than you are.

She walks up to **Priyangumanjari** *and looks her up and down.*

This home hasn't always been in this condition, princess! When I was still active, I used to keep it spick and span every day. Everything here hadn't gone to wrack and ruin like this. But, nowadays, even the two of us, mother and daughter, just lie here, as though we've gone to pieces. All this, because . . .

Out of breath again, she's unable to speak further. **Priyangumanjari** *moves away from her on the pretext of looking around the room.*

Priyangumanjari I can see that this house isn't in good condition. If Mallika could come with me, the problem would be solved easily. But now . . .

Biting her lip, she pauses for a moment, as though to think.

I'll still do whatever's possible before I leave. I'll instruct the builders to demolish this house, and in its place . . .

Mallika *recoils.*

Mallika Please don't do that. Please don't give the order to demolish this house.

Priyangumanjari *gives her a level look again.*

Priyangumanjari I was saying that only out of consideration for you. If it's inconvenient, then . . . it's all right. I won't issue such an order. Still, I want to do something or the other for you. I can't stay any longer now. I have to finish several essential tasks before tomorrow's journey. I didn't really have the time even now. But I felt it was necessary to visit you. He had gone for a ride towards the mountain peak, and while he was away, I came here. All right, then . . .!

Mallika *wrings her hands and lowers her eyes. In her anger,* **Ambika** *takes a couple of steps towards* **Priyangumanjari***.*

Ambika I wanted to say something to you, princess. I wanted to tell you that we people . . . we people . . .

She begins coughing, and her words are drowned out by the cough. **Priyangumanjari** *turns at the front door to look at her.*

Priyangumanjari I understand your pain. I'll certainly help you in any way I can. Right now, the attendants are waiting for me, so . . .

She looks at **Mallika** *with a sombre smile, shakes her head, and leaves. Limp with emotion,* **Ambika** *continues to look in* **Priyangumanjari**'s *direction. Then she practically collapses on to the window seat, picks up some manuscript pages, and holds them out to* **Mallika**.

Ambika Here, read the lines from *The Cloud-Messenger*. Didn't you say that the tenderness of his inner self was embodied in them? Haven't you seen an even more embodied form of that tenderness today?

Mallika *stares at her, as though transfixed.*

When he wants to pay you the true worth of your pure emotion today, why don't you accept it? The four walls of this house will be restored, and you'll be able to live in their household as a servant. What better fortune do you want?

Mallika The princess has her own outlook on life, Ma. How can someone else be held responsible for it?

Ambika But who's responsible for the princess's visit here? She undoubtedly came here in accordance with that person's wishes. The court's builders will renovate this house! Today he's in power, he has wealth. What better means could he have for acquainting us with that power and wealth?

Mallika But, Ma . . .

Ambika Ma knows nothing, understands nothing. Ma can't plumb the depths of feeling, Ma . . .

She starts coughing again, and can't speak further. **Vilom** *comes in from outside.*

Vilom Why are you so upset, Ambika . . .? The whole village is envying you your good fortune today.

He gives **Mallika** *a meaningful look. She avoids his gaze and moves to the other side.*

When the dust of royal feet blesses a house, people feel a great deal of pride. An occasion like this doesn't turn up in everybody's life, does it?

Ambika I've lived my life up to this day only to witness this occasion! How can such great good fortune fit into our mean little life?

She gets up abruptly.

Come. I'll go to the village and broadcast our good fortune in person to everybody. So many years of deprivation and pain have brought forth such big fruit that royal builders are going to renovate our house!

Vilom Sit down, Ambika! The village has no time to listen to you today.

He strolls over to the window.

The people of the village are busy at this time. They've got to put together a lot of different things for the guests who've come from elsewhere. Today, those guests want to collect and cart away even the stones of this place. The stones of this place are now considered extremely valuable.

Mallika   The stones of this place were valuable earlier, too, Arya Vilom. It's a different matter that no one grasped their value before now.

Ambika *angrily takes several steps towards* **Mallika**.

Ambika   So why don't you go and collect some for yourself?

It's possible that people may not leave a single stone in this place, and then there will be nothing left to support your emotion.

Mallika   Sit down, Ma, your condition isn't good.

Holding **Ambika** *by the arm,* **Mallika** *steers her to the window seat.*

Vilom   There's a lot of excitement all over the village. This is the most festive day in the life of the region. People aren't worrying about their animals today. They're busy putting together food and drink for the visitors. Among these materials are also some fawns that are being rounded up on the special orders of the princess.

Mallika   That's not true.

Vilom   Not true? The princess herself has ordered Indravarma and Vishnudutt to . . .

Mallika   That order could have some other meaning, too.

Vilom   Some other meaning? What other meaning can it have? Will the princess play with those fawns or will the artists of Ujjayini paint their likenesses? It's an entertaining spectacle that the artists from the capital city accompanying the royal family are wandering about today, creating copies of every object in our village. They won't leave a single tree, leaf or blade of grass here – of which they haven't created and carried away a copy.

Mallika   This, too, could have some other meaning.

Vilom *leaves the window and draws closer to* **Mallika**.

Vilom   When did I say that there's no other meaning? The meaning's very clear. They see every object here as a representation of strangeness, and they want to take that strangeness from here and display it to others. You, me, this house, these mountains – for them, these are all examples of the strange and the exotic. I, for one, commend their subtle and skilful vision, which can see strangeness even where no strangeness exists. I saw an artist today painting a portrait of his own shadow in the sunlight of this place.

Ambika   In the sunlight here they must find their own shadows unfamiliar! . . . Who was that demoness who used to catch hold of every creature by its shadow?

She starts wheezing again as she talks.

I wish I were that demoness, so that today I could . . . today I could . . .

Her coughing drowns her words. **Mallika** *goes to her and supports her by the shoulders.*

Mallika   I've told you, Ma, you should rest. Don't talk . . .
Arya Vilom, Ma isn't feeling well. Please let her rest now.

Vilom   Yes, take Ambika inside. The noise of the festivities in the village will disturb her mind even more. I came only to inform you about the celebrations. I'm surprised that Kalidas didn't consider it appropriate to visit you. I've heard that those people will actually leave tomorrow.

Ambika   He didn't think it appropriate to visit us because he knows that Ambika's still alive.

Vilom   But I believe he'll certainly come here once. He ought to come. No one breaks a bond in this manner.

He strolls over to the window again.

And, especially, no one who possesses a poet's tender heart. What do you think, Mallika? Shouldn't he come here once?

Mallika   Arya Vilom, I've requested you to let Ma rest right now. Your talk unsettles Ma's mind.

Vilom   My talk unsettles Ambika's mind? I believe that the sources of the disturbance lie elsewhere. Ambika knows the reasons why her mind is unsettled.

He looks out of the window.

I also understand those causes. That's why I come out and say many of the things that remain buried in Ambika's mind.

He turns to look at **Mallika**.

I know you find my presence disagreeable. That's nothing new. But I want to stay just a little longer.

He looks out again.

I see a horseman coming down from the mountain peak. It's possible that, this time, he'll want to stop here for a few moments. In that event, I'll also ask after his welfare. He and I have an old friendship.

Mallika *begins to lose control of herself.*

Mallika   Arya Vilom, in that case your presence here wouldn't be appropriate at all, from any perspective. If you'd like to meet him, this isn't the only place to do so.

Vilom *continues to look out of the window as before.*

Vilom   But what's wrong with this place? This is exactly where we met the day he left. The passage of time will be imperceptible if we meet in the same spot after so many years.

Mallika *goes up to* **Vilom**, *and, taking him by the arm, wants to draw him away from the window.*

Mallika I request you not to be obstinate right now about staying here . . . .

Vilom *does not budge from his position. The sound of hooves becomes audible in the distance.*

I'm asking you to please go away. This is my house. I don't want you to be in my house right now.

Vilom *remains standing as before. The sound of hooves keeps drawing closer.* **Mallika** *moves from the window to where* **Ambika** *is sitting.*

Ma, tell him to go away. I don't want any undesirable situation to develop here at this time. You're not well, and I don't want anything to happen that might have an adverse effect on your condition.

When **Mallika** *shakes her,* **Ambika** *reacts as though she has lost all power of mobility. Her brow is furrowed, and her eyes stare ahead without blinking. The sound of hooves draws very close.* **Mallika** *goes back to stand next to* **Vilom**.

Arya Vilom, I've told you to go away. You don't know that . . .

Having drawn very close, the sound of hooves begins to recede. **Mallika** *comes to a standstill, as though paralysed.* **Vilom** *turns slightly to look at her.*

Vilom I'll leave.

A low sarcastic sound escapes his lips.

I don't want to be the cause of any undesirable situation that might develop here. But may I know – what undesirable situation could arise?

He moves from the window to the centre of the room.

Well, Ambika, what undesirable situation could arise because of my presence here?

Ambika I knew it. I've known it ever since he left. If he'd come, I'd have been surprised. Now, I'm not surprised.

Her voice grows more shrill. **Mallika** *sits down on the window seat very slowly, as though she has lost her strength.*

Not surprised at all. I'm delighted that I was right about him. Life's only pure emotion! Tender emotion! Very, very tender emotion!

Vilom But I'm sorry. I've waited for this day for years. I also had faith in our friendship . . .

He gives **Mallika** *a meaningful look.*

Now, however, that trust is gone. Maybe the friendship was merely one-sided. He never thought us worthy of his friendship. And, then, friendship occurs only between like and like.

Mallika *stands up abruptly. Her eyes are glistening with the harshness of despair.*

Mallika Arya Vilom!

Vilom *looks at her as though he is toying with a child.*

I'm telling you again that you should leave. Otherwise, we'll really have an undesirable situation on our hands.

Vilom Is that so . . . ?

He looks at **Ambika** *with a smile.*

Then I should certainly leave. . . . Okay, Ambika! I worry a great deal about your health. So far as possible, please include ghee and honey in your diet. I've extracted some fresh honey recently. If you need some, I'll send it . . . .

Mallika We don't need any honey. Our home has all the honey we need.

Vilom Is that so? . . . Okay, Ambika!

He looks at both of them for a moment, then walks away, but pauses at the door.

. . . but if you do ever need any honey don't hesitate to ask.

He leaves. **Mallika** *stands subdued for a moment, with her head bowed. Unable to collect herself, she moves towards the inner room.* **Ambika**'s *expression changes from anger to hopelessness, and from hopelessness to compassion.*

Ambika Mallika!

Mallika *stops. But she hides her face in her hands without answering.* **Ambika** *rises, walks slowly towards her, and takes her in her arms.* **Mallika** *buries her face in* **Ambika**'s *shoulder. Her whole body trembles with grief but no sound escapes from her lips.* **Ambika**'s *eyes brim with tears; holding* **Mallika**'s *trembling frame close to herself,* **Ambika** *strokes her back soothingly. Then she begins to kiss the top of* **Mallika**'s *head, and to rub her cheeks against it, affectionately.*

You still want to weep? For that man? For that man who . . . ?

Mallika Don't say anything about him, Ma, don't anything . . . .

She breaks into sobs. **Ambika** *helps her sit down on the floor right there, and bends over her shaking back.*

End of Act Two

Act Three

After some more years.

The sound of rain and thunder. The curtain rises to reveal the same room. One lamp is lit. There is a great difference between the room's condition now and what it was earlier. Everything is decrepit and in disarray. There is only one large jar left, and it is broken at the edge. The window seat has been moved from its old position, and the tiger skin is no longer on it. The decorations painted on the walls, such as the swastikas, are barely visible. There are only one or two blackened pots near the stove. Soiled and tattered clothes are piled up in a corner. Initially, there is no one in the room. Then **Matul** *enters, in wet clothes and walking with a crutch. Looking all around, he sighs deeply and shakes his head in dismay. Then he moves to the middle of the room.*

Matul   Mallika!

Mallika's *voice is heard from the inner room.*

Mallika   Who is it?

Matul   It's me, Matul. Look at what the rain has done to Matul!

He begins to brush the water off his head and to squeeze it out of his clothes. **Mallika** *emerges from the inner room. Her clothes are torn in places, her complexion has darkened, and the expression in her eyes is a little strange. Her personality shows the same kind of deterioration as the room itself. The portion of the inner room that is visible when the door is open now contains a rickety crib, instead of a bed.* **Mallika** *shuts the door behind her.*

Mallika   Arya Matul – you, here, in this rain?

Matul   I had no refuge except your home, to escape from this rain. I thought that, no matter what, for Matul you're the same Mallika. . . . This monsoon rain will be the death of me! In the old days, when I could walk on two legs, I never worried about the rain, even the heaviest rain. But now the situation's awful – when I put my crutch forward, my foot slips backwards, and when I put my foot forward, my crutch slips backwards. If I'd known that I'd break my leg in the royal palace, I'd never have left the village at all. And, in my absence, those people turned my house into the kind of place where my feet slip all the time. Compared to the polished marble slabs I have now, my old clay floor was better, because at least it could grip my feet. Now I'm becoming homeless while I still have a home – I can't make it work either inside or outside. Just the sight of those white marble flagstones reminds me of the palace. Where I broke one of my legs!

Mallika   It will be hard for you to stand. Please sit down.

Matul *goes to the window seat, puts down his crutch, and settles down, as though for good.*

Matul If anyone were to ask me, I'd say that there can't be a more harrowing situation in the world than living in a palace. If you look in front, you see guards walking ahead of you. If you look back, you see guards walking towards you. To tell the truth, I could never figure out whether the guards were following me or I was following the guards. . . . And what was even more painful – the very people to whom I wanted to bow respectfully would, instead, bow to me. Bow to me . . .?

He gestures towards himself.

Tell me, what is there in Matul before which anyone should bow his head? Matul's neither goddess nor god, neither priest nor king. Then why should anyone bow to Matul and worship him? But, no – people were ready to worship not only Matul, but even the clothes that came off his back! And I used to touch my limbs again and again to check whether my body was still a thing of flesh and blood, or whether it had turned into the kind of smooth stone that one finds in the images of gods and goddesses in temples. . . . Since I came back here, my greatest joy has been that no one bows to worship me, and I don't have doubts about whether I'm the one walking in front, or whether there are guards walking ahead of me. The only thing I can't bear is this rain.

Mallika Shall I light a fire to dry out your clothes?

Matul *looks first at the stove, then all around him.*

Matul What a state you've allowed your home to fall into! Now that Ambika's no more, the house isn't in its proper condition. . . . Is it true that Priyangumanjari sent you some clothes and gold jewellery that you refused to accept?

Mallika I didn't need them.

She walks over to the pile of dirty clothes, pulls out the blank book from underneath, and begins to dust it off.

Matul And she had also told the builders to renovate this house.

Mallika I didn't think any renovation was necessary.

*She looks around for a place to keep the book. Then she puts it down near **Matul** on the window seat.*

Let me light a fire.

Matul No, the rain's stopping now.

Taking up his crutch, he walks over to the window.

It's only a light drizzle. If I can somehow drag myself home, I'll dry my clothes there. If the rain starts pouring down again, then . . .

*Moving away from the window, he draws close to **Mallika**.*

Have you heard any news of Kashmir?

She gives him a fixed and sombre look.

Mallika I stay at home all the time. How can I receive any news from anywhere?

Matul I've heard the news. I can't believe it – but, then, I also can. Nothing's impossible in politics. If it's impossible for such-and-such thing to happen, then it's just as possible for the same thing to happen. And it's also perfectly possible that what happens doesn't happen . . . .

Mallika *continues looking at him dazedly.*

Mallika But what's the news?

Matul The news is that the king has passed away. Rebel powers are rearing their heads in Kashmir. A wounded soldier who returned from there says that . . . that Kalidas has left Kashmir.

Mallika He has left Kashmir?

She sits down on the window seat as though she were still in a daze.

And he has gone back now to Ujjayini?

Matul No. He hasn't gone back to Ujjayini. The people of the capital city say that he has renounced everything, and has gone off to Kashi. But I don't believe it. He's so well respected in the city. If it wasn't possible for him to stay on in Kashmir, then he ought to have gone straight to the capital. But it isn't impossible, either. There's the life of politics – and then there's Kalidas! To this day, I haven't been able to figure out around what axis either of them turns. I believe the truth's always the exact opposite of whatever I'm able to grasp. And whenever I begin to arrive at the opposite, the truth flips into the opposite of that opposite. That's why, whatever I'm able to grasp is always untrue. From this, you can draw your own conclusion now, about what the truth is – whether he has renounced the world or whether he hasn't. My understanding is that he hasn't renounced the world – so the truth must be that he has, indeed, renounced everything, and has gone off to Kashi.

Mallika *picks up the blank book next to her and clutches it to her breast.*

Mallika No, that can't be the truth. My heart doesn't accept it.

Matul What did I tell you? Whatever I say can never be the truth! That's why I say nothing. If he has gone to Kashi, then I'm lying. If he hasn't gone to Kashi, then, too, I'm lying. . . . Does that satisfy you?

Matul *leaves in a huff, banging his crutch noisily.* **Mallika** *remains on the window seat, seemingly lost in thought.*

Mallika No, you haven't gone off to Kashi. You haven't renounced the world. That's not why I told you to leave this village. . . . I also didn't ask you to leave so that you could go and take on the burden of governance somewhere. When you did so, all the same, I still offered you my best wishes – even though you didn't accept them in person.

She looks at the blank book in her hands, as though with accusation in her eyes.

Even though I didn't remain in your life, you've always been an enduring part of my life. I never let you grow distant from me. You went on creating, and I continued to think that I was meaningful – that my life, too, has accomplished something.

She puts the book down on her knee.

And today will you reduce my life to meaninglessness in this way?

Placing the book on the seat, she gazes at it with fear, anxiety, and dejection.

You may be detached from life, but I can't be detached from it now. Can you look at life with my eyes? Do you know how these years of my life have been spent? What I've been witness to? What I was, and what I've become?

She rises and throws open the door to the inner room and gestures towards the crib.

Can you see this little creature? Can you recognize her? This is Mallika, who's growing up day by day, and, in place of Ma, I'm the one who's taking care of her now. . . . She's the child of my desolation. No one else could be the fullness, the feeling, that you were in me, but this womb of emptiness contains so many, many images of someone else! Do you know – I've lost my name and acquired an adjective in its place, and now, in my own eyes, I'm not a name but just an adjective.

Shutting the door, she walks towards the window seat.

The traders had said there is gossip in Ujjayini – that you spend a lot of your time in the company of courtesans. . . . But have you seen *this* face of the courtesan? Can you recognize me today? I go to the mountain peak even now and look at the garlands of clouds, just as before. I read lines from *A Gathering of Seasons* and *The Cloud-Messenger,* just as before. I haven't allowed the womb of my emotion to become barren. But can you measure the pain of my deprivation?

She sits down on the floor, with her elbows on the seat, and picks up the blank book.

No, you can't measure it. You once wrote that a single flaw hides itself in a crowd of virtues, just as the moon's blemish hides itself in a multitude of rays – but destitution can't hide itself. It can't hide itself even in a hundred good qualities. Not only can it not hide, it overshadows a hundred good qualities – destroys them, one by one.

As she speaks, she grows more deeply introspective.

But I endured all this. Because, even as I was breaking, I felt that you were making yourself. Because I saw myself, not in my own self, but in you. And today I hear that you're giving all this up, and renouncing the world? That you're detaching yourself from everyone and everything? Becoming indifferent? Is this how you're going to deprive me of my sense of power?

Lightning flashes, and the sound of thunder can be heard.

It's a day in the season of rain, just as before. The thunder's rolling, just as before. It's raining, just as before. I'm the same, as before. In the same house, as before. But . . .

Lightning flashes again and there are more sounds of thunder. The front door opens, slowly. **Kalidas***, with a look of devastation about him, opens the door and remains standing in the entranceway. In response to the sound of the door,* **Mallika** *looks towards it, and stands up abruptly.* **Kalidas** *enters the room.* **Mallika** *stares at him numbly.*

Kalidas Perhaps you don't recognize me.

One Day in the Season of Rain (*Ashadh ka ek din*)

Mallika *continues to stare at him in the same way.* **Kalidas** *surveys the room, then looks* **Mallika** *up and down, and walks over to the window seat.*

And it's perfectly natural for you not to recognize me, because I'm not the person you've known in the past. I'm someone else.

He sits down on the window seat and leans back on his arms.

And, to tell the truth, I'm a person I myself don't recognize! . . . Why are you standing transfixed like this? Are you very surprised to see me?

Mallika *shuts the front door, and advances distractedly towards him.*

Mallika   Surprised? I can't believe that you're you – and that this me, who's watching you, is really me!

Kalidas   I can see that you, too, aren't the same. Everything has changed. Or, it's possible that the change has taken place only in my vision.

Mallika   I can't believe that this isn't a dream . . .

Kalidas   No, it isn't a dream. The reality is that I'm here. After a journey lasting many days, I've arrived here – exhausted, broken, and defeated – to experience the reality of this place once more.

Mallika   You're soaking wet. I don't have any dry clothes for you, but I . . .

Kalidas   Don't worry about my being wet. . . . Do you know, to get wet in the rain like this can also be an ambition in life? It has been years since I got drenched. I don't want to dry off as yet. The walking had tired me out. For several days I was running a fever. But it's as though this rain has taken away all my weariness. . . .

Mallika *draws closer to him.*

Mallika   Are you very tired?

Kalidas   I was tired. I still need to rest, but the rain has lessened the exhaustion.

Mallika   You're really unrecognizable.

Kalidas *looks at her for a moment, then gets up and goes to the window.*

Kalidas   And who could recognize you, either? How this house, too, has changed! And I was hoping that everything would be the same – exactly as it was, in its place . . . But nothing's in its proper place.

He looks all around.

You've changed everything. Every single thing.

Mallika   I'm not the one who has made the change.

Kalidas *looks at her, then begins to walk about.*

Kalidas   I know you haven't made the change. But, Mallika . . .

He comes close to her.

. . . I didn't think this house would ever seem unfamiliar to me. The position and arrangement of every object in it was so settled. But, today, everything seems strange, and . . .

He looks into her eyes.

. . . and, even you. You, too, seem unfamiliar. That's why I say it's possible that the scene hasn't changed as much as my vision has.

Mallika You're tired – sit down. From the look of your eyes it seems that you're still not well.

Kalidas I've arrived here after many days of wandering from place to place. The reason why I didn't visit you when I was on my way to Kashmir is exactly the reason I'm visiting you today.

For a moment their gazes meet and lock.

Mallika I learnt from Arya Matul a short while ago that you'd left Kashmir.

Kalidas Yes, because my desire for power and status has left me. Today, I'm free of everything that has constricted me for years. In Kashmir, people think I've renounced the world. But I haven't renounced the world. I've only liberated myself from the persona of Matrugupta, so that I may live in the persona of Kalidas again. There was always an attraction pulling me towards the connection I broke off when I left this place. After my departure, I couldn't find anywhere else the intimacy I'd known with each and every thing here. I remember exactly the form and shape of every object here.

He looks around the room once more.

Jars, tiger skin, reed mats, clay lamps, wall decorations . . . and your eyes. What I'd seen of your eyes the day I left is still etched in my memory, to this day. I've been convincing myself all this while that, whenever I return, everything here will be exactly the same as before.

Someone knocks on the door. Taken aback, **Mallika** *looks towards the entranceway.* **Kalidas** *wants to go towards the door, but she stops him.*

Mallika Don't open the door. Just go on with what you're saying.

Kalidas At least go and see who it is.

Mallika It's a rainy day. It could be anybody. You go on talking. He'll go away.

The person at the door turns away, cursing in a drunken voice . . .
'. . . The door's always shut . . . *hunh* . . . the door's always shut!'

Kalidas Who was that?

Mallika I told you, it could be anybody. Anyone might need shelter in the rain.

Kalidas But I found his voice very strange.

Mallika You were talking about this place.

Kalidas I felt as though I knew the voice. As though, like all the other things here, it is also the altered form of some familiar thing.

Mallika You're tired and unwell. Sit down and talk.

Kalidas *sighs and sits down on the window seat.* **Mallika** *sits down on the floor at a little distance from him, with her arms resting on her knees.*

Kalidas I've thought many times about myself, Mallika, and every time I've come to the conclusion that Ambika was right.

He stretches his arms behind him, and raises his eyes to the ceiling.

Why didn't I want to leave this place? One reason was that I had no confidence in myself. I didn't know how I would feel in an environment of fame and honour, after living a life of deprivation and abuse. Somewhere in my mind was the anxiety that such an environment would overwhelm me, and change my life's direction. . . . And that anxiety wasn't quite baseless.

His eyes turn towards **Mallika***.*

You were very surprised that I was going to take up the governorship of Kashmir, weren't you? You must have found that very unnatural. But none of it seems unnatural to me. It was a natural reaction to a life of deprivation. Quite possibly, my reaction also contained a desire for revenge against all the people who'd abused me at will, who'd made me a laughing stock.

Biting his lip, he gets up abruptly and goes to the window.

But I also knew that I couldn't be happy. I tried to convince myself over and over again that the source of this shortcoming wasn't my environment, but my own self. If I could change myself, I'd be happy. But that didn't happen. I could neither change nor be happy. I was granted power and authority, I was given a great deal of honour, manuscript copies of whatever I wrote reached every corner of the country – but I couldn't find happiness. That environment and that way of life might have been natural for someone else, but they weren't for me. My field of action was different from a royal official's field of action. I felt over and over again that, by falling into the temptations of lordship and convenience, I'd entered that sphere illegitimately, and that I was far removed from the terrain on which I should have stayed. Whenever my gaze fell upon the horizon stretching far into the distance, I was pained by the perception that I'd removed myself from my own proper domain. I'd reassure myself that one day – tomorrow, if not today – I'd establish control over my circumstances, and divide myself equally between the two fields of action. But I continued to be moulded and driven by my circumstances. The tomorrow for which I was waiting never arrived, and I went on breaking, breaking, into pieces. And, one day. . . one day, I discovered that I was completely broken. I wasn't the person who was connected in any way to that large domain.

He falls silent for a moment. Then he resumes walking about.

I didn't want to pass through this place on my way to Kashmir. I felt at the time that this region, this range of mountains and valleys, would take the form of a mute question before me. Still, I couldn't resist the temptation. But I didn't experience any joy in being here. I was repelled by myself. I was also repelled by all those people who celebrated the day of my visit with festivities. That was the first time my heart and mind longed to be liberated. But it wasn't possible to be liberated then. I didn't visit you that day because I was afraid your eyes would make my restless heart even more restless. I wanted to save myself from such a situation. It could have had any kind of consequence. I knew what effect my failure to visit you would have on you, what others would say to you. Even so, I felt reassured that you wouldn't have any negative feelings in that respect. And I left with the hope that there would come a day when I'd be able to say all this to you, and convince you about the conflicts in my mind. . . . I didn't realize that conflict doesn't limit itself to just one person, that change doesn't move only in one direction. That's why I've a great sense of futility about being here today.

He goes back to the window.

People think I've written a lot while living that life and being in that environment. But I know I haven't written anything while living there. Whatever I've written was only the cumulative effect of my life here. These Himalaya mountains are the background of *The Origin of the Young God,* and the ascetic goddess Uma is you. The anguish of the imprisoned demigod in *The Cloud-Messenger* is my anguish, and his wife, stricken by the grief of separation from him, is you – even though I've imagined myself trapped on a mountain peak here, and envisioned you living in the city. In my play *The Recognition of Shakuntala,* you were the one who stood before me in the form of Shakuntala. Whenever I tried to write, I repeated the history of your life and mine, again and again. And whenever I sought to write at a distance from that history, my work didn't spring to life. The lamentation of Aja in my epic, *Raghu's Dynasty,* is nothing but a representation of my own pain, and . . .

Mallika *hides her face in her hands.* **Kalidas** *stops speaking suddenly, and stares at her for a moment.*

I wanted you to be able to read all this, but the connecting thread broke in such a way that . . .

Removing her hands from her face, **Mallika** *shakes her head in disagreement.*

Mallika The connecting thread never broke.

She picks up the manuscript pages wrapped in cloth, and places them in **Kalidas***'s hands.* **Kalidas** *looks through the pages.*

Kalidas *The Cloud-Messenger*! How did a copy of *The Cloud-Messenger* reach you?

Mallika I have all your works. I was able to get copies of *Raghu's Dynasty* and *The Recognition of Shakuntala* just a few months ago.

Kalidas You have all my works? But how did they become available here? Did . . .?

Mallika The merchants of Ujjayini sometimes travel along this route, too.

Kalidas And you can get these manuscript copies from them?

Mallika I asked them specially to get the copies for me. Each time it took a year or two to find a copy somewhere.

Kalidas And the money to pay for them?

Mallika It took a year or two to get a copy. There was plenty of time to save up the money.

Kalidas *sits down on the window seat with his head bowed.*

Kalidas The deprivations that have gnawed at me for years look even larger today, Mallika! I should have returned to this place years ago, so that I could get soaked in the rain, and then write – write everything that I haven't been able to write so far, and that has been gathering inside me for years like clouds in the season of rain . . .

Sighing deeply, he picks up the blank book lying on the seat, and begins to turn its pages.

. . . but is unable to come down as rain. Because it can't find its proper season. It can't find the right wind . . . What poem is this? These are merely blank pages!

Mallika I made these bark pages with my own hands and stitched them together. I thought that when you came visiting from the capital, I'd give you this blank book as a gift. That I'd say, 'Compose your greatest epic on these pages.' But, even when you visited once, you chose not to visit, and this gift simply lay around here. Now these pages are beginning to fall apart, and I feel hesitant to say that they're for you to write on.

Kalidas *keeps turning the pages.*

Kalidas You made these pages with your own hands so that I may write my epic on them!

Turning the pages, he pauses at one place in the bound volume.

Drops of water have fallen on the pages in various places, but there's no doubt that they weren't drops of rain. It seems that you've written a great deal on these blank sheets with your eyes. And not just with your eyes – in some places, the pages are soiled with beads of sweat, in other places, dry flower petals have left traces of their colour. In many places, your nails have peeled off their layers, your teeth have bitten them apart. And, in addition to these marks, the fading and discolouration caused by the summer sun, the dust of crumbling winter leaves, and the dampness of this house . . . In what sense are these pages blank any more, Mallika? An epic has already been composed on them – an epic with an infinite number of cantos.

He puts down the volume.

What new writing can be done on these pages now?

Rising, he goes to the window. He looks out for a few moments, then turns back towards **Mallika***.*

But there's life still ahead of us. We can begin again from the beginning.

The sound of a baby crying and whimpering is heard from the inner room. **Mallika** *gets up quickly and walks towards it, visibly anxious and perturbed.* **Kalidas** *watches her go, looking as though he were stunned.*

Kalidas   Mallika!

Mallika *pauses, and looks at him.*

Who's crying?

Mallika   This is my present – my here and now.

She goes inside. **Kalidas** *comes and stands in the middle of the room, as though he were frozen.*

Kalidas   Your present?

Someone knocks on the front door, then kicks it open. **Vilom** *appears in the entranceway, cursing at the door. His clothes are muddy. He enters, swaying a little.*

Vilom   On a wet day, brother Vilom, you've slipped and fallen, and fallen straight into a ditch. . . . I've told you so often, don't ever climb up too high. But why would brother Vilom listen? When he first came, the door was shut. He went away and slipped and fell. He came back, and the door was shut. And suppose he'd gone away again? Today is the kind of day when . . .

Seeing **Kalidas**, *he stops mid-sentence. He looks like someone examining a minute object very carefully.*

Who knows what's happened to these eyes of mine? Sometimes unfamiliar figures look very familiar, and sometimes even familiar figures don't look familiar . . . Now, this is a very familiar figure, but I just can't recognize it. I know this figure well, but the personality seems new . . . Hey, brother, do you know me?

Mallika *emerges from the interior and, catching sight of* **Vilom**, *freezes at the door of the inner room.*

Kalidas   Your appearance has changed a lot, but you're still the same person today.

Vilom   I'm acquainted with this voice, and also these words.

He tries to fix his eyes upon **Kalidas**, *and to look closely. Then he suddenly bursts into laughter.*

So, it's you – you? . . . All my troubles from falling and hurting myself have vanished! I've had such a desire to set my eyes upon you, for so long. Come . . .

He opens his arms towards **Kalidas**, *but the latter moves away.*

You won't embrace me? Because my body is soiled? Or do you just detest me? But the connection between you and me can't be broken off so easily. You'd said, hadn't you, that we're very close to each other. Didn't you say that? In all these years I haven't let any distance creep into our closeness. In fact, I believe that we're even closer now.

He turns towards **Mallika**.

Why, Mallika, am I not right? . . . Why are you standing there as though you are frozen? Vilom's no longer an uninvited guest in this home. Now he enters it by right. No? Now he can welcome Kalidas, and offer him hospitality in this house. No?

He turns to **Kalidas** *again.*

You'll say how much of a matter of chance this is – that we met in this house back then, and that we're meeting here again today. But, believe me, it isn't a matter of chance. Whenever you would have come to visit, this is where we would have met.

He turns towards **Mallika** *once more.*

You haven't yet begun the formalities of welcoming Kalidas as a guest? To have a guest in your home after years and to not welcome him properly? Do you know – know how much Kalidas loves the fawns of this region . . .?

He turns back towards **Kalidas**.

There's a little fawn in this house, too . . . Haven't you seen Mallika's little girl? Her eyes are no less beautiful than a fawn's. And do you know what Ashtavakra says? He says . . .

Mallika *steps forward quickly.*

Mallika   Arya Vilom!

Vilom *laughs.*

Vilom   You don't want Kalidas to know what Ashtavakra says!
But I'm not convinced by his observation. That's why I was about to say, it's possible that Kalidas may be able to look and tell how far Ashtavakra is right. Do the little girl's features really resemble Vilom's features, or . . .?

Hiding her face in her hands, **Mallika** *goes to the window seat and sits down.* **Vilom** *moves close to* **Kalidas**.

Come – will you look?

Kalidas   Go away from here, Vilom!

Vilom   Go away?

He laughs.

From this house, or from the province itself? I've heard that governance is a very mighty business. There's a great deal of power and privilege in lordship.

Kalidas   I'm telling you that right now you should leave.

Vilom   Just because you've come back? . . . Because the land you left many years ago seems to be yours again today? . . . Because your rights are perpetual?

He laughs.

You talk as though life has no motion, no vitality, outside you. All that exists is you – there's no one else. But time isn't heartless. It has empowered others, too. Has given them rights. Time didn't stop short on the threshold of this house, bearing oblations of incense and food without actually offering them. It has given others opportunity! It has built something. . . . Are you repelled by what time has built? Because you can't see yourself where you wanted to see yourself?

Vilom *stares at* **Kalidas** *for several moments, and laughs again.*

You want me to leave immediately. I'll leave. Not because you're ordering me to leave. Only because you're a guest here today, and a guest's wish must be honoured.

He walks towards the front door, but pauses near it and looks back at **Mallika**.

Make sure, Mallika, that nothing's lacking in our hospitality. We don't know whether a guest who's visiting us for the first time in many years will ever come back.

He gives both **Mallika** *and* **Kalidas** *a meaningful look and leaves.* **Mallika** *uncovers her face and looks at* **Kalidas**. *Both remain silent for a few moments.*

Mallika   What are you thinking about?

Kalidas *walks over to the window.*

Kalidas   I'm thinking that that was a day in the season of rain exactly like this one. Clouds were amassed in the valley exactly like this, and an untimely darkness had set in. I had seen a wounded fawn in the valley, and picked it up and brought it here. You had attended to it.

Mallika *gets up and goes near him.*

Mallika   You're thinking about something else, too!

Kalidas   And I'm thinking that the expanse of lowlands at the foot of the mountains is still the same. The path that leads to the mountain peak is also the same. The moisture in the wind is as it was before. The sounds in the environment are also as they were before.

Mallika   And?

Kalidas   And that it's the same pulsating consciousness within me. The same heart that surges with emotion. But . . .

Mallika *looks at him in silence.* **Kalidas** *moves from the window to the seat, where he picks up the blank book.*

   . . . but, at that time, this epic of blank pages hadn't been written yet.

Mallika   You were saying that you want to begin again at the beginning.

Kalidas *sighs.*

Kalidas   I said that I want to begin from the beginning. Perhaps it was a confrontation between desire and time. But I see that time is more powerful, because . . .

Mallika   Because?

The baby's crying is audible from the interior once more. **Mallika** *rushes into the inner room.* **Kalidas** *puts down the volume on the seat and speaks as though he were answering her question, but only to himself.*

Kalidas   Because time doesn't wait.

Lightning flashes, and the sound of thunder is heard. **Kalidas** *looks all around once and goes to the window. It begins to rain. Returning to the seat, he picks up the blank book and looks at it one more time, then sets it down again. He casts a glance towards the inner room, then goes to the entranceway. He pauses there for a moment, as though lost in thought. Then he leaves, and shuts the front door behind him. The sound of thunder and rain increases. After a few moments,* **Mallika** *emerges from the inner room, holding the baby close to her breast. Not seeing* **Kalidas**, *she runs to the window.*

Mallika   Kalidas!

Still clutching the baby, she goes from the window to the entranceway, and throws open the front door.

Kalidas!

She begins to move towards the threshold, but, looking at the child in her arms, comes to a dead stop. As though broken in spirit, she goes to the window seat and sits down. Hugging the child even closer to herself, she begins to weep as she kisses it. Lightning flashes again and again, and the thunder continues to roll.

The End

Whirlpool (*Aavart*) (1978)

Datta Bhagat

Translation by George Nagies, Vimal Thorat and Eleanor Zelliot

Datta Bhagat (1945–) is a Marathi playwright, critic, and Professor at the Dr. Babasaheb Ambedkar Marathawada University. A leader in the field of *Dalit* Theatre, he has authored several critically acclaimed plays whose chief objective is to give a voice to *Dalits*, people who belong to marginalized caste groups, and highlight the challenges they pose to upper-caste myths and ideologies. His critical contributions include *Dalit Chetna aur Marathi Dalit Rangmanch* (*Dalit Consciousness and Marathi Dalit Theater*).

Originally written in Marathi and published in 1978, *Whirlpool* is about *Dalit* identity and caste stratification in post-independence India. It foregrounds these themes by showing the social exclusion and mistreatment of three generations of a *Dalit* family – Tukaram, his father, and Tukaram's son, Monahar – by the upper castes. The play exposes the caste system through the sacrificial killing of Tukaram's father sixty years ago, who was deemed responsible for a cholera outbreak in the village because he had touched the feet of a Brahmin. Thus, it throws light on the perpetration of abuse historically and points out the ongoing violence that is justified through rituals and socially sanctioned customs even though constitutionally caste discrimination was banned. The play is informed by the influence of Dr B. R. Ambedkar, a lawyer and an architect of the Constitution of independent India, who advocated for the 'Annihilation of Caste' for the empowerment of *Dalits*. The influence of Ambedkar can be seen in the play's questioning of the law by alluding to three types of systems that dispense justice: the village *panchayat*, Ram Rajya (the Kingdom of Rama), and a modern court with a *nyayamurti* or judge where unjust verdicts are handed out. The mock trials in these differential court-like settings raise the question of rights by providing commentary on overt discrimination through the denial of temple entry and access to wells for drinking water, to *Dalits*. As such, they prompt readers and audiences to think about equality and 'the anguish of an age-old inheritance of suffering; and highlight the contradictions between constitutional law that abolished caste discrimination and the continuing caste hierarchies that strip human beings of dignity based on 'customary practice'.

Bhagat dramatizes these themes through the conventions of *Tamasha* – a popular theatrical form that engages with audiences through music, singing, and dancing. To this end, the Stage-Manager and the Jester, who introduce the importance of *Dalit* literature, deploy musical instruments such as the *dholak* (drum) and *tuntuni* (stringed instrument) to communicate with the audience through various forms of role-playing.

Ultimately, the play emphasizes the need to acknowledge and hear *Dalit* voices because in 'a democracy, everybody has the right to speak.' But does the Jester and Stage Manager's insistence that they must keep moving 'in circles' offer a way out of the quagmire of caste politics that the play highlights?

Reference

Bhagat, Datta. *Whirlpool*. Translated by Georg Nagies, Vimal Thorat and Eleanor Zelliot in *Modern Indian Drama*, edited by G. P. Deshpande. New Delhi: Sahitya Akademi, 2000.

*The stage is empty. The voices of the dholak (small drum) and the tuntuni (stringed instrument) resound. Slowly the rhythm quickens. To the increased rhythm the Sutradhar (**Stage-Manager**) and behind him the vidusak (**Jester**) enter the stage. They are one with the rhythm. They together cry out 'ha, ha, ha' make a gesture and stand fixed in the middle of the stage. The background music stops.*

Stage-Manager Johar, Mai-Bap, Johar.[1]
I am the Mahar of Your Mahars.
I am so hungry I come for Your leavings.
I am full of hope; I am the slave of Your slaves.
Cokha says: I have brought a bowl for Your leftover food.

Jester Hey, hey, hey!

Stage-Manager Why, what happened?

Jester Why are you harping on that same old theme again?

Stage-Manager It's not like that at all. *Johar* is ancient, but its meaning is modern

Jester Fine! And what is its meaning?

Stage-Manager *Johar* is ancient, but there is a new meaning.

Jester Oh yes, I got that! But what is the new meaning?

Stage-Manager New meaning? Now, why am I supposed to know that? Nowadays this is called Dalit literature.

Jester What kind of affliction is that?

Stage-Manager You don't know of Dalit literature?

Jester No, not at all.

Stage-Manager I don't know either.

Jester Vety well.

Stage-Manager A definition cannot be given, but whatever happens. there is this Dalit literature.

Jester I don't understand.

Stage-Manager You don't understand? Even if you have understood, what will you do? Definition is just definition.

Jester All right. And yet, if I knew, it would be better.

Stage-Manager It's a belch, isn't it?

Jester Is this something to ask about?

---

[1] *Johar* was the traditional greeting of a Mahar (a Dalit caste of Maharashtra) to his superiors. Here God Vitthal is addressed with Mai-Bap (*mother and father*). The whole verse is actually an *abhanga* (*Bhakti-song*) by Cokhamela, a saint who lived in thirteenth-/fourteenth-century Maharashtra.

Stage-Manager Now tell me . . .

Jester Hey, everybody knows that.

Stage-Manager Even so, give a definition, won't you?

Jester Oh no, a definition cannot be given.

Stage-Manager But belching you do understand, don't you?

Jester Oh yes, now I have understood.

Stage-Manager What have you understood?

Jester That what the meaning of Dalit literature is.

*The **Jester** looks to the right side of the stage.*

Stage-Manager You have understood, haven't you? Very well. Hey, what are you looking at over there?

Jester I'm waiting.

Stage-Manager For whom?

Jester Who should I be waiting for? Hey, the greetings and salutations are finished, so why haven't Radha and the Gopis appeared yet?

Stage-Manager Oh my, how backward are you?

Jester Meaning what? Has Radha appeared before I came?

Stage-Manager No, it's not like that at all. Nowadays the revered Datta Bal[2] has forbidden the Radha-Krsna tale.

Jester What Datta Bal is this that prohibits the entry of the God?

Stage-Manager Not the God! He has prohibited making fun of Radha and Krsna.

Jester Very well.

Stage-Manager What's very well?

Jester Who prohibited that? Datta Bal, is it?

Stage-Manager There revered Datta Bal.

Jester How can Bal understand such a meaningful matter?

Stage-Manager It's not like that! Ridiculing God Krsna is unacceptable to him.

Jester Ridiculing God Krsna is unacceptable to him?

---

[2] Datta Bal is a self styled saint figure, popular during the 1970s. He pleaded to purge Tamasa a folk play of its traditional Radha-Krishna scene, which is a very significant formal element of Tamasa. He felt it was blasphemous.

Stage-Manager Oh yes, it's unacceptable to him.

Jester That's really very nice.

Stage-Manager What do you mean?

Jester Now that God Krsna will not appear, I'll have the chance of teasing Radha.

Stage-Manager What terrible things you say.

Jester In my college, teasing the girls angered the principal a lot, and now you speak about teasing Radha in a play as if it was something very terrible. As if you were the principal's father!

Stage-Manager Now it's enough of your chit chat. Keep quiet, won't you?

Jester Let me speak a little louder now. During the nineteen month of the Emergency I kept quiet, didn't I?

Stage-Manager Take care!

Jester What happened? Has she come? [*Looking for Radha.*]

Stage-Manager Be quiet, that's the meaning of take care.

Jester I thought Radha has come when you said take care.

Stage-Manager Stop that crazy talk.

The dialogue becomes rhythmical.

Jester Done so.

Stage-Manager Begin telling the story.

Jester Done so.

Stage-Manager We will go a little further. (*They both advance four steps. They stop and look at each other.*)

Jester Further we cannot go. We cannot go beyond this row of lights.

Stage-Manager We will go back a little.

Both go four steps backwards and then stop suddenly. Having turned around they look at each other.

Jester We cannot go back any further. We cannot cross the back curtain.

Stage-Manager Why do you behave like that, *my lion* [=my hero]?

Jester All these circumstances have done me in.

Stage-Manager What's the meaning! What's the matter?

Jester The Yesibai-Tamasa has come to the village.[3]

---

[3] Tamasa is the principal form of folk theatre in Maharashtra.

Stage-Manager So let it be.

Jester It has slunk into the theatre.

Stage-Manager So let it be.

Jester It's called *loknatya* [people's theatre].

Stage-Manager So let it be. What is so wrong about that?

Jester Why are you so disturbed? It's like getting a bubbly high drinking lemon soda. But look, all friends look down on that Vithabai's act.

A song is sung in the style of Vithabai. [Vithabai is a famous female performer, who was honoured by the president of India.]

Stage-Manager If Tamasa becomes a little high class, what's wrong with that?

Jester High class? What mother's son can refuse that? But then it will be a drama, not Tamasa. (*He sings in a rhythmical voice.*) Going forward we burn on the stage lights, going backwards we hit the wall.

Stage-Manager So where shall we go? What shall we do? Tell me your opinion.

Jester We cannot stay here.

Stage-Manager We cannot Stay here.

Jester We must go back.

Stage-Manager We must go back.

Jester We must go forward.

Stage-Manager We must go forward.

Jester We must not go forward, brother, we must not go backwards.

Stage-Manager We must not go forward, brother, we must not go backwards.

Jester We must move in circles.

Stage-Manager Oh yes, we must move in circles.

Jester We must move in circles, move in circles.

Stage-Manager We must move in circles, Let's go together.

They begin to dance in circles.

Jester Hey, stop, stop my friend. Look, we have come a long way. Oh, fine.

Stage-Manager Then hey, is that Sonapur?

Jester Is it near Bamani?

Stage-Manager Definitely it's near Narsi-Bamani.

Jester Narsi-Bamani, that means our Namdev's[4] Narsi-Bamani?

Stage-Manager Do you think Namdev was your classmate?

Jester No, no! Wasn't Namdev in the BA course [*studied*]?

Stage-Manager Will it break your tongue if you call him Namdev Maharaj?

Jester To address a historical person only by his name is today's fashion.

Stage-Manager You are talking about future things, but actually we have come to a point in time very long past.

Jester Past? How long past?

Stage-Manager We have travelled thirty-one years backward.

Jester Is it so?

Stage-Manager Do you think I'm lying? Look at this, this *dindi (group of devotees)* is probably the *pava (little group of devotees)* of Thakur Maharaj.[5]

Jester Hey, yes, my friend. Today his stopping-place is here in Sonapur. Tomorrow it will be Bamani, and the day after tomorrow it will be Narsi. In Narsi all the tents will be gathered together and from there all will go to Pandharpur- hey! Will we go to Pandharpur?

Stage-Manager What?

Jester (*in a devotional mood*) To meet with God Vithai. Nowadays she resides in Pandharpur. (*He sits down suddenly and is about to talk about Vithabhai. The* **Stage-Manager** *stops him halfway . . .*)

Stage-Manager Yes, yes, yes.

Jester What happened?

Stage-Manager Hay, this is not that Tamasa dancer Vithabhai. The meaning of Vithabhai is Mother Vithoba.
(*They namaste to the invisible Vithai and sing:*) Mother Vithai is the devotee's mother.

'Jnanraj Mavli, Tukaram', with these cheers the dindi *enters. In front there is the maharaja, behind him the bearer of the musical instrument, behind him the banner-bearer, who is a very old man. The* **Jester** *and the* **Stage-Manager** *go and meet with the dindi. When the bhajan singing has stopped the maharaja comes forward.*

Maharaja Sidnak! (*A man comes forward from the dindi.*)

---

[4] Namdev is the name of a fourteenth-century saint who founded the tradition of pilgrimage to Pandharpur.
[5] The dindi is part of a palkhi, a procession on its way to the pilgrimage centre of Pandharpur. The main dindi carries the footprints of the saint celebrated by that group. Each caste has its own dindi. Thakur Maharaj heads the dindi of the Marathas.

Sidnak Yes please. (*Having touched the* **Maharaja**'s *feet he politely stands a little aside. Afterwards all in turns follow* **Sidnak**'s *example.*)

Maharaja Sidnak, we have arrived in Sonapur, haven't we?

Sidnak Yes maharaj, every year we stop here, by the Pipal tree at this crossroad. Tukaram Baba always comes here to join us.

Jakhu My goodness, how can we ever forget this Pipal tree? This railway track didn't exist then.

Jester You keep very old matters in mind.

Stage-Manager What did you think, that this old bone is of today? [=*He is very old man.*]

Jakhu It was a vety bad season, you weren't born yet, I was a youth then, do you understand?

Jester That means fifty or sixty years ago, doesn't it?

Jakhu Why fifty or sixty years? It's exactly sixty years since. This Tukaram, who'll come here to join us, he was ten years old then. At the time of this affair this ox-cart's track didn't exist yet. The dindi of Cintaman Maharaj comes down this road. And on this road Tukaram's father came along, and he went straight to touch the feet of the maharaja.

Jester Brother, this was a time of devotion to the saints.

Jakhu What, you're talking about devotion? Tukaram's father was beaten up.

Jester He was beaten up? How did that come about!

Jakhu Hey, Cintaman Maharaj is a *Bhamburda,* and this *yeskar* low caste grabbed and touched the feet of the maharaja . . .

Jester Oh, when Tukaram's father got beaten up, nobody did anything?

Jakhu He did, didn't he? He got beaten up, but why? Because he abandoned the customs of his caste. Hey, Tuka says, when you're low caste, you've got to eat dirt.

Jester But why did he lower his head to the feet of the maharaja?

Jakhu What can we do? Pandurang himself appeared before him in a dream.

Jester And why in that case Pandurang didn't save him?

Jakhu The God was putting him to trial.

Jester What was the trial?

Jakhu The test was still to come . . .

Jester What happened then?

Jakhu The cholera broke out in the village.

Jester The cholera?

Jakhu   Yes brother, cholera comes like a curse.

Jester   And else?

Jakhu   What else? On the first day Cintaman Maharaj departed for the other world.

Jester   Alas! And then?

Jakhu   In two days the whole village was finished.

Jester   What happened next?

Jakhu   What should have happened? There was a message from the Goddess through the mouth of the *bhakta* [*devotee, worshipper*], saying that she demanded Tukaram's father as a sacrifice.

Maharaja   Oh my God, your will is unfathomable.

Jakhu   Oh maharaja, in this well over there Tukaram's father threw his body. Brothers, he was a great devotee.

Maharaja   Pandurang, Pandurang . . .

Jakhu   From that time onwards the Bhamburda Maharaja never again travelled this road. He has taken the upward road. [*i.e. has gone to heaven*]

Maharaja   Sidnak, has Tukaram not yet arrived?

Sidnak   I will go to the village and look for him.

Maharaja   The warkaris [*devotees*] of Pandhari,
Who keeps count of piety?

While he says that all stand in a row as before. **Sidnak** *walks around them and comes to stand behind the back of one of them. Those who are included in this dindi stand with their backs to the audience.*

Sidnak   Tukaram baba, what has happened? Tukaram baba, Tukaram baba . . .

Tukaram (*stepping out of the row*)   Who is there? Who is it at this time of the evening?

Sidnak   Why, Tukaram baba, have you forgotten what day it is today? Won't you come to Narsi this year?

Tukaram (*steps out of the house*)   Heaven forbid! How could I possibly forget that?

Suddenly he lowers his head to **Sidnak**'s *feet.*

Sidnak   You forgot it just like that. The maharaja did worry.

Tukaram   The *Josi* [*astrologer*] of our village said that today's lunar mansion is Tuesday. Therefore I was of the opinion that you will come on Sunday, but now you are two days early.

Sidnak   The lunar mansion is not Tuesday's but Sunday's, and on Sunday we have to go to Narsi.

Tukaram It seems as if Josi Baba got something wrong.

Sidnak We will look into that later. It's getting late. The maharaja is sitting and waiting at the other side of the village.

Tukaram Oh yes, I will call together everybody. Uncle Pira, hey Uncle Pira, who is there? Tell the dindi has come, go quickly. Gopala, hey Gopala

One person emerges from the row touches the feet of **Sidnak** *and stands away politely.*

I don't *see* Manohar, so call him, Uncle Pira, ...

Piraji Tuka, Manohar is not listening to anyone. Who knows what someone who has been to Pune and Bombay has learned there.
And then he sits here and teaches it to the boys . . .

Gopala Piraji, but he won't tell them something bad, will he?

Piraji He tells them to give up the caste duties in the village. He is following Bhim Baba [*Dr Ambedkar*] now.

Manohar What's wrong with that? God gave you two hands. So toil and labour.

Piraji And who will remove the dead cattle of the village? [*a traditional duty of the Mahars*]

Manohar The one to whom it belongs. Who calls for a *Bhangi* [*sweeper*] to wash the bottoms of the children.

Piraji But why? Why should we change?

Manohar People say that you don't live cleanly and that you therefore contaminate them. That you eat fish and meat and that you will desecrate the deity. I instructed the children of all the nearby villages. They live cleanly. They don't eat fish and meat – therefore we are fit to go to the Hanuman temple.

Piraji That's what I've heard, too. It's true.

Manohar What have you heard?

Piraji That you will desecrate the Hanuman deity.

Manohar Oh no, we will go to the temple. We will worship the deity.

Piraji What if the big people get to know?

Manohar We will tell them. Not today, but on the day the dindi will come.

Piraji The dindi has come already, Manohar. The maharaja is already on the road. The maharaja is waiting for our arrival.

Manohar How did that happen? The Josi said that today's lunar mansion is Tuesday.

Gopala It means that the Josi Maharaja has deceived us.

Manohar It doesn't matter. For this task I needed his help, but without his help, anyway, we will enter the temple.

Piraji Tuka, make this child of yours understand. This will set the village afire.

Tukaram What is his fault? Jnanoba, Cokhoba, Savata, didn't they all sit in one row? [*with the upper caste people, at a meal.*]

Piraji But these were saints, mahatmas!

Manohar Therefore their conduct should be exemplary for us. We should follow in their footsteps. Going to the Pandharpur temple together with my people, I will worship the deity, God lives in all of us. So how can our touch desecrate the God?

Piraji But don't you know your village?

Tukaram What can they do? They will boycott us, like they have done before. But there is no tyranny now. The chief sahab[6] will set everything right.

Sidnak Tukaram baba, we can talk later. The maharaja is waiting?

Tukaram Hey, Gopal Baba, take the water-pot and now let's go quickly . . . Let's go. Piramama . . .

A song: 'You noble pilgrims'.

All 'Merciful mother and father.'

Tukaram 'How much kindness you have given us, oh God.'

All 'What can we say, you are far above us'

Shouting 'Jnanoba Mavli, Santaram Mavli, Tukaram' they all form a dindi and the procession goes its way. Lights dim and all stand with their backs to the audience as before. The **Jester** *and the* **Stage-Manager** *step in the middle of the stage.*

Jester My lion, we have come a long way.

Stage-Manager Yes, we have arrived in Sonapur.

Jester Have you heard what Piramama and Manohar were talking?

Stage-Manager Yes, heard it.

Jester Yes, and the public heard it, too.

Stage-Manager That's true.

Jester This mad Tukaram sides with his son.

Stage-Manager Yes, and what can be done?

Jester He wiil be beaten up for nothing.

---

[6] 'Chief sahab' means the Police Inspector.

Stage-Manager Yes, he will be beaten up. But why is this so important?

Jester What?

Stage-Manager Don't worry, the village people have come to beat him up.

Jester The village people have come to beat him up? Where are they? (*He acts as if he were running away.*)

Stage-Manager Stop. Hey brother, think for a moment, if the village people have come to beat him up, then what is going to happen to us? (*He mimes running away.*)

Jester Very well. And then we will go to the hospital. Ravsaheb Shriman Dheknaji Dhamdhere, the president of the welfare society, will visit the injured. A splendid picture in the newspaper.

Stage-Manager Whether there is something else or not, now I have understood the politics behind it . . .

Jester He is one wheel of Baba's chariot [*Baba's chariot: Dr Babasaheb Ambedkar's movement*]. The wheel turns, and politics turn with the wheel. Well now, tell me, what did Tukaram say about the chief sahab in the meantime?

Stage-Manager It was during Mughal rule. Will you listen?

Jester Don't tell it to me, tell it to the public.

Stage-Manager Well now, listen. (*Singing*)
I heard the tale of what happened in Sonapur.
The tale of the quarrel between Baji the goldsmith and Candar Patel.
It was not a big matter, but enough for a quarrel.
In the struggle of the two Tukya got caught up.
Sonar claimed the embankment, the Patel was besides himself with rage.
He seized Sonar's fields and wrought havoc on them.
They summoned Tukya, he came, the village council was convened.
'Speak in my favour' the Patel said to him, with threats.
Bear in mind that we have the accounts of your debts of many generations.
Speak, to whom does the field belong?
Your speech will tell that your master is the Patel.
   The superintendent came to the village.
   He summoned Tukya.
   The superintendent said: I'm taking an oath before God.
   To ensure the respectability of the law.
   Tukya spoke the truth,
   And favoured Sonar.
Boiling with anger the Patel said that the Mahar's Baluta[7] is finished.
Nobody protected them, and they got beaten up.

---

[7] Baluta is a relationship between the Mahar and the village, i.e. certain prerequisites such as a little land, grain, etc., for specific duties, in this case, land boundary decisions.

Jester Therefore Tukaram had called the Chief Sahab?

Stage-Manager The Chief Sahab scolded Candar Patel, trashed his servants [*Patel's servants who conspired with him*] and went the way he had come.

Jester When Tukaram was beaten up, what were the other people doing?

Stage-Manager What were they doing when Tukaram's father was thrown into the well? That very – (*upon the last word the standing dindi turns around and begins to sing a bhajan: 'Let the head be cut, let the body break . . . [. . . but the truth must he told]' The* **Jester** *and the* **Stage-Manager** *are included in the dindi. The people of the dindi stand with their backs to the audience as before when two persons step out as if they have met on the road.*)

Kisan Ram Ram Mahadubhai.

Mahadu Ram Ram.

Kisan Today you are early going to your field.

Mahadu Yes, I'm thinking of going to Narsi tomorrow.

Kisan Has it reached your ears what nonsense Tukaram's son is speaking?

Mahadu What has happened?

Kisan He was away from the village for four years . . .

Mahadu I know that.

Kisan He has gone to Dehu, to Pune, to Bombay. Having seen some half wrong, half right things he has come here and now tells these things to everybody.

Mahadu What is he telling?

Kisan Well, the untouchable Mahar boys listened to him and now are bent on entering the Vithoba temple of Pandharpur.

Mahadu Hey hey! Is it so? Has the Kaliyug come?

Kisan Therefore Tukaram Maharaj said – listen, the fruit of Kaliyug is the origin of future misfortune. Four classes, eighteen castes will dine all togther.

Mahadu What is going to happen next?

Kisan What do you expect? The Pujari will lock the temple and he will run away.

Mahadu What a good thing to do.

Kisan There will be no benefit in it.

Mahadu Why?

Kisan They'll break the padlock and then they will push inside.

Mahadu When the deity is enraged it'll become known. When Tukaram's father had touched Cintaman Maharaja's feet the whole village was shaken because of the cholera.

Kisan   I was too little at that time.

Mahadu   But I understood a bit.

Kisan   What happened then?

Mahadu   What should have happened? Police Inspector Candar Patel is a very dangerous man. He was feared even when there was the tyranny. He summoned the *Potraj*.[8] Through the Potraj there was a message from the Devi, and the message was: 'I want Tukaram's father offered as a sacrifice. He is at the root of all the sins.'

Kisan   The Mother Devi really said so?

Mahadu   How stupid are you? What Mother Devi . . .? The Patel had intimidated the Potraj. What power has the Potraj to contradict the Patel.

Kisan   Well, well. And then . . .?

Mahadu   And then what? With array and pomp, striking up music, they all went to Tukaram's house. There Piraji tied his hands and his feet and threw the sinner into the deep well there.

Kisan   You destroyed that sin. Now what are you going to do with that other sin?

Mahadu   With what other sin?

Kisan   With the sinful Manohar. I heard he's going to enter our temple.

Mahadu   What we did to his grandfather, that's what we're going to do to him.

Josi   There, he has made full preparations. Sit here, keep talking.

Mahadu   Kisan?

Josi   This lad, Manohar, just today has gathered four boys together.

Starts moving.

Mahadu   Where are you going right now?

Josi   We've also made some preparations, haven't we, some preparations for going to the cremation ground. The dindi will come, and the lads took the firm resolve to enter the temple that day.

Mahadu   That means today . . .?

Nosi   No, the day after tomorrow . . . I told them the wrong day of the week, so they're two days late, otherwise the story of our village would have reached Pandharpur. All their preparations are useless, as the dindi has come early.

Mahadu   Otherwise they would have entered the temple.

Josi   This rascal not only called the lads from Sonapur, but from all the surrounding

---

[8] The Potraj is servant of the goddess Mariai and functions as a trance-oracle.

villages. They were all coming. Now come. We are prepared for the day after tomorrow.

Kisan   *Josi* Maharaja, you acted very shrewdly.

Josi   What shrewdness is there in what I did?

Kisan   What else can it be called than shrewd? You alerted all the villages.

Josi   Yes, you're right. But that wasn't because of my shrewdness. I only followed Candar Patel's orders. My goodness, how could we dare to disregard his orders?

Mahadu   He is as trustworthy as Piraji was.

Kisan   But the Patel has . . .

Josi   . . . no idea of all this? The arrangements for later on are already complete, too. The work left with us now is only to light the torch.

Kisan   Whose . . . ?

Josi   Nobody's. His plan was to enter the temple, wasn't it? That's what we've heard from himself, right?

Mahadu   Look, these people have just come.

Piraji, **Tukaram**, **Manohar** *and* **Gopal** *step out from the row, singing a bhajan. Seeing the* **Josi Maharaja** *they are taken aback and remain standing a little away.*

Kisan   Where are you going, brothers?

Piraji   Thakur Maharaja's dindi has come, hasn't it?

Josi   But that means that they're two days early. It seems as if they've confused the lunar mansions [=*the days of the week*].

Tukaram   The maharaja would never make a mistake regarding the lunar mansions [=*the current date*].

Josi   Hey, why? What do you mean to tell us? Do you mean to say that we can't read the calendar?

Mahadu   Tukya, you've become very proud. Is it your maharaja who performs the village josi's duties?

Kisan   Do you mean to insult our Josi Maharaja?

Manohar   Why do you accuse us? Who did we insult?

Kisan   Shut up, rascal. You don't understand a thing. Tukya, has your father ever read the calendar?

Manohar   Don't mention my grandfather, Patel.

Mahadu   Yes, yes, don't mention that matter, Kisan. Have you forgotten how the cholera has knocked down the village? If you bring out that matter again the cholera will strike once again.

Tukaram Why do you speak about my father, Patel? He suffered the fruits of his own deeds.

Kisan And today you will suffer the fruits of your son's deeds.

Tukaram What has he done?

Kisan As if you didn't know.

Mahadu Hey, Kisan, if you go too far he will possibly call the chief sahab. And it's still the chief sahab's rule here.

Kisan He won't live until the chief sahab gets here.

Manohar What are these threats good for? Tell me my faults.

Kisan You know your faults quite well. You contrived a plan.

Manohar Are you talking about us entering the temple.

Kisan Now you're talking straight.

Manohar And that's why the Josi Maharaja told us the wrong lunar mansion?

Kisan That's the truth.

Manohar After all the preparations had been finished I was the one to tell everything.

Kisan Which preparations? You mean to desecrate our deities?

Manohar If we enter the temple will it desecrate your deities?

Kisan As if you didn't know.

Manohar Your deity is that impotent? It will be polluted?

Kisan But why don't you have your own temple?

Manohar Isn't that temple ours, too?

Kisan Oh no, it isn't.

Manohar Is God the patrimony of any one caste?

Mahadu This lad won't teach us *brahmajnan* [*divine knowledge*]. You're defiling us.

Manohar You're all talking about bodily impurity. But the soul is pure and shining. Bodily impurity originates from the body. Show me that religion that teaches that the body is born pure.

Mahadu Hey, Tukya, look, your son is full of wisdom, take care of him, otherwise . . .

Manohar Is it in this society an offence to have knowledge?

Mahadu What is to be must be plenty. Now say 'I won't go to the temple', beg Josi Maharaja's pardon and then go . . .

Josi   Yes; beg forgiveness, and do so by rubbing your nose on the ground [*i.e. with abject entreaties*].

Piraji   Let us pass by, mai-bap. He made a mistake, we beg your pardon, and now let us go home.

Manohar   What for do you beg their pardon, Piraji dada? As yet we didn't commit a sin.

Josi   No sin? You mean saying that we don't read the calendar right is not a sin?

Mahadu   You mean to say our religion is debased?

Manohar   We didn't say all these things.

Josi   How falsely he speaks!

Piraji   Beg their pardon, Tukya, that's what I beg from you, rubbing my nose on the ground.

Sidnak   The maharaja is waiting, make haste, tukaram baba.

Manohar   What maharaja? Devotion to whom? Do what you think is right for you. Shall we look on silently, whatever happens? A deity that is desecrated by our touch is not our deity. That religion that keeps us away is not our religion. It's better to live one day the life of a lion than to live a thousand days as a meek sheep, that's the message that was given to us.

Mahadu   Pirya, tie his hands and feet . . .

Manohar   That's not necessary. We will go wherever you tell us. But I want to make it known that it is not in your power to make a decision on justice and injustice. Not even the goddess who is pretending to enter the body of the potraj, not even she has the power to decide on justice or injustice. It's the people who rule, that's what Gandhi and Nehru say.

Mahadu   That may be the case there, but here it's Candar Patel who rules. Pirya, have you tied them or not?

Piraji *acts like tying them.* **Sidnak** *emerges from one side, the rest from the other side, then they stand in a row as before. When they've formed the row they sing a bhajan. Slowly the dindi joins them in this song.*

Where are you busy my father, Pandurang of Pandhari . . .
In your court are holy middlemen making people's lives miserable
Society becomes meaningless
Only fear is left
Oh master, stop your self satisfaction
Deny the false worship.

When the song is finished only the dindi is in motion. **Sidnak** *steps out, panting heavily.*

Sidnak   Maharaja, there are dire difficulties. (*This debate is going on while cheering shouts of 'jnanba tukaram' begin in a low voice.*)

Maharaja Why, what happened?

Sidnak Tukaram baba has been brought before the pancayat.[9]

Maharaja But why?

Sidnak His boy has been talking about entering the Hanuman temple.

Maharaja The Bhamburda temple?

Sidnak Yes, my maharaja.

Maharaja Who is this rascal?

Sidnak Tukaram's Manohar.

Maharaja Tukaram's Manohar?

Sidnak Yes, my maharaja.

Maharaja (*beginning a bhajan*)
Hari, Hari, what can we say now? How can we say it? Hey,
We have the right only of leftovers.
The bhakti of the saints is very good.
Vithoba's name is easy to chant.
My only wish
Is to be without caste, says Cokha.
God will fulfil my wish life after life
Pundlik varda Hari'ri Vitthal. Jnanoba Mauli Jnanraj Mavli Tukaram.[10]

Delighted the dindi leaves. Only the **Stage-Manager** *and the* **Jester** *remain on stage. They're dancing.*

Jester Jnanoba Mauli Jnanraj Mauli Tukaram.

Stage-Manager Jnanoba Mauli Jnanraj Mauli Tukaram.

Jester Manohar Mauli Piraji Mauli Tukaram.

Stage-Manager Manohar Mauli Piraji Mauli Tukaram.

Jester Piraji Tukaram.

Stage-Manager Piraji Tukaram.

Jester Tukaram, Tukaram.

Stage-Manager Tukaram, Tukaram.

Jester Does he become a Ghasiram?

Stage-Manager Ghasiram, Ghasiram.

---

[9] village court.
[10] a chant of all the names of the Vithoba cult.

Jester (*holding himself up suddenly*)   Hey, why are we talking about this Ghasiram? He is the *kotval* [*chief police officer*], isn't he?

Stage-Manager   Oh yes, definitely. The one *kotval* who takes revenge on Nanasaheb in Tendulkar's play.

Jester   How did this fellow come here?

Stage-Manager   He didn't come here, but he was brought here, but what for?

Jester   There's no meaning in it.

Stage-Manager   No meaning in it? Why, what happened?

Jester   Tukaram will never become Ghasiram.

Stage-Manager   Meaning what?

Jester   That means I'm asking what else can there be? Is Tukaram now captured and tied up or not?

Stage-Manager   They have taken him, haven' they?

Jester   But why?

Stage-Manager   Because he has insulted the Josi Maharaja.

Jester   Who told the wrong lunar mansion?

Stage-Manager   Josi Maharaja did.

Jester   To whom?

Stage-Manager   To Tukaram, devotee of Vithoba.

Jester   So who is at fault?

Stage-Manager   Josi Maharaja is. (*He is alarmed.*)

Jester   Yes, yes. Don't panic. The punishment is nineteen months in jail . . . Have you understood?

Stage-Manager   Yes, yes. Got it.

Jester   Tukaram called the chief sahab to the village. The distribution of the Baluta to the Mahars began, but what did Tukaram get?

Stage-Manager   He got beaten up by the Patel's servants.

Jester   Now that Manohar talks about entering the temple, what'll he get?

Stage-Manager (*silent*)

Jester   Wherever one goes, the dhak leaves remain three [= *there is poverty and helplessness*]. Tukaram's father, Tukaram, Tukaram's son Manohar, they are always the victims.

Stage-Manager   Meaning what?

Jester In what manner does the spinning top move? Gar, gar, gar, but on one spot only. Tomorrow Manohar's child will move around like that, too.

Stage-Manager I don't understand.

Jester Tukaram is a very straightforward, honest person, isn't he?

Stage-Manager It seems so, yes.

Jester Just like Tukaram, Sakharam and Gangaram are straightforward and honest.

Stage-Manager Maybe, maybe.

Jester Whosoever's name is – ram, that person is straightforward and honest.

Stage-Manager Oh, I understand. Go on.

Jester Then instead of being made Tukaram or Gangaram, why wasn't he made Ghasiram?

Stage-Manager I have no objection.

Jester I haven't either, but it hasn't happened like that. . . .

Stage-Manager Why?

Jester Because beginning with Sambuk, it seems to everybody as if Rama's killing of Sambuk was to his own good.

Stage-Manager Now you're moving into very deep waters.

Jester Oh no, I've gone into the Ramayana.

A throne is brought quickly. There are cheers of 'Ramacandra ki jay' [May Ramacandra be victorious]. The **Jester** *seats himself in the manner of Ramacandraji. From the cheering crowd two servants come and stand waiting to either side of him. One holds a royal parasol. The* **Jester** *accepts with great dignity the cheers from the crowd.*

Ministers, Friends, people –

A man makes an effort to enter.

One Have pity, my Lord, have pity.

Jester Gatekeeper, give way to this petitioner. Let him come in.

One My Lord, I was looted. Rescue me. (*Kneeling in entreaty.*)

Jester Why, petitioner, speak out, what's the matter?

One My Lord, I'm a poor Brahman.

Jester What's the matter, Brahman? We will rescue you. Which kind of difficulties have befallen you?

One My little son has died, my Lord. In this *Ramrajya* [*the kingdom of Rama: a perfect world*] I was made wretched.

Jester For what reason?

One In the kingdom there is such a sin perpetrated that my son has died.

Jester Brahman, give us your blessing, we'll free you from your worries. We'll search for the origin of this evil. We'll search every corner of the kingdom and find the cause of this evil.

Stage-Manager As you will, maharaja . . . .

Jester The responsibility for the distress of this poor Brahman is ours. I order that you now go. Search every part of the kingdom.

Stage-Manager Your order, maharaja.

In the meantime the tied **Manohar** *is dragged in forcibly.*

Jester What's going on, my servant.

Servant Maharaja, this *Nisada* [*a low-caste man, an outcaste*] practised ascetic penance in a wood near Ayodhya. And this unfortunate creature wasn't ready to come here.

Jester What's your name?

Manohar Sambuk.

Jester You're a Nisada?

Manohar Yes, sir. . . .

One Visva Samraksak [*all-protector*] Bhagvan [*worshipful Lord*] he is the sinner because of whom the son of this poor Brahman has died. The wrongful penance of this Sudra is at the root of this evil.

Jester You were practising ascetic penance?

Manohar Yes, I was.

Jester You also know that this is wrong?

Manohar Yes, I do.

Jester (*standing up*) Counsellors, remove this sinner from here. And then behead him.

He descends from his lion's seat (throne). With cheers of 'Ramacandra ki jay' [May Ramacandra be victorious] all exit. The throne is still in its place. While the crowd is cheering, a chair is brought and placed facing the throne. It's a chair of an old type. The **Jester** *seats himself on this chair and spreads his legs.*

Jester Attendant, hey, attendant . . .

Stage-Manager Yes, master.

Jester Hey, why do you stand there pitched like a pole of a collapsing roof?

Stage-Manager I'm just waiting for Mahadurav and Kisanrav.

Jester Hey, they will come, won't they? Is Josi Maharaja worried because of that?

Stage-Manager Now they've all come, haven't they?

Kisan   Ram Ram, Patel.

Kahadu   Ram Ram.

Josi   Ram Ram.

Jester   Josi Maharaja, why do you look so annoyed?

Mahadu   Something bad happened.

Jester   What happened?

Kisan   Hey, wasn't Tukya's son about to desecrate our deity?

Mahadu   Tukya said that Josi Maharaja cannot read the holy calendar.

Jester   Have you heard that with your own ears?

Kisan   Do you think I'm telling lies?

Jester   So, why did you come with empty hands? Why haven't you grabbed him and brought him here?

Mahadu   He's down below.

Jester   Bring him before me.

Stage-Manager   Hey, bring them here.

Piraji *brings the tied* **Tukaram** *and* **Manohar**.

Jester   Tukya, is this your son?

Tukaram   Yes, sir.

Jester   Is it true what Kisan says? That child was about to ascend the stairs of our temple?

Manohar   It's true.

Jester   This lad has gone to Pune and Bombay and has become very brave. Eye, look straight into my eyes and answer me.

Josi   He isn't ready to apologise, either.

Jester   How can he apologise? He thinks the government is his.
Hey, but what is his? The government is in Delhi, and Delhi is very distant.

Josi   Why are you silent now? You used to speak very arrogantly to me.

Jester (*getting up*)   Throw these two into the vat with the boiling sugarcane juice immediately. And yes, the Josi Maharaja will go to the city and tell the doctor that our two workers fell into the sugarcane vat while they were making sugar and burnt to death.
Go quickly. (*All go.* **Manohar** *cries out loudly.*)

Manohar   That's injustice. We are innocent. The people of the village will throw us into the sugarcane vat and burn us to death.

Only the **Stage-Manager** *and the* **Jester** *remain on the stage. One more chair is brought for the nyayamurti* [*embodiment of justice, the judge*]. *The* **Jester** *seats himself on this chair in the manner of a nyayamurti. In front of the chair there is a table. Two witness boxes are brought.*

Stage-Manager   The complainants Manohar and Tukya are present.

The accused Manohar and Tukya are present. (**Manohar** *comes and stands in one witness box.*) The witness Pirya Saknaji is present. (**Piraji** *stands in the witness box.*) Two lawyers are present. According to the rules the oaths are taken.

Lawyer   Piraji, look, your testimony is of ultimate importance in this case.

Piraji   Yes, sir.

Lawyer   Are these accused persons known to you?

Piraji   Yes, sir. This is Manohar Savai, and that's Tukya Savai, his father.

Lawyer   Since when do you know them?

Piraji   We were born in the same village and we grew up there. We are related to each other and we used to serve the same master.

Lawyer   Which master?

Piraji   Raybhan Patel.

Lawyer   For how many years?

Piraji   It was twelve years.

Lawyer   Does he have a sister?

Piraji   One.

Lawyer   Your Eminence, to ask the witness questions of this kind is inappropriate in this court.

Lawyer   Your Eminence, here the witness's testimony is of utmost importance.

Jester   Well, . . . Proceed.

Lawyer   How old is his sister?

Piraji   She may be some twenty or twenty-two years old.

Lawyer   Has she been married?

Piraji   No.

Lawyer   Why not?

Piraji   Because her family lives in great poverty. There was no money for a marriage.

Lawyer   How do you know?

Piraji   I was there when these two asked the Patel for money.

Lawyer What did the Patel say?

Piraji He said they won't receive any money, maybe later they would.

Lawyer And then?

Piraji Manohar said to me that if the Patel won't give them any money, he will inform the newspaper that the Patel tried to assault the honour of their sister.

Lawyer What did you do then?

Piraji I tried in every manner to convince them not to do so, but who has, on the one hand, done twelve years of service and who has, on the other hand, not received even five or six-hundred rupees is likely to be very angry.

Lawyer What happened next?

Piraji Infuriated the two of them went to the Patel's mansion.

Lawyer Did you see that?

Piraji Usually I stay there overnight. On that day I was there, too.

Lawyer What happened next?

Piraji They knocked on the door. And then among the two of them and the Patel there was a lot of pushing and shoving around the doors.

Lawyer Who did then tear out Tukya's eyes?

Piraji Nobody tore them out. He did it to himself.

Lawyer He himself?

Piraji Yes, he himself. The Patel had closed the doors because he wanted to avoid a quarrel, then the two were jostling against the doors. In these doors there are very big spikes. Tukya jostled himself forcefully against the doors. The doors opened but the spikes were thrust into his eyes.

Lawyer What were you doing?

Piraji I was holding the doors closed together with the Patel.

Lawyer Your Eminence, the testimony of this witness makes it utterly clear that Raybhan Patel did not harm to Manohar Savai or Tukaram Savai, but that he rather closed the doors in order to avoid a quarrel and to protect himself. In the course of that Tukaram lost his eyes out of his own carelessness and misfortune. But the complainants gave a false account before the court and falsely accused Raybhan Patel, therefore I request you to mete out punishment to them.

Jester (*to the* **Lawyer**) Do you want to cross examine the witness?

Lawyer (2) No, thank you.

Jester Piraji, you can go. (*When* **Piraji** *has left* **Kisan** *steps into the witness box.*)

Kisan Your Eminence, we want justice.

Jester Are you in the record of cases?

Kisan Yes, your Honour.

Jester What's your name?

Kisan Kisan Vald Mahadu Rankhambe.

Jester Your village?

Kisan Uranganv.

Jester Proceed with the case.

Kisan Your Eminence, we are poor Kunabis[11] from Uranganv. We have never been in any sort of trouble.

Jester Then why have you come here?

Kisan Under provision 302 we have been accused of murder.

Jester Really? Who did so?

Kisan This uncle and nephew, sir. Their surname is Saranvare. His father was a very virtuous man. The cholera had come to the village. The people died one by one. Then this saintly man sacrificed his own life by taking *jalsamadhi* [*drowning himself*]. Thus he eliminated this tribulation from the village. But now they say that we pushed him.

Jester The record says that the hands and feet of the body were tied with ropes.

Kisan We did not tie him, your Eminence. He himself tied his hands and feet. That's in order to keep worldly attachments from rising while taking jalsamadhi.

Jester Oh, I see.

Kisan Yes, sir. Now you see.

Jester Indicted Manohar and Tukaram, you've heard all the accusations that were made against you. I give to one of you the opportunity to put forward a defence. Considering your stages of life I give this opportunity to Manohar, the representative of the younger generation. Manohar, do you want to speak?

Stage-lighting is now solely on **Manohar**.

Manohar Yes, your Eminence, today I will tell what's on my mind.

To express the anguish of an age-old inheritance of suffering is the grave purport of my speech.

I'm the world ruler of poverty. I'm the Arya Chanakya of the politics of the destitute. My hopes and desires were crushed under the rock of tradition. The challenging shout of my soul has never passed my lips. Your barriers kept the Sarasvati of my tears from

---

[11] a community of landless agriculturalists.

flowing. But today I will speak out. The words of revolt which flowed in my blood age after age are now suddenly taking shape and becoming visible. The blood clotted by sad and dire suffering gushes out today in fiery words. I'm the same sinner Sambuk who crossed the boundaries of your Aryan religion. The power of my ascetic practices was sinful in your mind. I'm the one who has never acted against the wishes of Sita, the lord of the kingdom of the fourteen thrones, the ten-necked Ravana. Even though, when Yuddhistira climbed to heaven and all others fell by the way, his eyes filled with tears when he saw a sick dog. But now the Suryaputra asks for brotherhood and nobody cares. The poison of the traitor Indra's abhorrence runs in my nerves. The dream of Visvamitra to make a different world was destroyed by Visnu. I'm that dear Mahar child carried so lovingly by Eknath. I am that Chokhamela whose bones, buried under the wall of Mangalvedha cried out the name of the Lord. Oh Lord, – come and save me – I am the sense of hope in this song. I'm the one [*Dr Ambedker*] who challenges the father of the nation [*Gandhiji*].

I'm that Savai who in exchang for speaking the truth had to give his eyes. I'm that Saranvare from Uranganv who accused those people who sacrificed my grandfather. I'm the spark that will set afire a storehouse of wood five thousand years old. There were several bodily veils, time has taken many turns, but today I've reached here. Today I'm standing at that turn of time where I will enter the temple. If you consider this sinful, then I'm committing a sin, but I want that turning like a spinning top to come to an end. The moving in circles on one spot should be ended. Your honour, if I've incurred guilt, well, then that's it. I'm a spinning top, a spinning top turning in circles on one spot.

The light on **Manohar** *dims and the whole stage is lighted.* **Tukaram** *stands there as before. They both leave the witness-box. The assembly now takes its decision. They wear bright white caps, but there seem to be blue and ochre-coloured caps, too.*

Jester Brothers, does it seem to you as if this father and son have incurred guilt? (*The* **Jester** *speaks in the manner of a leader. From the congregation 'yes, yes, yes' is heard.*) All right, all right. It is said that the *pancayat* [*village court*] is supreme. There is democracy nowadays. If you say so then we will send them to the police-post, but the good name of our village Sonapur . . . .

All No, no, no . . .

Jester All right, then speak, what punishment ought to be given to them?

Kisan Expel the two from the village.

Jester But don't forget, they're our brothers, whatever may have happened

Mahadu Banish those Mahars, if you won't, cut off their hands.

Jester The days of tyranny are gone. Nowadays there is democracy. Say something constructive.

Piraji (*wearing a blue cap. With lowered gaze he looks here and there. All watch him. When he gets up he says*)   Sarpanc [*head of the pancayat*]!

Kisan Ey, Pirya, sit down.

Josi Sarpanc, it seems to me that the two ought to be punished.

Piraji (*again standing up*) Sarpanc, send them to the police-post instead.

Mahadu Ey, Pirya, sit down. We know you have been elected, but it doesn't mean you've become a wise and different person. Sit down.

Jester Let him speak, let Piraji speak out. In a democracy everybody has the right to speak.

Piraji Sarpanc, it seems to me as if we should forgive them once again.

Jester (*standing up*) Brothers, (*whispering is heard*) I've heard the opinions of all of you. Whatever has happened, Tukaram and Manohar are our brothers. (*Whispering is heard.*) When our brothers make a mistake they are beaten, expelled from the village, punished. But these are the old, worn-out punishments. Gandhibaba says that there should be *Ramrajya* [*the kingdom of Rama: a perfect world*] now. (*Whispering is heard.*) We won't judge them. We won't punish them.

According to what Mister Piraji has said we will forgive them. (*Whispering sound.*) Wait – a man that is forgiven carries his head high. Again he will commit a fault. Therefore there ought to be punishment. An entirely customary punishment. In accordance with the orders of our most benign government we will dig a public well in our village. Water is to be found only two to four hands [*one to two meter*] deep. This well will belong to all of us. The little work which remains to be done these two will do. (*Whispering sound.*) That way the village will benefit, and they will benefit, too. Tukaram and Manohar, is that acceptable for you?

Piraji (*falling in*) Of course it is acceptable, master, what else could they say. They don't have any common sense left.

Jester Now Kisanrav Patel will make all the arrangements. Won't you, Kisanrav?

Kisan All the arrangements will be made.

Jester The meeting is closed. Start the work.

All begin to dance holding hands and forming a circle. They surround **Tukaram** *and* **Manohar**. *In the middle the two act as if they were digging a well.*

Jester Hey, why do you but clap your hands? Shout: May Mahatma Gandhiji be . . .

All . . . victorious!

Jester Remove poverty![12]

All Work hard. Work quickly. (*All begin to dance, clapping hands in rhythm. Between the* **Jester** *and* **Kisan** *there is a communication of signs and winks going on. Red light falls on* **Tukaram** *and* **Manohar**. *The* **Jester** *and the* **Stage-Manager** *come forward.* **Kisan Patel** *stands a little away immersed in thought. The stage-lighting*

---

[12] an election slogan Indira Gandhi once used.

dims. The singing and clapping of hands is done in such a manner as if it was from a distance.)

Stage-Manager (*in rhythm with the applause*)   What have they done? What have they done?

Jester   They're digging a well. They're digging a well.

Stage-Manager   How many workers dig the well?

Jester   Two workers dig the well. Two Mahars dig the well.

Stage-Manager   To whom does the well belong? To whom does the well belong?

Jester   It belongs to the village. To all the villagers.

Jester   To whom does the water belong? To whom does the water belong?

Stage-Manager   It's the villager's water, not the Mahar's.

Jester   The poor were deceived. The Mahars were deceived.

Having ignited some sticks of explosives **Kisanrav** *flees, warning all: get out, get away, get away from here. All run away. When* **Manohar** *and* **Tukaram** *try to come out of the well nobody helps them, but just then there is the sound of an explosion to be heard. The two of them fall down wounded. The* **Jester** *and the* **Stage-Manager** *stand fixed stone-like. The exhilarated dindi enters, in its own manner. There are Vitthal-cheers: 'We will wave the banner of God's name.' The dindi goes off.* **Tukaram** *and* **Manohar** *join the dindi and they all exit. Only the* **Stage-Manager** *and the* **Jester** *are on the stage and there is a dead quiet. Slowly the rhythms of the dholak* (*small drum*) *and the tuntuni* (*stringed instrument*) *start.*

Jester   We cannot stay here.

Stage-Manager   We cannot stay here.

Jester   We must go back.

Stage-Manager   We must go back.

Jester   We must go forward.

Stage-Manager   We must go forward.

Jester   We must not go backward, we must not go folward, brother.

Stage-Manager   We must not go backward, we must not go forward, brother.

Jester   We must weave in circles.

Stage-Manager   We must weave in circles.

Jester   Weave in circles, whirl around, weave in circles.

Stage-Manager   Weave in circles, whirl around, weave in circles.

As they move in circles, whirling around like a spinning top, the curtain falls.

The Lone Tusker (*Ottayan*) (1991)

K. N. Panikkar

Translated by K. S. Narayana Pillai

Panikkar (1928–2016) was a playwright, actor, translator and director who authored more than twenty plays in Malayalam and translated plays from Sanskrit and English into Malayalam. Born in the village Kavalam in Kerela, he received an undergraduate degree in economics and a law degree from Madras Christian College, following which he practiced law from 1955 to 1961. His contribution includes founding the theatre group Sopanam in Thiruvananthapuram and serving as the secretary of Kerela Sangeeth Natak Academy. Even more important was his bringing regional folk theatre forms into the space of national theatres and establishing the relevance of these forms for urban audiences exposed primarily to proscenium stages. He received many accolades including the Sangeet Natak Akademi Award in 1983, a Sangeet Natak Akademi Fellowship in 2002, and the Padma Bhushan, one of India's highest civilian honours, in 2007.

The play foregrounds the story of the lone tusker, a socially marginalized character, to highlight the themes of exploitation, injustice and power relations. The playwright uses vivid imagery, verse and theatrical conventions from the community of *Chakyars* or artists who perform *Kootha* and *Koodiyattam* in Kerela temples. To this end, the play begins with an announcement by a *Chakyar* named Parameshwaran about his role: to perform a *Lokdharmi* (people's theatre) play and through that narrate 'a tale of worldly affairs.' What is the purpose of this announcement? Is it a theatrical device to engage audiences and prompt them to think about the role of folk and traditional theatre? Is it to secure the place of drama as central to the social life of the *Chakyar* community, and a means of livelihood for them? What does the playwright's deployment of regional traditional theatre, music and dance suggest for a modern national audience, especially given his conscious foregrounding of the distinction between *Lokadharmi* (people's theatre) and *Natyadharmi* (embellished and stylized), in the play?

The play forces readers/audiences to think about the complex relationship between form, language and genre in the effective representation of social marginality and class power to which Panikkar was committed; therefore, he foregrounds popular theatrical elements as embodied by Parameshwaran who communicates the politics of power through the aesthetics of bodily maneuvers, dance, stylized movement and music, instead of spoken dialogue alone.

Reference

Panikkar, K. N. *The Lone Tusker*. Translated by K. S. Narayana Pillai. Calcutta: Seagull Books, 1991.

Chakyar *enters. [The Chakyars form a community of artists who perform the Koothu and Koodiyattam plays in the Koothampalams of Kerala temples.] He carries a knapsack on his back. He appears to be on a long journey.*

Chakyar My name is Parameshwaran. Well-versed in the art of speech, and being incarnated in a family of Kusilavas and Sutas, I took up acting as my profession. And today I propose to enact an extremely and entirely enjoyable story for the benefit of the audience. At the outset let me tell you that compared to my other plays this play is peculiar in more than one respect. You probably got that impression from the way I began. It is a purely *Lokadharmi* play; by this I simply mean that the story really took place. It is a tale of worldly affairs. I will certainly do my best to make it a *Natyadharmi* play; in other words, I shall try to add the necessary embellishments, clothe it in attractive costume and enact it in a suitable manner, nay in the most befitting and appropriate style. If you are to experience this *Natyadharmi* quality, a bare representation is not enough. Shouldn't I render at least one verse? For that I have undergone voice training and am more or less ready. I shall recite the verse in due course. Just because I have to recite a verse I must not make it worse.

Now, I don't want to leave another peculiarity of the play unsaid. This is my own story, which means that it could be yours too.

For,

> there reflects a different image
> on the Sun
> in each of the bowls filled
> with water
> the sun is one and the same, the
> images many,

let us all be one as we enter my story.
Also let us see if by elaboration, we may make ambiguous

> what has already been said,
> Between you and me
> Do not differentiate, we are all one
> spirit with manifold forms.
> We might say that both you
> and I exist,
> or it may be that

neither you nor I exist.

Now that I have stated a few simple maxims, I shall start narrating the story in the *Natyadharmi* style of articulation in which I have trained myself. I do promise that later I shall move onto the enactment of the play in the proper manner. Let me start with the verse:

> One of bravado one day,
> the lone adventurer that I am,
> at the end of a performance sacred I
> picked up my knapsack

and left the place,
And while travelling thus alone, by the
force of my sins of the past
I was trapped in a jungle as dusk fell
I was struck by the storm raging within.

Having recited the verse and enacted its meaning, he turns to one side and indicates having seen a forest.

Oh! What shall I do now? Whither shall I go in this wild jungle? A dreadful forest without even the scent of man! Oh! God, it is a pity that I am trapped here at this untimely hour. (*Looking into the distance with rapt attention.*) Is that nor a herd of grazing elephants that I see yonder? Or are these elephants but a cluster of hillocks hugging the darkness? There is also a towering tusker who has broken away from the herd. He is running along in rut. Had I been at home, how interestingly could I have described the odour of the rutting and the swinging gait of this elephant in rut! But now – alas the tusker is aiming at me and running forward. At this critical moment all my histrionic talents are benumbed. Not only that, I am also learning new lessons.

But will this humble actor live long enough to re-enact them in a manner beneficial to the world at large? Come what may, let me try a bit of acting in front of this elephant. If I am blessed enough, the elephant may be frightened by my performance and go back. In that case I won't have to give up my life; that would mean that the art of acting has triumphed.

He pretends to be an elephant and dances to the accompaniment of drumbeats. While the performance is going on, a **Woodsman** *appears on the stage. Even after his arrival, the* **Chakyar** *continues dancing. The* **Woodsman** *also acts as if he sees a real elephant in front of him.*

Woodsman   Are you an elephant, you wretched fellow?

Chakyar   Yes, I am a lone tusker in rut that has lost its way, I strayed away from a herd of elephants grazing at a distance. I feel that I have become incapable of staying with the herd.

Woodsman   Aren't you in rut? Let me see if I can put you in chains. (*Acts as if he is beating the* **Chakyar**.)

Chakyar   Oh, my dear Woodsman, don't beat me. Please don't.

Woodsman   Don't I have to chain you? (*Continues to 'beat' him.*)

Chakyar   Oh no. you need not. My rut has subsided. I am now a lone tusker well trained and disciplined. I don't think I need to be tamed ... I promise I shall adjust myself to any company, why did you beat me like that? Please don't beat me. Did you beat me up in order to chain me? It is quite unnecessary. Night is approaching and the scene is a desolate forest. And I, a lone tusker, no shelter for me. And then I have the good luck to meet someone resembling a human being. Therefore you may chain me anywhere you like.

The Lone Tusker (*Ottayan*)

Woodsman (*looking at the knapsack of the* **Chakyar**) What is this, fellow?

Chakyar A knapsack.

Woodsman What kind of knapsack?

Chakyar The same as everyone has.

Woodsman There must be something in it, pick it up yourself. (**Chakyar** *puts it across his shoulder.*) Now move along. Hm move on.

He strikes the **Chakyar** *from behind. The latter walks along in a circle imitating the gait of an elephant.*

Chakyar (*turning around*) Where are you taking me?

Woodsman Aren't you afraid? After all, I am a woodsman.

Chakyar My beloved woodsman, I am really frightened. I am quite sure that within my mind I am afraid. Don't you get the impression that I am afraid? you should have got that impression. Or is it because I am not acting? (*Turning to the audience.*) In such helpless condition, how can anyone act?

Woodsman Really? Then move on to our dwelling. (*Both of them resume walking in a circle.*) There you'll find Mooppanar.

Chakyar Mooppanar! What's he? Animal or man?

Woodsman Neither. Just Moopanar.

Chakyar Will he eat me up, my dear woodsman?

Woodsman Why not? The sin of killing will be washed off by the eating.

Chakyar Then I'm going to be killed? My beloved friend, kindly free me here. It is better for me to be devoured by some wild animal than to go to your dwelling.

Woodsman No, you won't be let free. (*Grabs hold of the* **Chakyar**.)*

Chakyar I shall run away and escape even without my own knowledge. (*Runs.*)

Woodsman Stop there! (*He seizes the* **Chakyar** *and brings him back.*)

Chakyar (*falling at the* **Woodsman**'*s feet*) My beloved woodsbaby * save me, please save me. Pray let me off without doing me any harm!

Abruptly the **Chakyar** *stops acting his part, moves downstage and speaks to the audience as if he is discoursing.*

Uttering such words, I fell at the feet of the woodsman and entreated him not take me to his dwelling. At that time, just about an hour of daytime was left. It was in the middle of a forest, hence it was impossible to tell the exact time. Still had the light started fading away completely? No; but wasn't there some dimness here and there? Oh yes, there was. Or was the light fading within my mind? That was the truth. The inner light was completely gone: As to what happened afterwards

Both the characters enact their respective roles as indicated in the following verse.

In fear I walked on,
> The woodsman struck me hard;
> I paused in grief;
> he roared from behind in command
> Thoughts of the guardian deity in mind,
> I gave myself up to such justice
> as the forest proffers.
> My fear and grief

Vanished.

Chakyar *falls down, A second woodsman,* **Mooppanar** *(the head of the clan), more dreadful than the first one, enters with touch in hand. Both of them stand behind the* **Chakyar***, with raised swords. They laugh aloud jubilantly. But the* **Chakyar** *is not frightened at all.*

Woodsmen (*moving their swords in a ritualistic manner around the* **Chakyar***'s head*)

> For Kali, Kuli and Kalan,
> for the subject, for the king, for the blessed victim,
> for blood for *vatha* and *kotha*,
> ride on my sword and come.
> Oh Kali, Tirukali, Bhadrakali

Chakyar Who are you? What are you doing? You must tell me the truth. Are you gods of death? If so, it is good that we have met. When do you return? I shall go with you

Mooppanar Where?

Chakyar To your country.

Woodsman Open your knapsack, let me see what's in it

Chakyar There's nothing in my knapsack; nothing suitable for you.

Mooppanar All the same, open the knapsack, you! (*Brandishes his sword. They push the* **Chakyar** *about as if he is a plaything.*)

Chakyar Ha, but why such flirting with me, beloved? If you think I won't open the knapsack even after such humble entreaties from both of you, you are indeed two pigheads. It is wrongly said that you are animals. You have no intelligence at all.

Woodsman (*shouting*) Remember, we can follow what you say!

Mooppanar (*in a still louder voice*) Your throat will be split open, you dog. Open your knapsack, hm, open it.

Chakyar *opens his knapsack. In it there are two or three withered red garlands. Apart from these there are bracelets and a headdress. The* **Woodsman** *examines these items one by one. At last he takes out a pair of kuzithala or small cymbals.*

Woodsman What is this, you loner?

Chakyar   It is the *kuzithala*. How did it happen to be in my knapsack? This is the *Kuzithala* on which my Nagiyar, my beloved one, used to keep rhythm with her lotus hands (*caresses the kuzithala*). She made a mistake in the rhythm during the performance. So, I quarreled with her and came away. Still there is her *kuzithala* in my knapsack

Woodsman   What is this for?

Chakyar (*striking the kuzithala rhythmically*)   To give tala. Hearing it, even people like you with all the darkness of the forest, their heads can dance.

Woodsman (*snatches away the kuzithala from the* **Chakyar***, beats rhythm on it and dances*)   It is fine, very fine, you loner.

Chakyar *takes back the kuzithala and plays on it for some time. The rhythm inspires the two* **Woodsmen** *to dance in ecstasy*

Mooppanar (*extricating himself from the effects of the rhythm*)   Stop this playing, stop it.
(*To* **Woodsman**.) Shouldn't we do away with him? Take up the sword. Brandish it.

Together they make the **Chakyar** *stand with his head bent.* **Woodsman** *is about to cut off his head.*

Chakyar   Wait a bit. You, woodsmen, what are you doing? What have I done to deserve this? Beat the rhythm on the *kuzithala*?

Mooppanar   No. Mother Kali wants blood. She wants your crimson blood. Hm. Bend forward now.

Chakyar (*pretending to be afraid*)   This might be better than being swallowed by wild animals. (*Diplomatically*.) Still, it is only a short while since we got acquainted. Shouldn't we get to know each other? Shouldn't we establish an intimacy? After that, you may beat me up, or kill me or do whatever you like.

Mooppanar   Who are you? Tell me the truth.

Chakyar   I? You may consider me an animal from the country. Since you have dedicated to offer me as a sacrifice to Kali, I must certainly be an animal. (*To the audience:*) If it becomes necessary to play the role of an animal, what can I do but play it?

Woodsman   What is your occupation?

Chakyar   Drama

Mooppanar   Drama? Then do some drama

Chakyar   It is impossible to 'do' drama as and when you ask me to; do you understand me, wild cats?

Mooppanar   What did you call us? Let me hear it again.

Chakyar   It's a very respectable term – wild cats

Woodsman   Are you willing to do drama? If not, I will spill your blood. (*Lifts the sword.*)

Chakyar   Don't do that. I shall do drama. But it requires some preparation.

Mooppanar   What do you require?

Chakyar   Both of you must at least be ready to see it. Are you ready?

Mooppanar   I am ready.

Woodsman   I am also ready.

Chakyar   Then half the work is over. The light of that torch will suffice. Look here friends, it is not enough on your part to be merely ready to see the play. Watch me closely with your whole mind involved in the performance. (*The **Woodsmen** remain motionless, closely watching the **Chakyar**.*) In this forest, you have only caves to dwell in, isn't it so? I shall build a nice house for you. (*The **Woodsmen** look at each other approvingly.*)

Woodsman   A house? Very good. Build it, build it.

Mooppanar   Oh yes, build the house, build it by all means. You are a clever guy.

Chakyar (*mentions one by one the various steps connected with the construction of a house and simultaneously enacts it in time to drum beats*)   First of all the ground must be cut into and made ready. Then the foundation has to be built by piling up stones one by one. After that, the walls have to be built up.

Don't we need some timber for the construction? Look, you have a bulky tree over there. That may be cut down. And now, work on the timber. Let me prepare the door frames. I shall fix the door myself. Now you have the really difficult work. The beam has to be lifted and put in position. That is indeed very hard work, How can I do it alone? I am only a loner. Please join in this task. Hm, hold it up.
Eldiyya – lift it together
Aaisa – not alone – aaisa
Elamalira – aaisa

Chakyar *enacts lifting a log. In the background the drumbeats come faster. Now the* **Woodsmen** *seem to be carried away by illusion. They join hands with the* **Chakyar** *in lifting the log, and start behaving as if they are bringing the entire weight. Then the* **Chakyar** *releases his hold and comes downstage.*

Chakyar (*to the audience*)   See the wild cats lifting the beam. Two guys supporting such a weighty beam – you can guess their strength.

Are they two lizards perched on the ceiling? They seem to bear the weight of the entire ceiling. However, I have won, and they have lost; I don't propose to make such a claim. For I am after all a loner. Let the two stand there like this, bearing the whole weight. Meanwhile, I shall recite a verse, close this drama and then join them in bearing the weight. The audience may utilise that time to leave this theatre.

Who has won and who has lost,
I am not eager to learn;
to wish all happiness to you,
Bharatavakya will be sung.

Chakyar *and the* **Woodsmen** *act as if they are carrying the log forward. Their movements are in rhythm with the drumbeats.* **Chakyar** *plays the role of an elephant carrying the log.*

The End.

Seven Steps Around the Fire (1999)
Mahesh Dattani

Mahesh Dattani (1958–) is a playwright, actor and director. He was born in Bangalore, where he received his early education at Baldwin Boys High School, and later attended St. Joseph's College where he studied economics and history. Dattani has written numerous critically acclaimed plays in English, many of which have been performed in India and internationally. Through his plays, Dattani represents stories about marginalized characters and communities such as *hijras*, women and courtesans, and themes of gender and class discrimination. For his enormous contribution to Indian drama, he received the Sahitya Akademi Award in 1998.

Seven Steps Around the Fire was first broadcast as a Radio Play by BBC 4 in 1999 and saw its first staged performance at the Museum Theatre, Chennai (by the MTC production and The Madras Players) in August 1999. Another performance was staged at the India Habitat Centre in Delhi. Its Canadian premiere took place in Mississauga, Ontario, in September 2013, by Sawitri Theatre Group at Meadowvale Theatre. The importance of *Seven Steps* lies in it being the first full-length play about *hijras*, a group that the Supreme Court of India recognized as the 'third gender' through a ruling in 2014. Despite this recognition, *hijras* continue to face violence, social exclusion and harassment, which often threatens their lives and livelihoods.

Dattani's play unravels stories about the *hijra* community through a murder plot that brings together characters from different gender groups in conversation about solving the murder mystery and, in the process, exposes the problems emanating from journalism, social work, police brutality and gender power-relations that circumscribe their lives. Commentaries on the *hijras* about their daily activities and places where they live reveal the multidimensional aspects of their lives and lived experiences. This representation accords a layered complexity to this community, challenges stereotypical representations in popular culture, film and everyday conversations, and exposes the paradox that marks their presence at weddings and childbirth as auspicious while simultaneously relegating them to the margins of society. 'May you have a hundred sons' is a blessing the *hijras* shower upon the young couple Subbu and his wife, when they arrive to sing at their wedding. Ironically, the phrase also points toward the history of gender preference and heterosexual marriage. What other insights does the play provide? On *hijras*? On the socially limited role that Uma's husband envisions for her as his wife, even though she enjoys the privileges of a middle-class life and through her education as a PhD researcher? As Uma helps the *hijra* Anarkali escape the false accusation of the murder charge and begins to nurture a relationship with the *hijra* community, she not only starts to overcome her slanted perceptions about *hijras* but also acquires a consciousness about her own complicated identity. Is the murder plot an effective strategy for exposing the complex web of social relations that contribute to various levels of entrapment for the various genders?

Because the play's audience is primarily an English-speaking urban audience, the outreach of its message throughout India may be perceived as limited. Nonetheless, its performance across national and international venues raises an important question: What advantages can the English language provide in raising awareness about the *hijra* community, across global/multicultural audiences? While several playwrights such as Gurcharan Das, Cyrus Mistry, Girish Karnad and Manjula Padmanabhan contributed to post-independence Indian drama in English, it was Dattani's plays that put Indian

English drama on the international literary map, dealing with marginal figures and issues of social justice. Is the critique of using the English language justified given that English was a colonial introduction? Or does it signal the need to recognize the heterogeneity of Indian theatre that continues to be produced in multiple languages?

Reference

Dattani, Mahesh. 'Seven Steps Around the Fire', in *Collected Plays I*. New Delhi: Penguin, 2000.

Seven Steps Around the Fire was first broadcast as *Seven Circles Around the Fire* by BBC Radio 4 on 9 January 1999. The cast was as follows:

Uma Rao	Priyanga Elan
Suresh Rao	Rehan Sheikh
Constable Munswamy	Shiv Grewal
Anarkali	Rikki Beadle Blair
Champa	Saeed Jaffrey
Salim	Amerjit Deu
Mr Sharma	Nitin Chandra Ganatra
Subbu Sharma	Ajay Chabra
Director	Jeremy Mortimer
Music	Eero Hameenniemi
Production Assistant	Vivien Rosenthal

The play was first performed on stage at the Museum Theatre, Chennai, by MTC Production & The Madras Players on 6 August 1999, with Anuradha Ananth, Victor Paulraj, Kartik Iyer, Sourabh Ahuja, Sudhir Ahuja, P.C. Ramakrishna and Asim Sharma, directed by Mithran Devanesen.

Sanskrit mantras fade in, the ones chanted during a Hindu wedding. Fire. The sound of the fire grows louder, drowning the mantras. A scream. The flames engulf the scream.

Interior. The office of the Superintendent of Police.

Whirring of fan (stays throughout the scene). Rustle of paper. Footsteps approaching.

Munswamy   You may see the hijra now if you wish, madam.

Uma   Will she talk to me?

Munswamy (*chuckling*)   She! Of course it will talk to you. We will beat it up if it doesn't.

Rustle of paper. Pause.

Madam, if you don't mind me saying, why is a lady from a respectable family like yourself . . .?

There are so many other cases. All murder cases. Man killing wife, wife killing man's lover, brother killing brother. And that shelf is full of dowry death cases. Shall I ask the peon to dust all these files?

Uma   No. Maybe some other time. I think this particular one is of interest to me at this time.

Munswamy   If you don't mind me saying, what is the use of talking with it? It will only tell you lies. I will bring it.

Uma   No. Can I meet her in there?

Prison gates clang shut.

Interior. The male section of Central Jail, Bangalore.

Banging of metal plates on the floor. Quite a din. **Munswamy** *runs his stick on the bars of the prison.*

Munswamy   Quiet! Quiet!! (*A whack on an arm followed by a yowl.*) Quiet, I says. You sons of . . . loafers. Do you know who this madam is? She is the daughter-in-law of the Deputy Commissioner and the wife of our Superintendent!

Silence.

(*Taps on bars with his stick.*) Now come on, come on. Do namaskara to madam.

Silence.

Uma   Er – namaskara.

A chorus of meek male namaskars.

Munswamy   Madam, once again I request you to take up some other case. Look at this man. He cut off his wife's nose. He will give you an interesting story.

Uma   I would like to meet Anarkali.

Titters from the prisoners.

Where is she?

Munswamy Anarkali! Come here.

Anarkali (*from far*) No! I don't want to meet any journalist.

Munswamy I will come inside and beat you up, you worthless Pig!

Anarkali I am not in the mood.

Uma I am not a journalist.

Anarkali I don't care if you are the mother of all the whores in Bangalore. I said I am not in the mood!

Munswamy Why do you want to bring this shame on your family, madam? I beg of you go home.

Uma Anarkali! Please, help me.

Anarkali Go away. After servicing all these sons of whores, my mouth is too tired to talk.

Uma God!

Munswamy (*nearly in tears*) Madam! I beg of you! If Sir finds out I let you in here, he will have me transferred!

Silence.

Uma All right. Perhaps I better look at some other . . . case.

Munswamy Yes! Come, madam, you can sit comfortably in the office. Will you like some tea or Pepsi?

Anarkali Wait. (*Approaches.*) Are you really the wife of the big munswamy? Or is this man lying so I will talk to you?

Munswamy Go away. Madam is no longer interested in your filthy lies.

Anarkali I didn't kill her. She was my sister!

Munswamy (*hits the bars with his stick*) Ai! Go back! (*Hits harder.*) Back!

Anarkali Would you kill your sister?

Munswamy (*hits the bars again*) Back! Beat it! Kick the hijra!

The other inmates begin to beat **Anarkali** *up.*

Anarkali (*hitting back at first*) Ai! Don't touch me!

The other inmates scream with pleasures as they beat up **Anarkali**.

Aaagh! Aaaagh!

Uma (*her voice almost drowned by the anarchy*) Stop! Stop it! (*Fade out.*)

Interior. The bedroom of Suresh and Uma.

A Hindi movie fight scene blaring from a TV set in the next room.

Suresh   That is just the sort of name a hijra would fancy. (*Chuckles.*) Anarkali!

Uma   Why do they put her in a male prison?

Suresh   They are as strong as horses. Wear the purple one.

Uma   I wore that last night.

Suresh   Again.

Silence. **Uma** *opens the wardrobe.*

Good.

Uma   She is being beaten up by all the male prisoners.

Suresh   How do you know?

Uma   She told me. (*Takes a nightie off a hanger.*) Munswamy brought her into your office, just as you instructed.

Suresh (*gets up*)   Good. (*Goes towards the bathroom.*) Don't believe a word of anything it says. They are all liars. (*Opens the bathroom door and steps in.*)

Uma   Yes. Why did you arrest her?

Suresh (*off*)   Didn't you go through the file? (*Sound of gargling.*)

Uma   Yes, I know she is arrested for the murder of her sister, but . . .

Suresh *chokes with laughter as he is gargling, and coughs.*

Suresh (*off*)   What's that you said? Sister? (*Re-enters.*) There is no such thing for them. More lies. They are all just castrated degenerate men. They fought like dogs every day, that Anarkali and . . .

Uma   Kamla.

Suresh   Look, it is one thing that I am allowing you to go through these cases for your thesis, but don't feel any compassion for them. They will take advantage . . . Keep your soft heart for me.

Uma   What is the evidence against Anarkali?

Suresh   Come here.

Silence. **Uma** *lies down on the bed.* **Suresh** *moans with pleasure as he kisses her.*

Hmm. Uma, I really love you. You know that.

Uma   Yes.

Suresh   Hmmm. Uma . . . Open your eyes . . .

Cut to

Uma (*voice-over*)   Case 7. A brief note on the popular myths on the origin of the hijras will be in order, before looking at the class-gender-based power implications. The term hijra, of course, is of Urdu origin, a combination of Hindi, Persian and Arabic, literally meaning 'neither male nor female'. Another legend traces their ancestry to the Ramayana. The legend has it that god Rama was going to cross the river and go into exile in the forest. All the people of the city wanted to follow him. He said, 'Men and women, turn back.' Some of his male followers did not know what to do. They could not disobey him. So they sacrificed their masculinity, to become neither men nor women, and followed him to the forest. Rama was pleased with their devotion and blessed them. There are transsexuals all over the world, and India is no exception. The purpose of this case study is to show their position in society. Perceived as the lowest of the low, they yearn for family and love. The two events in mainstream Hindu culture where their presence is acceptable – marriage and birth – ironically are the very same privileges denied to them by man and nature.

Not for them the seven rounds witnessed by the fire god, eternally binding man and woman in matrimony, or the blessings of 'May you be the mother of a hundred sons'.

Fade in **Anarkali**. *Whirring of fan.*

Interior. The office of the Superintendent of Police.

Anarkali   We make our relations with our eyes. With our love. I look at him, he looks at me, and he is my brother. I look at you, you look at me, and we are mother and daughter. Oh, brother, give me a cigarette, na.

Munswamy   Shut up. And don't call me brother.

Anarkali   Just one, na. (*Very sexual.*) I will do anything for you, brother. Give, na.

Munswamy   Chee! Who would want to . . . (*Flustered.*) I – I don't smoke.

Anarkali   If you had a beautiful sister, you will give her a cigarette for a fuck, no?

Munswamy   Just because madam is here . . .

Anarkali   You are not a sister-fucker?

Munswamy   Just talk to madam and then I will see to you.

Anarkali   I don't want to talk to madam! I want a cigarette!!

Uma   I think there are some here. My husband must be keeping his Gold Flakes here somewhere . . . (*Opens a drawer.*) Aha!

Anarkali (*delighted*)   Oh!

Uma   Here.

Anarkali   One for the night. One for the morning.

Uma   Keep the whole pack.

Munswamy   Madam!

Anarkali   Maachis. Maachis.

Munswamy   What will Sir say?

Uma   Nothing. You will replace the pack.

Anarkali *strikes a match.*

Munswamy   If Sir finds out . . .

Uma   How will he know? Unless you tell him. And if you do, I'll just tell him I caught you stealing his cigarettes.

Munswamy   Madam!

Anarkali *laughs loudly.*

Uma   Here. Buy a pack for Sir, and one for yourself.

Munswamy   M-madam . . .

Uma   Quickly before Sir comes back.

Anarkali *inhales, enjoying her cigarette.*

Munswamy   Yes, sir.

Munswamy *exits.* **Anarkali** *blows smoke.* **Uma** *coughs a little.*

Anarkali   So you are really the wife of the Superintendent?

Uma   Yes. I teach at Bangalore University.

Anarkali   Oh.

Uma   I teach sociology.

Anarkali (*smokes*)   Very good.

Uma   I am doing my paper on class- and gender-related violence.

Anarkali   What do you want me to do? Shall I come to sing and dance when you pass exam?

Uma   I have told you a little bit about myself. Now tell me something about you.

Anarkali   What is there to tell? I sing with other hijras at weddings and when a child is born. People give us money otherwise I will put a curse on them. (*Laughs.*) As if God is on our side. (*Smokes.*) I did not do anything to Kamla. She was my sister.

Uma   Why did you fight with your sister?

Anarkali   You never fought with your sister?

Uma   I . . . don't have a sister.

Anarkali   Not even one?

Uma   I have cousins, but we didn't grow up together.

Anarkali (*sympathetically*)   Oh. (*Smokes.*) If you were a hijra, I would have made you my sister.

Uma   Oh. Thank you.

Anarkali   But you are not a hijra, no?

Uma   No.

Anarkali   So you will not be my sister.

Pause.

Uma   Of course we can be sisters!

Anarkali   Where are you and where am I?

Uma   But . . . I wish you could understand . . . This is just what I am trying to do with my paper!

Anarkali   What paper?

Uma   One day you will understand. Anarkali, I would love to be your sister, if you will be mine.

Anarkali   Oh! You are only being kind. Don't hurt my heart.

Uma   No, I mean it.

Anarkali   Look at me.

(*Pause.*) Oh! My sister! You are my sister, no?

Uma   Yes.

Anarkali   Get me out of here.

(*Pause.*) Sister, I did not kill Kamla. You believe me, no?
(*Pause.*) You don't believe me? You doubt your own sister?

Uma   Er – no. I don't . . . But what can I do?

Anarkali   You are the daughter-in-law of the DCP and you ask me what you can do to save your sister?

Uma   Look, I am here to gather some information for my thesis . . .

Anarkali   Then say that. Don't pretend to be my sister.

Uma   I don't have any power!

Anarkali   I will tell you who killed her.

Uma   You mean . . . you know?

Anarkali   But don't tell your husband.

Uma   Why not?

Anarkali   They will kill me. But I will tell you because you are my sister.

Uma   Look, I – I don't think I want to get involved . . .

Anarkali   Go away! You are worse than all those journalists!

Uma   Maybe you should tell my husband. They will protect you.

Anarkali   You are innocent fool.

Uma   Look . . .

Anarkali   But you are my sister. If you do not want to help me, it is all right.

Uma   I do . . .

Anarkali   Maybe you are more unhappy than I am.

Uma   Look, I want to help you but I don't know how.

Anarkali   If you give them money, they will release me.

Uma   But I can't bail you out!

Anarkali   Please, sister! I will die here. Help me get out, then I will run away.

Uma   You can't do that! You have to report to the police station.

Anarkali   They will kill me also if I tell the truth. If I don't tell the truth, I will die in jail.

Pause.

Uma   My husband won't let me.

Anarkali   You don't have any money?

Uma   No . . .

Anarkali   Get it from your father. Say it is for your baby.

Uma   I don't have any children.

Anarkali   Oh, sister! Make up some excuse!

Munswamy *enters.*

Munswamy   Madam, Sir is coming. Please, put this packet where you found it.

Opening of drawer.

Uma   Wait. There were three short of a full pack. Anarkali, here take these – one, two and . . .

Shutting of drawer.

Munswamy   And you! Stand up and stop smoking!

Anarkali *stands up.*

Madam, I hope you are finished with this . . .

Uma   Leave us alone for a few minutes.

Munswamy *exits.*

Anarkali   Give me a hundred rupees, sister. Quickly.

Uma *fumbles in her bag.*

You will help me go away?

Uma   Here. That is all the money I have. Even if I wanted to, I couldn't explain to my husband why I am paying for your bail.

Anarkali   Go to Champa. Go behind Russel Market in Shivajinagar and ask for the hijra Champa. Give her the money.

Uma   Anarkali! (*Pause.*) If you loved your sister Kamla, why did you scar her face with a butcher's knife?

Pause.

Anarkali   I would do it to you also. If it will save your life.

Uma   What do you mean?

Pause.

Anarkali   She was beautiful. Very beautiful.

Footsteps.

That is why Salim's wife put fire to her beautiful skin and burned her to the other world.

Creak of swing doors as **Suresh** *enters, followed by* **Munswamy**.

Salaam, Saab.

Suresh   I hope this thing didn't give you any trouble.

Uma   No. She is very well-behaved.

Suresh   Are you through with it?

Uma   Yes, I am for now.

Suresh (*snaps his fingers*)   Take it away.

Munswamy (*clicks his heels*)   Sir! (*Snaps his fingers.*) Come!

Anarkali   Salaam, saab . . . Salaam, memsaab.

Footsteps. Creak of swing doors, twice. Footsteps fade.

Suresh   Did you get what you want?

Uma   Not really.

Suresh   You look tired. I will have Munswamy take you home.

Uma   Yes, I am a bit tired. But if you don't mind, could you ask him to take me to my dad's home?

Suresh   Why not? It has been a long time. I hope that bud of a pomegranate didn't frighten you. What did it tell you?

Uma   She is a real liar, as you said. The usual stuff. Hard luck stories.

Suresh That is the sort of crap that finds its way into your academic papers.

Uma Well . . . Mine is going to be different.

Fade in traffic noises.

Interior. A car driving through busy roads.

Pause while traffic noises are heard.

Uma (*thought*) Nobody seems to know anything about them. Neither do they. Did they come to this country with Islam, or are they a part of our glorious Hindu tradition? Why are they so obsessed with weddings and ceremonies of childbirth? How do they come to know of these weddings? Why do they just show up without being invited? Are they just extortionists? And why do they not take singing lessons?

(*Pause.*) Is it true? Could it be true what my mother used to say about them? Did they really put a curse on her because they did not allow them to sing and dance at their wedding? Or was that their explanation for not being able to have children of their own? Or . . . a reason to give to people for wanting to adopt me?

Pause.

Munswamy Madam, close your window. At this traffic light, there are too many of them.

Uma Oh, don't worry. I can handle them. I always carry coins.

Munswamy (*disapproving*) You are too kind, madam.

Uma No, I don't think so.
(*Pause.*) Who found the body?

Munswamy What? Oh, you are still thinking of . . . The body was found by some passer-by, after four days. The temple priest complained about the stench. It was thrown into the pond after being burned.

Uma Didn't the hijras report Kamla missing to the police?

Munswamy Hah! As if they care! After we found out the body was a man's without . . . that the body was a hijra's, we called them. Then they came. They were more interested in the jewellery.

Uma Jewellery?

Munswamy So much jewellery she was wearing when she died! Even a bride does not wear so much. That too gold. All stolen, I am sure. How will hijras get so much gold if they can only beg for a few rupees?

Uma (*thought*) Then is it true? That they are criminals? Am I making a fool of myself? Even so, I've got to find out for myself . . . Who knows? Some of those people out there might be . . . they just might be . . .

(*Speech.*) Things haven't changed much, have they? Look at those pavement dwellers there. They have been around as long as I can remember.

Munswamy Madam, there are a lot of changes. My father was also a constable. Let me tell you that I am seeing more in today's world than my father.

Uma Really? Such as?

Munswamy More crime. So much crime and the police cannot do anything.

Uma Why? Because they don't know who the criminals are?

Munswamy Everyone knows . . . (*Pause.*) And beggars. More and more beggars. God knows what all they do. They are spies all of them. How else do the thieves know where to loot and when? Madam, don't pity any of them. They are not worth it.

Silence.

Uma When I was small . . . my mother always carried small change. When we stopped at the traffic lights . . . she would throw the coins as far as she could on the pavement . . . I would watch while they fought with each other for the coins. The lights would change, and we would drive away. When she died, I took her jars of coins – there were four pickle jars filled with worthless paisas . . . I stood on the verandah and threw them over the walls.

Munswamy Madam, be careful. The hijras will come running now.

Uma There are no hijras. Children! Just children.

Munswamy Same thing. Beggars only, no?

The car stops at the signal. Screaming of little children. **Uma** *throws the coins far. The screams increase in intensity as they fade away.*

Good idea! Very good idea.

Fade out traffic.

Interior. Ramaswamy's home.

Munswamy What shall we do? Shall I take you to your home?

Uma Maybe he is still at the university. Er – I think I will wait for him.

Munswamy (*clears his throat*) Madam, I have received instructions to wait for you and take you back. Your father-in-law is expecting some guests . . .

Uma Let me call to see if he has left. (*Picks up phone and begins to dial. To* **Munswamy**.) Would you like an ice cream? Go into the kitchen and ask the maid for some.

Munswamy No, no. It is okay.

Uma (*on the phone*) Could you put me through to the Vice Chancellor's office? . . . This is his daughter, Uma Rao . . . Tell him it's urgent . . . (*To* **Munswamy**.) Try the ice cream. It is really good.

Munswamy No. It's okay.

Uma   Why don't you get some for me? In there. Almond and pistachio. Just tell Mary.

Munswamy   Er – okay. (*Exits.*)

Uma   Hello? Dad? How are you? . . . At home, your home . . . Things are fine, don't worry. I was just passing by and . . . Oh, nowhere in particular. I have Suresh's car and one of his constables, so I thought I might drop in and surprise you. How are you? . . . Oh. I hope you are taking your medication . . . I wish I could come back and live here with you . . . I just might . . . Well, you taught me to do exactly what I want to do, and one day I just might . . . He is doing well . . . I did go. There is nothing wrong with me. He needs to go for a check up. In many ways I am quite glad. I–I don't think I want any . . . I don't know. Look, I have to get back . . . I was wondering – could I borrow some cash from you? Suresh is busy right now and I don't want to disturb my father-in-law for these things . . . Good question. About 50,000? . . . It's to buy a present for Mr Sharma's son's wedding. Subramanyam – Subbu. You do remember him, don't you? I–I just thought it might be good idea to buy him something different . . . I haven't decided yet. Since I am free now, I thought I will go to the old bazaar and get it over with . . . Can I have it right away? I know where you keep the key . . .

Munswamy (*enters*)   Madam, your ice cream.

Uma (*on the phone.*)   Thank you! . . . No, I better rush. I will see you some other time. Bye. (*Hangs up.*)

Munswamy   It is very nice. Mary gave me a little bit to taste.

Uma   If you like it, you may have it. I will be right down. Just freshen up a little.

Munswamy   Then are we leaving.

Uma   Yes. But we won't be going home.

Munswamy   Then where?

Pause.

Uma   Constable Munswamy.

Munswamy   Sir!

Uma   I had a very, very long meeting with my father right now. Understand?

Munswamy   Y–yes, madam. But where are we going?

Uma   You will know in good time. In the mean time, have your ice cream while I . . . freshen up.

Exterior. In the car.

Door slams shut. The car starts up.

Munswamy   Where are we going, madam?

Uma   Take me to Shivajinagar.

Munswamy   Why?

Uma   We are going to visit Anarkali's friend, Champa.

The engine of the car is switched off.

Munswamy   No. No . . . madam.

Uma   But we must! Don't you want to help Anarkali?

Munswamy   No. My duty is to protect you, madam.

Uma   Then you must go where I go.

Munswamy   Yes, but . . .

Uma   So what are we waiting for? Hurry up, I have to be back home soon.

Munswamy   I don't know what Sir will say.

Uma   Who is going to tell him? You?

Munswamy   It is my duty, madam. If he finds out, he will suspend me.

Uma   Take your cap off . . . Now you are not on duty. Let's go.

Munswamy   N–no, madam . . .

Pause.

Uma   Very well, I will go on my own.

Munswamy   It is dangerous for you to go there. Please understand! If something happens to you, then I am responsible.

Uma   Constable Munswamy!

Munswamy   Sir!

Uma   To Shivajinagar.

Pause.

Munswamy   Madam, I will take you to your residence. Those are my orders.

Uma   You will take the car to my residence.

Uma *opens the car door, gets out and slams the door shut.*

Munswamy   Madam! Wait.

He opens the car door, gets out and slams the door shut. Traffic noises increase as we have exterior acoustics.

Uma (*yelling*)   Rickshaw!

Munswamy   Please! Madam, what will I say to Sir?

Autorickshaw drives up and comes to a halt near **Uma**.

Uma   Get your car out of the way. You are blocking the traffic. (*To the driver.*) Shivajinagar, and make it quick.

Uma *gets in. The autorickshaw drives away.*

Munswamy (*shouting at beggars*)   Ai! If you touch the car, I will put you in jail! Get away, you beggars!

He opens the car door, gets inside, shuts the door and starts up the car. Music. Traffic noises. Bazaar or market noises under **Uma**'s *voice-over.*

Uma (*voice-over*)   The invisible minority. Behind Russel Market, everyone knew where to find them, although I couldn't see any hijras on the streets. They only come out in groups and make their presence felt by their peculiar loud hand clap.

Autorickshaw comes to a halt.

(*Speech.*) How much?

Car door bangs shut in the distance.

Munswamy (*approaches* **Uma**)   Madam!

Uma   What are you doing here? (*To the driver.*) Keep the change, thank you.

Munswamy   Why are you . . .?

Autorickshaw drives away.

Why do you have so much money in your bag? Oh – why are you inviting so much trouble?

Uma   Go home. I don't need you.

Munswamy   No. I will not leave you now.

Uma   Oh, all right. But stay about a hundred yards away from me. I don't want you scaring all the hijras away.

Munswamy (*sighs*)   Yes, sir.

Fade in soundtrack of music and singing of hijras. The singing is interspersed with loud clapping of hands.

Interior. The living room of Champa.

Champa   Come in.

Uma *parts a curtain which sets off bells tinkling.*

Uma   Namaskar.

Champa   Sit down.

Uma   Thank you . . . So, you are Madam Champa.

Champa *guffaws.*

I am sorry if I said something . . .

Champa (*booming*)   Don't say sorry!

Uma I–I'm . . . confused.

Champa Who are you? And why do you visit us?

Uma I want this meeting of ours to be kept a secret.

Champa Hah! . . . So you are not a journalist.

Uma No.

Champa We did not kidnap your son. Ramu came to us of his own free will. If you want, you can take your son away.

Uma I don't have any children.

Champa (*shows sympathy but only for a moment*)   Oh! Poor woman . . . How did you come to know of our meeting? Did the police send you?

Uma Er – no. Anarkali sent me.

Champa Anarkali? But she is . . . She is not in town.

Uma I know where she is. I met her there.

Champa Oh. So you are a social worker. Say that.

Uma Yes . . . I am a social worker.

Champa Please excuse me, madam. I did not know that . . . You see us also as society, no?

Uma Of course. I mean – you are.

Champa Good. But don't do any good work for that bitch Anarkali!

Uma Oh.

Champa She deserves to be where she is! I hope she dies.

Uma Oh . . . Why?

Champa I am the head hijra, and I will decide who the guru will be after me. Anarkali will never be the guru. I will burn this place down before she sits here.

Uma Oh.

Champa But first, you tell me. Why are you here?

Uma Well, er . . . Well . . . Just to let you know that Anarkali is well. And I hope she will be released shortly.

Champa Hmm. You are hiding something from me.

Uma No. Why should I?

Champa What is in that bag?

Uma Why? Why do you ask?

Champa Why are you holding it so tightly?

Uma I–I didn't notice that I was. (*Plonks her bag beside her.*) There.

Champa You have a lot of money in that?

Uma (*laughs in embarassed manner*) Yes, but . . .

Champa Are you mad? Hold the bag tightly. You should not bring so much money in to such places.

Uma I thought it would be safe.

Champa You said Anarkali sent you.

Uma Yes.

Champa Why?

Uma Actually, she said you will help her, but . . .

Champa Of course, I will help her. Did I say I won't help her?

Uma No . . .

Champa If I had the money I would throw it on that Superintendent's face and get her back. Sons of whores, all of them.

Uma Oh.

Champa I know I said she should die in jail. But, after all, I am the head hijra and she is my daughter.

Uma Yes. Then I guess . . . Well . . .

Champa Have you brought money for her bail?

Uma Yes.

Champa Oh, may you have a hundred children! I knew that you are really a social worker.

Uma You will bail her out?

Champa What a question to ask!

Uma She – she didn't really kill Kamla, did she?

Champa What difference does it make whether she did or no?

Uma I certainly don't want to help anyone who is a murderer!

Champa Yes, yes. That won't suit you. No. She did not kill Kamla. They were sisters.

Uma If I gave you the money, will you go to the court and get her release orders?

Champa Did I come begging to you – 'please give me money to save my daughter'? Huh?

Uma (*opens her bag*) Here.

Champa (*leans over*)   Aah, these old bones! How much is it?

Uma   Enough for the bail amount and some more for your trouble.

Champa   Oh! May you have a hundred sons! As soon as that bitch is out, I will make her the head. Now that Kamla is gone, who else do I have?

Uma   Wait a minute. You mean – Kamla was your first choice?

Champa   Kamla was everyone's first choice.

Uma   And Anarkali, your second? I mean, now that Kamla is dead, Anarkali stands to gain from Kamla's death?

Champa   Yes. But what can I do? There is nobody else who I can . . .

Uma   Can I have my money back?

Champa   Why? What is your problem now? Anarkali did not kill Kamla, I am telling you!

Uma   But it seems like she may have.

Champa (*fiercely*)   I know she did not kill her! Why can't you understand?

A commotion outside. **Salim**'s *voice rises above the sound of protests.*

Quickly! (*Throws the bundle of money to* **Uma**.) Put it in your bag.

Uma *puts the money in her bag hurriedly.*

Uma   Maybe I should leave. Thank you for your hospitality.

Salim *storms in, sending the bells tinkling wildly.*

Champa   I told you not to show your face here!

Salim   Shut up, you old bag! I told you to send me her things. Where is her trunk?

Champa   Quiet, you fool! I have a guest here. A memsaab. Madam, this is Salim. Do salaam to madam.

Salim   Salaam.

Champa   Now go away.

Salim   First give me her trunk.

Champa   I have the right to Kamla's clothes and jewellery even if you gave them to her!

Salim   You can keep all that. Let me first go through her trunk. And I didn't give her anything.

Champa   Then who gave her all that? The Prince of England?

(*Pause.*) Now don't make a noise in front of my guest. Do you know who she is?

Salim   No.

Champa   She is . . . she is . . . Tell him, madam. Tell him who you are.

Uma Er . . . I am the daughter-in-law of the Deputy Comissioner of Police.

Pause.

Champa Madam!

Salim I am sorry to disturb you, madam. I–I will . . .

Champa And don't come to my house like this. Don't you know we have important guests like this all the time?

Salim I am very sorry.

Uma Why do you want to go through Kamla's things?

Salim It is okay. I will leave now.

Uma No. Wait!

Salim *leaves in a hurry. Tinkling of bells.*

Who is he?

Champa Please don't mind him, madam. That Salim is ashamed to say that he used to come for Kamla every day. Now, madam, before anyone comes, give me the money for poor Anarkali quickly. I will hide it in my room.

Uma What was he looking for? Unless you answer that question, I am not giving you the money. Not only that, I will tell my father-in-law that you killed Kamla. (*Pause.*) They will arrest you and Anarkali will be the head hijra while you rot in jail.

Champa A photograph.

Uma What kind?

Champa I don't know. He says he wants a photograph that Kamla has. Of Kamla and him together.

Uma Where does Salim live?

Champa In Palace Orchards. He is the bodyguard of the minister.

Uma Which minister?

Champa I don't know. It is a big white house with big walls. His son is getting married next week.

Uma I know which one you mean. Now, Champa, it is very important for me to look through Kamla's things.

Pause.

Champa Come with me.

Film music from a radio with a lot of crackle.

Interior. Cramped quarters. Kamla's room.

Champa Ai! Get out! All of you.

Grumbles as the occupants leave, taking the radio with them.

This is her trunk. I don't give the key to anyone. All the jewellery belongs to me. (*Unlocks and opens a rusty tin case.*) Everything that she owned is in here, madam. I myself put it all there.

Uma Then you must have seen the photograph.

Champa There are some photos in this.

Uma *opens a tin box.*

Uma Who is this beautiful young man?

Champa Kamla. Before she became Kamla. (*Going through the pictures.*) These were his first father and mother. Afterwards I am her father and mother . . . This one we took together after she became my daughter . . .

Uma But where is the one with Salim?

Champa I don't know, madam. I really don't know.

Uma Was he planning to take Kamla away?

Champa I don't know.

Uma Yes, you do. That would not have suited you at all. You would lose an earning member of the family. You did not want that to happen.

Champa That is true but only because she will not be happy in the outside world.

Uma But the real reason you wanted her dead was to warn others, who may wish to leave the fold, of the consequences.

Champa That is not true! We had fights. But Anarkali and me – we are not killers.

Uma Anarkali couldn't have killed her. Kamla was running away anyway, leaving the way clear for her. Oh no. One person who wanted her dead is yourself. She defied your authority.

Champa She was my only daughter! (*Pause.*) Take your money and get out of my house! Go! This is my house! (*Pause.*) You don't know! You don't know!

Uma What? I don't know what?

Pause.

Champa You don't know how much we all loved her.

Interior.

Music. Sound of a telephone being dialled.

Uma Professor, this is Uma Rao!. Do you have some time to discuss my paper? . . . Well, I will be brief. I am wondering whether I could leave out the case study on the hijras . . . Well, it all seems a little too sordid and I find it more and more difficult to do thorough research . . . I know there is very little written about them, and now I understand why . . . But there is no way I can win their trust! Maybe there is, but I don't know . . . How important is it? . . . Oh . . . I guess I will have to . . . If my family throws me out, I hope that doctorate will come in handy.

Exterior. In a car.

Munswamy   Madam! We cannot go to the minister's house!

Uma   Oh, be quiet! We are not going to meet him. He is in America. Don't you read the newspapers? Remember to do exactly what I told you.

Munswamy   B–but, madam, I am not on duty.

Uma   Who is to know?

Munswamy   Still, if Sir finds out I am using the police car . . .

Uma   How will he know? Unless I tell him . . .

They drive on.

Exterior. The gates of the minister's residence.

Munswamy (*commanding*)   Ai, watchman! Open the gates! We are here on official work. To the servants' quarters.

The gates open. They drive in. They get off.

Who is Salim amongst you?

Salim   I am Salim, sir. Salaam, madam.

Uma   I would like to have a word with your wife.

Salim   My wife?

Munswamy   Go on. Don't waste time. Call her here.

Salim   But, she is not here, sir.

Munswamy   Don't lie.

Salim   She has gone to her village.

Uma   Why did you send her away?

Salim   I did not send her away. Her mother is not well, so she went to . . .

Uma   Salim, please do understand, we do not want to arrest her. We just want to ask her some questions.

Salim   W–what questions?

Uma   You know perfectly well what about. You do not want us to talk about it in front of these people do you? . . . Now let me talk to your wife. I know she is hiding in there somewhere.

Pause.

Salim Madam, please come in to the main house. I will bring my wife to you.

Uma How is Subbu?

(*Pause.*) What's wrong? Why do you look so frightened?

A voice booms from behind.

Mr Sharma What do you want and who sent you here?

Munswamy S–s–s–sir!

Mr Sharma I will have you two arrested unless you have official permission to be here.

Uma (*hiding her nervousness*) Mr Sharma, I am afraid that we may not have permission, but we are here in your own interest.

Mr Sharma And who may you be?

Uma I am Uma Rao.

Mr Sharma So?

Uma I am DCP Rao's daughter-in-law.

Mr Sharma I will verify that right away.

Uma Please don't call my father-in-law!

Mr Sharma Oh. Why not?

Uma I was meaning to call you, but I thought you were away in America. Look, can we talk in private?

Clinking of tea cups.

Interior. The living room of Mr Sharma.

Mr Sharma Hmm. You are doing all this for your thesis?

Uma (*sighs*) I don't know. I think so.

Mr Sharma So you feel that Salim was having an affair with this . . . person, and his wife found out?

Uma Possible. I am just checking out her story. One of the hijras who has been arrested says it could be Salim's wife who killed Kamla.

Mr Sharma It is all very disgusting.

Uma It is very difficult to get to the truth. They are all so used to lying. I am sure the hijras know, but they are not telling.

Mr Sharma One of them must have done it. They do fight amongst themselves a lot.

Uma That is . . . probable. But somehow . . .

A voice from the staircase.

Subbu   Are you going to arrest Salim?

Mr Sharma   Go back to your room, Subbu. You are unwell.

Subbu   Please don't arrest him. He is a good man.

Mr Sharma   Nobody is arresting anybody. (*To* **Uma**.) My son Subbu. He is unwell. A bit tired with all the wedding preparations.

Uma   Hello, Subbu. Congratulations. Remember me? We met at . . .

Subbu   I hate weddings. I don't want all this. I don't wish to go ahead with this.

Mr Sharma   Subbu, please go back to your room.

Uma   I am sure your father has found a wonderful person for you, Subbu. You must go ahead with it.

Subbu   Do you think so? Everyone says I should.

Uma   Of course, you should.

Mr Sharma   Well, I must say goodbye now. I do hope you will make it to the wedding.

Uma   We are all looking forward to it. Thank you for your time. A pleasure to meet you, Subbu.

Subbu   Please don't arrest Salim. He is a good man.

Interior. The bedroom of Suresh and Uma.

Uma   Some more tea?

Suresh   Hmm? No.

Pouring of tea into cup.

Uma   What are we buying for Subbu?

Suresh   Who?

Uma   For Subbu on his wedding day.

Suresh   Oh. Sharma's son. I don't know. You decide. Does it have to be very expensive?

Uma   No. But I would prefer to give him something special.

Suresh   Your father called.

Uma (*stirs her cup*)   When?

Suresh   Yesterday some time, I can't remember when. He said something about money. (*Puts down paper.*) Why do you need so much money?

Uma   I don't. It's for something else. I have it all with me right here in my bag. (*Picks up bag and unzips it.*) See . . . I was a bit concerned about Subbu's wedding present. After all, my father knows the Sharmas quite well. And so do you and your parents. (*Zips up her bag.*) So I thought they might appreciate a Persian rug.

Suresh   Fine. Buy whatever you think is best.

Pause.

Uma   I went to the doctor again. Your mother insisted she takes me.

Suresh   What did they say?

Uma   Nothing . . . They want to see you.

Suresh   I don't think so.

Uma   Just a test for your sperm count.

Suresh   I don't have to go . . .

Uma   Would you like to go shopping with me?

Pause.

Suresh   Why did you ask your father for the money?

Uma   Oh, no particular reason. I was visiting him and . . .

Suresh   You should have asked me. Have I ever refused you any money?

Uma   We could go shopping together.

Rustle of newspaper.

Suresh   Are you through with your research?

Uma   Not yet. I think I would like to have some more time with Anarkali.

Suresh   That would be difficult.

Uma   Oh, please! It is important. My guide is very impressed with her case. He feels it will go a long way in making my paper relevant.

Suresh   No. What I mean is she . . . he is no longer in our custody.

Uma   Where is she?

Suresh   She left. Someone came and bailed her out.

Uma   Oh . . . When was this?

Suresh   A couple of days ago. Some old hijra. Made quite a scene. Said she had pawned her jewellery or some such thing . . . Are you feeling all right?

Uma   But she will report to the police?

Suresh   Maybe. Who knows? If she runs away to another town, who can trace these people? Anyway, we only arrested her because there was no one else. There is no real proof against her. It could be any one of them.

Uma   I – I must go . . . shopping.

Fade in bazaar noises.

Exterior. Bazaar.

Uma *walks through the bazaar. The noises fade as she enters a narrow lane. Film music can be heard from a transistor. A dog barks.* **Uma** *knocks on a door. A window opens.*

Champa (*from window*)   Go away!

Uma   Champa, let me in. I want to talk to you.

Champa   Madam, you should not mix with people like us.

Uma   I am sorry if I offended you in any way. Please do let me in. I must speak to Anarkali.

After a while, the door opens.

Champa   What do you want now?

Uma   Help me in getting the murderer of Kamla arrested.

Champa   How can I help you?

Uma   Anarkali must have taken the photograph from Kamla's box.

Champa   Shh! Come in.

They go in.

Interior. The living room of Champa.

Uma   She was the only one close to Kamla. If you don't have it . . .

Champa   What use is the photograph?

Uma   If Salim wants it so badly, it must be important.

Champa   Listen to me, madam. Forget it.

Uma   No. I feel I owe it to you and Anarkali and . . . and . . . all of you!

Champa   We don't know anything about any photo!

Uma   What about Anarkali? Where is she?

Champa   She is not here. Now please go before anyone sees you here.

Pause.

Uma   Who are you scared of? Salim?

Champa   No. Not Salim. There are others more dangerous than he.

Uma   Who?

Champa   I don't know.

Uma You do. But you don't trust me.

Champa Not even your father-in-law can put them in jail.

Uma Please! Let me speak with . . .

Champa You want to meet Anarkali? Come, come inside. Come.

They walk to another room.

Uma (*gasps*) Anarkali.

Anarkali (*in pain, barely audible*) Hello, sister.

Champa They broke her nose.

Anarkali Come closer. (**Uma** *moves closer to* **Anarkali**.) Does your husband know you are here?

Uma No.

Anarkali Why did you not tell him?

Uma (*after a while*) He wouldn't allow me to visit you.

Anarkali Then what will you do knowing who killed Kamla?

Uma Tell my husband to make an arrest.

Anarkali One hijra less in this world does not matter to your husband.

Uma Trust me, and tell me. Who is it?

Pause.

Anarkali You will be there at the minister's son's wedding?

Uma Yes.

Anarkali With your husband?

Uma Yes.

Champa Anarkali!

Pause.

Anarkali Don't put your own position in danger. Go home.

Champa Madam, do as she says. Go home to your husband.

Pause. **Uma** *leaves. Music. We follow* **Uma** *into the street. The dog barks again. The bazaar noises grow. The music overpowers the noise of the bazaar.*

Exterior. In the car of Suresh and Uma.

Fade in car in motion. Occasional honks from other vehicles.

Suresh You look good.

Uma It's the sari you bought me for Diwali.

Suresh   You should have worn your diamonds.

Uma   This is only the wedding ceremony. I will wear them for the reception.

Suresh   I think we have lost them.

Uma   No. There they are . . . At least, the car following them.

Suresh   One day, I too will have a five-car escort . . . There is talk, that father will become the Comissioner soon . . . So what did you buy for them?

Uma   A huge carpet. From us. Your parents are giving them a chandelier for their new home.

Suresh   Do you think the carpet is flashy enough?

Uma   It takes three servants to carry it.

Suresh *applies the brakes. The car skids a bit.* **Suresh** *honks loud and long.*

Suresh (*mutters*)   Bloody beggars!

Cut traffic. Fade in wedding music.

Exterior. At the wedding.

Music. Chatter of guests.

Suresh   Who was that waving to you?

Uma   That was Mrs Nair, the liquor baron's wife. And that's his brother with her, visiting from Canada. Do you want me to introduce them?

Suresh   No, no. Excuse me. I think I will say hello to Mr Birla.

Chatter of guests continues.

(*Fading.*) Hello, Mr Birla . . .

Uma *wanders about.*

Mr Sharma   Looking for someone as usual?

Uma   Oh!

Mr Sharma   I am sorry, I didn't mean to startle you.

Uma   No, no. I wasn't . . .

Mr Sharma   You had that searching look again.

Uma   Did I? How can you tell?

Mr Sharma   I have seen it in many people. It is usually a spiritual search that I see.

Uma (*laughs*)   And is that what you see in me?

Mr Sharma   Yes. I see a search for the truth.

Uma   Do you think I will find it?

Mr Sharma If you look in the right place.

Uma Which would be?

Mr Sharma You know the saying about the musk deer? He searches everywhere for the source of the heavenly fragrance, not realizing it is contained within his own body.

Uma *laughs.*

You don't believe it is true?

Uma And yourself? Have you found what you have been searching for?

Mr Sharma Yes. My son is getting a wife from a fine family. I am happy to see that he is entering the phase of the householder.

Uma And you feel the truth lies in that?

Mr Sharma For him, yes. My truth is in ensuring he is on the right path . . . Come. The time is auspicious.

Cut chatter to fade in Sanskrit marriage shlokas being chanted. Occasionally the fire crackles as butter is thrown into it.

Don't they look fine together? This is the happiest moment for any parent – watching their child perform these rites.

The crackle takes on an ominous proportion and so do the chants. The chants recede to a distance.

Salim Madam, you should not be seen here near the servants' quarters.

Uma I want to meet your wife. Where is she?

Salim She does not know anything about what you want to know.

Uma You brought Kamla here night after night. Surely she must know.

Salim Go back to the wedding!

Quick footsteps as someone approaches.

Uma What are you doing here?

In the distance, **Mr Sharma** *is being congratulated: 'Congratulations!', 'Sharma saab, congratulations', 'May you be a grandfather soon!' The group of hijras approach, clapping loudly. They wear dancing bells on their ankles.*

Champa May God bless this house with many children!

Anarkali May God always smile upon this house!

Uma Look! That's Anarkali!

Suresh Ssh!

Uma Oh! I can't be bothered!

Champa Salaam to all! We will bless this marriage with our singing and dancing.

One of the hijras begins to beat on a drum.

Mr Sharma Stop! Stop it!

They stop beating the drum.

Who invited you here? Where are those security people?

Suresh I will check. (*Walks away in a hurry.*)

Champa Do not be so angry, sir. It is a happy occasion.

Mr Sharma Shut up. Get rid of them, someone.

Uma No. Wait! You can't do that.

Mr Sharma Are you taking their side?

Uma No. It is bad luck to turn away a hijra on a wedding or a birth.

Champa Thank you, my daughter. May you have a hundred sons!

Mr Sharma Do you really believe in that?

Uma Mr Sharma, what have you got to lose? The marriage ceremonies are done. You should be happy. Just let them dance a little. Is that asking for too much?

Suresh (*approaches with security guards*)   I will have you all suspended for this! Here they are. Throw them all out. (*To the hijras.*) Get out of here, or I will lock you all up in jail!

Mr Sharma Er . . . maybe I overreacted. After all, their presence is expected. I will just give them some money . . .

Champa Thank you, sir, but we must sing and dance to bless this house and the handsome couple.

Mr Sharma Well, all right. Just one number and you will get your baksheesh.

Anarkali Where are the newly married? They must be here.

Mr Sharma Oh!

Uma Please! It is important!

Mr Sharma Request the young couple to come here.

The hijras begin to dance, singing a crude Hindi film song. The singing is largely drowned as the drumbeat and the dancing bells are unrealistically overpowering. It builds to a crescendo.

Subbu No!

A short scuffle.

Suresh What the . . .?

Some gasps.

Mr Sharma Subbu!

Subbu Stay away!

Suresh Subbu, give it back to me!

Anarkali Subbu, no!

Mr Sharma You keep out of this!

Subbu I am leaving you all! You can't keep me away from Kamla.

Uma Subbu, forget what I said. Please, let us talk.

Mr Sharma Son, please put that gun down. Let us talk.

Subbu No.

Mr Sharma It was a mistake. I am sorry, son. (*Calls out.*) Salim!

Uma Subbu, I am sorry. I did not know.

Salim Subbu, sir, please . . .

Subbu Salim, I trusted you. You promised.

Anarkali Subbu, I have a gift for you.

Salim You stay away from him!

Mr Sharma It's okay, Salim. Anything, just . . .

Anarkali See. See, Subbu.

Subbu W–what is it?

Anarkali A photo . . . Take. These people cannot take this away from you.

Salim Give that to me.

Subbu No. It's mine. Only I shall have it. Give it to me.

Champa Give it to him. Take it, my son.

Anarkali *walks up to* **Subbu** *and gives him the photograph.*

Suresh Now, give me the gun.

Subbu Stay away! (*Backs away and begins to cry.*) You killed her!

Silence except for **Subbu***'s sobs. A gunshot. Some screams.*

Mr Sharma No-o-o!

Interior. Living room of Champa.

Tinkle of bells as **Uma** *walks in.*

Anarkali Madam!

Uma I am so glad you are here.

Anarkali I am not going anywhere. I am now the head hijra. Champa has retired. She is leaving to spend the rest of her days in her sister's house in Bombay.

Uma Why didn't you tell me?

Anarkali Would you have believed me? Anyway, what is the use of all that? What does it matter who killed Kamla? She is dead . . . So many times I warned her. First I thought Salim was taking her for his own pleasure. When she told me about Subbu, madam, I tried to stop her. I fought with her. I scratched her face, hoping she will become ugly and Subbu will forget her. He wanted to marry her . . . I was there at their wedding . . . She gave me that picture to show to Champa. I saw the men coming for her. I told her to run . . . (*Cries for a while.*) Here, madam, take this.

Uma What is it?

Anarkali A special mantra is in the locket. Champa gave this to me for you. Wear it and you will be blessed with children. Sister! May you and your family be happy! Now go away, and do not come here again. Please go, sister!

Silence.

Interior. The bedroom of Suresh and Uma.

Uma . . . The photograph was what Mr Sharma was after. A Polaroid picture that Subbu and Kamla had taken soon after their private wedding in some remote temple . . . A picture of Kamla as a beautiful bride smiling at Subbu with the wedding garland around him. The poojari probably didn't know that Kamla was not a woman. Of course Mr Sharma couldn't have it – totally unacceptable. So he arranged to have Kamla burned to death. But Salim had to tell him about the picture. Mr Sharma simply had to have that picture. He sent Salim to threaten Anarkali and Champa . . . He did get the picture eventually . . . after losing his son. What a price to pay! And now he will be arrested and tried for murder.

Suresh I don't know . . . (*Pause.*) How do you know all this?

Uma I have my resources.

Interior. The office of the Superintendent of Police.

Whirring of fan.

Suresh Sir, that is the truth. I have my resources to verify all this. Of course, they are all sworn to secrecy so . . . And Mr Sharma's gratitude will be expressed in ways that will be, I am sure, more than adequate . . .

Whirring of fan stays for a while.

Uma (*voice-over*) They knew. Anarkali, Champa and all the hijra people knew who was behind the killing of Kamla. They have no voice. The case was hushed up and was not even reported in the newspapers. Champa was right. The police made no arrests. Subbu's suicide was written off as an accident. The photograph was destroyed. So were the lives of two young people . . .

Music.

Further Reading

Bharata-Muni, *The Nāṭyaśāstra*.
Bhasa, *The Vision of Vasavadatta*.
Bhatia, Nandi, *Acts of Authority, Acts of Resistance: Theater and Politics in Colonial and Postcolonial India*.
Bhatia, Nandi, *Performing Women/Performing Womanhood: Theatre, Politics and Dissent in North India*.
Bhatia, Nandi, *Modern Indian Theatre: A Reader*.
Dattani, Mahesh, *Collected Plays*.
Deshpande, G. P., ed., *Modern Indian Drama: An Anthology*.
Karnad, Girish, *Collected Plays*.
Karnad, Girish, *Hayavadanna*.
Karnad, Girish, *Nāga-mandala: Play with a Cobra*.
Karnad, Girish, *Tughlaq*.
Kumar, Kusum, *Listen Shefali*.
Mee, Erin, ed., *Drama Contemporary: India*.
Mukherjee, Tutun, ed., *Staging Resistance: Plays by Women in Translation*.
Sharma, Tripurari, *The Wooden Cart*.
Sircar, Badal, *Evam Indrajit*.
Tagore, Rabindranath, *Three Plays (Red Oleanders, Tapati, and Formless Jewel)*.
Tendulkar, Vijay, *Collected Plays in Translation*.
Wells, Henry W., ed., *Six Sanskrit Plays in English Translation*.

Bibliography

Atamjit, ed. *Plays from a Fractured Land (Punjabi Partition Drama in Translation)*. New Delhi: Sahitya Akademi, 2021.
Bhagat, Datta. *Whirlpool*. Translated by Georg Nagies, Vimal Thorat and Eleanor Zelliot in *Modern Indian Drama*, edited by G. P. Deshpande, New Delhi: Sahitya Akademi, 2000.
Bharata-Muni. *The Nāṭyaśāstra*. Translated and with introduction and notes by Manomohan Ghosh. Calcutta: Manisha, 1995.
Bharata-Muni. *The Nāṭyaśāstra*. English Translation with Critical Notes by Adya Rangacharya. New Delhi: Munshiram Manoharlal Publishers, 2010.
Bharati, Dharamvir. *Andha Yug*. Translated by Alok Bhalla. New Delhi: Oxford University Press, 2005.
Bharati, Dharamvir. *The Blind Age (Andha Yug)*. Translated by Tripurari Sharma. New Delhi: National School of Drama, [2001?].
Bhasa. *The Shattered Thigh and Other Plays*. Translated by A. N. D. Haksar. India: Penguin, 1993.
Bhatia, Nandi. *Acts of Authority, Acts of Resistance: Theater and Politics in Colonial and Postcolonial India*. Ann Arbor: University of Michigan Press, 2004.
Bhatia, Nandi. *Performing Women/Performing Womanhood: Theatre, Politics and Dissent in North India*. New Delhi: Oxford University Press, 2010.
Bhatia, Nandi. *Modern Indian Theatre: A Reader*. Delhi: Oxford University Press, 2009.
Chatterjee, Sudipto. *The Colonial Staged: Theatre in Colonial Calcutta*. London: Seagull Books, 2007.
Dattani, Mahesh. 'Seven Steps Around the Fire', in *Collected Plays I*. New Delhi: Penguin, 2000.
Deshpande, G. P., ed. *Modern Indian Drama: An Anthology*. New Delhi: Sahitya Akademi, 2000.
Dharwadker, Aparna Bhargava. 'Introduction', in Karnad, Girish, *Collected Plays Volume Three*. New Delhi: Oxford University Press, 2020.
Dharwadker, Aparna Bhargave. *Theatres of Independence: Drama, Theory, and Urban Performance in India since 1947*. University of Iowa Press, 2005.
Jahan, Rashid. *Behind the Veil*. https://archive.org/details/behindtheveilplayenglish/mode/2up.
John, Joya. 'Plays of Datta Bhagat'. *Muse India* (21). https://web.archive.org/web/20100104135355/http://museindia.com/showfocus10.asp?id=1030.
Kalidasa. *Shakuntala*, in Arthur W. Ryder, ed., *Translations of Shakuntala and Other Works*. London: J. M. Dent & Sons, Ltd., 1912.
Karnad, Girish. *Collected Plays Volume Three*. New Delhi: Oxford University Press, 2020.
Karnad, Girish. *Hayavadana*, in Siyuan Liu and Kevin J. Wetmore, Jr., eds, *The Methuen Drama Anthology of Modern Asian Plays*. London: Bloomsbury, 2014.
Karnad, Girish. *Nāga-mandala: Play with a Cobra*. Delhi: Oxford University Press, 1990.
Karnad, Girish. *Talé-Danda*. Translated from the original Kannada by the author. Delhi: Ravi Dayal Publisher, 1993.
Kumar, Kusum. *Listen Shefali*. Translated by B. T. Seetha in *Staging Resistance: Plays by Women in Translation*. New Delhi: Oxford University Press, 2005.
Lal, Ananda, translator. *Rabindranath Tagore: Three Plays*. New Delhi: Oxford University Press, 2001.
Lal, P. *Great Sanskrit Plays*. New York: New Directions, 1964
Mee, Erin. 'Chapter 7: Modern Indian Theatre', in Kevin J. Wetmore, Jr., Siyuan Liu, and Erin Mee, eds, *Modern Asian Theatre and Performance 1900–2000*. London: Bloomsbury, 2014. 169–94.

Mee, Erin. 'Chapter 8: Theatre of Roots: Post-Independence Theatre in India', in Kevin J. Wetmore, Jr., Siyuan Liu, and Erin Mee, eds, *Modern Asian Theatre and Performance 1900–2000*. London: Bloomsbury, 2014. 195–238.
Mee, Erin, ed. *Drama Contemporary: India*. Baltimore: The Johns Hopkins University Press, 2001.
Mee, Erin, B. *Theatre of Roots*. London: Seagull Books, 2008.
Menon, Jisha. *The Performance of Nationalism. India, Pakistan, and the Memory of Partition*. Cambridge University Press, 2012
Mukherjee, Tutun, ed. *Staging Resistance: Plays by Women in Translation*. New Delhi: Oxford University Press, 2005.
Panikkar, K. N. *The Lone Tusker*. Translated by K. S. Narayana Pillai. Calcutta: Seagull Books, 1991.
Rakesh, Mohan. *One Day in the Season of Rain*. Translated from the Hindi with an Introduction, an Afterword, and Notes by Aparna Dharwadker and Vinay Dharwadker. Gurgaon: Penguin Books, 2015.
Sircar, Badal. *Beyond the Land of Hattamala and Scandal in Fairyland*. Translated from the original Bengali by Suchanda Sarkar. Calcutta: Seagull Books, 1992.
Sircar, Badal. *Evam Indrajit*. Translated by Girish Karnad. Calcutta: Oxford University Press, 1974
Sircar, Badal. *Three Plays: Procession/Bhoma/Stale News*. Calcutta: Seagull Books, 1983.
Tagore, Rabindranath. *Chitra*. New York: The Macmillan Company, 1916.
Tagore, Rabindranath. 'The Post Office', in Siyuan Liu and Kevin J. Wetmore, Jr., eds, *The Methuen Drama Anthology of Modern Asian Plays*. London: Bloomsbury, 2014.
Tagore, Rabindranath. *Three Plays / Rabindranath Tagore*. Translated and with an introduction by Ananda Lal. New Delhi: Oxford University Press, 2001.
Tendulkar, Vijay. *Collected Plays in Translation*. New Delhi: Oxford University Press, 2003.
Thapar, Romila, ed. *Śakuntalā: Text, Readings, Histories*. New Delhi: Kali for Women, 1999.
Wells, Henry W., ed. *Six Sanskrit Plays in English Translation*. London: Asia Publishing House, 1964.